THE GEEK OF CHIC

AN AMERICAN DREAM ITALIAN STYLE

FEDERICO MARCHETTI

Co-written by *Daniela Hamaui*

Translated from the Italian by *Richard Dixon*

Post Hill

PRESS

A POST HILL PRESS BOOK
ISBN: 979-8-89565-060-8
ISBN (eBook): 979-8-89565-061-5

The Geek of Chic:
An American Dream Italian Style

Cover design by Paper Paper

Co-written with Daniela Hamaui
Translated from the Italian by Richard Dixon

This is a work of nonfiction. All people, locations, events, and situations are portrayed to the best of the author's memory. This book reflects only the authors' personal views and is not endorsed in any manner by Richemont, its affiliates, and/or its past or current management.

Post Hill Press
New York • Nashville
posthillpress.com

Published in the United States of America
1 2 3 4 5 6 7 8 9 10

To my mother, a great lover of books,
who would never have imagined that I would
have written one, and to Maggie, my daughter,
to whom I leave an album of memories

TABLE OF CONTENTS

FOREWORD

By Giorgio Armani

I had not a moment's hesitation when Federico asked me to write the introduction to his memoir for young dreamers and innovators. I accepted immediately because of my feelings of esteem for him and the affinity and vision that binds us. In Federico I can see something of myself: my ideals and my way of acting and thinking. In him I recognize loyalty, enterprise, leadership quality. He is someone whose opinions are important to me, so much so that I wanted him on my group's board of directors.

Federico has made it alone, imagining much and working more, arriving from Ravenna, where he was born, to London, and from there to become part of King Charles III's task force. Along the way he created YOOX, being one of the first to sense the potential of fashion on the web, inventing a reality that hadn't existed until then. Commitment and determination have been his instruments, courage his driving force, intelligence and the readiness to seize opportunities his merit. Those who want to break the mold have to take risks, swim against the tide, walk untrodden paths. Risk requires courage, and a touch of recklessness: You throw yourself in, without too much thought, otherwise you'd come to a halt. I too have done the same.

I think the only way of transmitting to future generations the sense of commitment and also the enjoyment of risk, as well as the importance of imagination, is through personal example. I don't believe in textbooks, and even less in commonplace formulae. Federico thinks as I do. The following pages are exactly this: a series of events described by the person who has experienced them. I'm quite sure that standing up for what you've done, showing your face, gives a truth and authenticity to everything. Showing your face and using your pen: there's no other way to create a captivating story.

INTRODUCTION

History is not a collection of ifs, yet my own history is full of them. If I hadn't fallen in love with America from the time I was a child selling Mickey Mouse comics on the beach, if I hadn't completed a training program at Lehman Brothers in New York, if I hadn't done an MBA at Columbia University, if I hadn't sensed the revolutionary power of the internet—in other words, if I hadn't discovered that technology and the American Dream were two pillars on which to place all my energies—then I probably wouldn't be here to describe my adventures. But there are many other ifs: If I hadn't been Italian, if I hadn't been born in a city like Ravenna where beauty is everywhere, if I hadn't absorbed all the culture, history, uniqueness, and wealth of my country's heritage, if I hadn't adored fashion and discovered how Made in Italy had become the most sought-after brand of all, I wouldn't have tried to revolutionize the whole luxury fashion sector by inventing one of the world's first projects for online sales.

At the start of the twenty-first century, doing business online was futuristic; there were no models to refer to. You had to invent something that didn't exist, you had to work out what road to take, to explore new territories, like American innovators had done centuries before. One of the modern-day pioneers was certainly Steve Jobs; he had created Apple, one of the most revolutionary companies, but had decided to do things his own way. Not many people know that he came to Italy in 1985 to meet Mario Bellini, the architect who designed some of the most extraordinary and colorful typewriters. Jobs had heard him several years before, in 1981, at the International Design Conference at Aspen in Colorado—along with the movie director Bernardo Bertolucci (winner of nine Oscars several years later for *The Last Emperor*) and the automobile designer Sergio Pininfarina—and had discovered the simplicity and beauty of Italian design. On his arrival in Milan, he tried to persuade Bellini to design for Apple but although no agreement was reached, Jobs was inspired by the Italian Idea (which was the title of his speech at Aspen). He blended design and precision, aesthetics and functionality, and created his Macs which entered our lives with an alluring charm. They were useful but also beautiful. Technology, which is cold and rational by its nature, could therefore be seductive. Jobs's "Think different" was also that. I followed this idea almost unconsciously, creating a company that was tech and warm, functional and exciting, digital and cultural, full of surprises, of amusement, of novelty. I was selling online but wanted to amaze my customers, to entertain them, to capture their imagination. I blended American speed and adrenaline with Italian sensibility, with my city's mosaics—those that inspired even the Memorial Church at Stanford University, from which so many American innovators have come—and with the aesthetic expertise that brings millions of tourists every year to visit Italian centers of art and discover the sculptures of Michelangelo, the paintings of Raphael, and the codex of Leonardo da Vinci. Feeling and rationality, passion and innovation, sensibility and utility. Future and past, fun and reliability, reason and sentiment. And I could continue with these contrasts that have been fused together to give my company a personality so definite and different from the others that it has been unrivalled for so long. Fashion is ethereal, sensitive, exclusive, elitist, made with superb fabrics and styles devised by creatives who love their creations, who won't part with them unless they know where they will be going, unless they know who will wear them and whether they will be in good company. The leading brands didn't understand that around their clothing was a cold, mechanical environment devoid of emotion: Amazon, in fact, never managed to interest them. They needed a magical colorful room in which customers could dream and do their shopping while someone undertook with extreme precision and with the full potential of digital technology to build a high-performance network capable of satisfying their desires.

If I had miscalculated the ingredients, if I hadn't been so obsessed by beauty and by the Italian spirit, if I hadn't devised a creative project completely different from all the others, if I hadn't ended up acquiring my aesthetically glamorous English competitor thereby creating an Anglo-Italian group which had thousands of employees and was an undisputed world leader, I would still be that kid with imagination who dreams about the future, but I wouldn't be able to claim to have fulfilled an American dream Italian style. And I wouldn't have been able to tell my story here. This book isn't a simple biography or an academic textbook. It's a story in which heart and reason each find their own space and their own purpose, and where stories about personal experiences are interwoven with practical advice for entrepreneurs of the future.

Books are like Russian dolls. Each story contains many other stories within it, whether large, small, surprising, familiar, or so completely new and unexpected that it stirs our curiosity. *The Geek of Chic* is the story of a kid born in a northern Italian town who had a love of beauty. He wanted to create a modern technological company but felt that without creativity the business would be dull and lifeless. He wanted to brighten it with colors and feelings and was convinced that by merging form and function he could invent something new and outstanding.

1

Time and I work together. We share moments that I cannot miss. Time has always fascinated me.

I was born in the north Italian town of Ravenna, in the Romagna region, and its sea and tranquility are imprinted on my imagination. Then I flew to New York and its frenetic pace became my adrenaline. I've always been conscious of time, of when the moment is just right to do something, or when it's better to wait. I chose the spring equinox of 2000 to found my company YOOX, at a time when selling fashion online seemed like an episode out of *Star Trek*. I decided that the summer solstice was the perfect day to open online. I defied a freezing December day in 2009, after the collapse of Lehman Brothers, to list it on the Stock Exchange, and chose Cyber Monday of 2020 to leave my position as CEO.

The right moment has been a constant feature of my life. Many things have happened because I opened that door at that moment, on that day, at that hour. 1969 was also the right year to be born.

Apollo 11 was launched from Kennedy Space Center at 13:32 on July 16, 1969.

It would take five more days before the commander, Neil Armstrong, and the pilot of the lunar module, Buzz Aldrin, prepared for the Moon landing. At 20:17 on July 21, they called:

"Houston, Tranquility Base here. The Eagle has landed." Six hours later, at 2:56, Armstrong began his walk on the Moon with the words: "That's one small step for man, one giant leap for mankind." Aldrin followed him nineteen minutes later. The two men started moving slowly, planted the American flag, collected rock samples, and raised an incredible dust, which remained suspended for a long time. Richard Nixon, the US president, called them from the White House, and Armstrong and Aldrin left various things before their departure, including an olive branch and a plaque with the words: "Here men from the planet Earth first set foot upon the Moon July 1969, A.D. We came in peace for all mankind." The year 1969 marked the beginning of a new age—an age of searching for new galaxies to reach and to conquer. The world was no longer enough.

I'm a child of those times. I love space and science fiction. I'm the product of that restlessness toward the future. I'm fascinated by unknown lands, by daring adventures never yet attempted. I'm an explorer and a navigator; I feel the world is too small for me and, since my earliest childhood, I have only one desire: to escape, to travel, even just in my imagination. I feel sure there's much to discover outside and, as someone who's afraid of the unknown, I want to know about what I don't know, I want to learn about what I don't understand, to invent what doesn't exist, to become what I am not. And I will always be like that.

I'm always looking ahead—my sights have always been set on the future. That's why 1969 is the perfect year for me. The Moon landing, in fact, is not the only event that interests me. Something even more symbolic and sensational took place on October 29 when the computers of UCLA and of Stanford Research Institute at Menlo Park were linked for the first time. No one could imagine the full significance of this connection. They called it Arpanet, and at first it seemed an event like so many others, an experiment between academics. In truth, it was the embryo that gave birth to the internet, the invention that would change my life and the world as we now know it. It would mark the prelude to the third industrial revolution that brought the twentieth century to a close and opened the new millennium. It marked the beginning of the age of connection, of smartphones in the hands of over five billion people, of computers on every desk around the planet, and of artificial intelligence. And, for me, it marked the time when technology became a central factor for innovation and creativity.

But before returning to my birth in 1969, I'd like to tell you something about where I come from. To do this we must go back in time, to Ravenna in the early 1950s. Italy, at the time, had been beaten down by recent history. On the heels of losing almost half a million men in WWI, we were on the wrong side of history in WWII. War, fascism, occupation, and civil strife left the Italian economy in shambles. Poverty was common, especially in the rural south and northeast. Peasant women often still dressed in somber, ankle-length mourning attire in honor of war dead and many people outside the major cities still rode about on donkeys, as they had for thousands of years. Rome, Naples, Milan, Turin, and Genoa all still bore the marks of heavy bombing—and damage to their collective psyches to match.

It would have been almost unimaginable to Italians at the time—my parents' generation—that they would witness a dramatic transformation within a decade. The late 1950s and early 1960s marked the start of a so-called "Economic Miracle" that reshaped our country forever. Auto-based industries in the north (Ferrari, Alfa Romeo, Ducati, Fiat, Pirelli) and craft and design businesses making fine furniture, glassware, textiles, and ceramics helped Italy build an international reputation synonymous with quality and craftmanship. Citizens were now consumers, and quality of life and buying power quickly increased; people moved to the cities in vast numbers and a cosmopolitan culture emerged. Young people inspired by American films and music began to challenge traditional norms and values. Italian cinema flourished too, with directors like Vittorio De Sica and Federico Fellini producing timeless films that also reflected the social and cultural changes of the time.

My parents, Lidia and Giancarlo, will witness all of this soon, but back in 1950 they are still kids. She is thirteen and in middle school. He is sixteen and at commercial school. Lidia is still young, and her parents keep an eye on her. Giancarlo collects her from school on his Lambretta motor scooter but must ask her father's permission before taking her out. He's handsome, amusing, quiet, and Lidia is in love with him. He lost his mother when he was twelve. He and his two brothers nursed her to the end. She died one evening in her bed, in front of them. Her absence would leave an indelible mark. Giancarlo is sad, but he's keen to grow up, to become independent. He's in love with life, one look is enough for girls to fall for him, and the Rimini discotheques are his hunting ground. Elegant, mysterious, a dandy, a communist, he likes dancing with other girls but then returns to Lidia, who waits and is besotted with him. They get married. Lidia is beautiful and vaguely resembles Ingrid Bergman; he looks perfect and irresistible in his wedding suit. Both find work. After her college exams she becomes a switchboard operator while Giancarlo takes a job with a road transport company and then, a few years later, works for the Corriere Romagnolo courier service, which sends him to Milan. Lidia follows him and gets a job with the STIPEL telephone company. They live in via Pellegrino Rossi, on the outskirts of the city. These are difficult times for Lidia; she feels isolated, and each morning has to take two trams to reach Piazza Affari. She sits on the wooden seats, tearful, reads the novels of Vasco Pratolini that keep her anxiety at bay, keep her mind occupied, but her only wish, her only dream, is to return to Ravenna. Someone in the street where she lives in Milan keeps singing "Romagna Mia," and she feels all the more homesick and pained about her husband who has become ever more distracted, drawn by other temptations, in a city she finds cold and distant. "They were the worst three years of my life," Lidia always says, finding herself now pregnant with my older brother, ignored, unable to see ahead. She decides to return to Ravenna, even at the risk of going back alone. Meanwhile, Giancarlo has tried setting up his own business and has failed, so he follows her. There they are again in Romagna, the region she is proud of, where her family have lived since the 1500s. He starts working for Fiat as a warehouse keeper while Lidia, after the birth of Fabrizio, resumes work as a switchboard operator for the TIMO telephone company in Piazza Kennedy. It's a hectic office with much coming and going, she enjoys talking to the customers, they provide company. There aren't yet many private houses with telephones; people often call the switchboard operators for a number, or to make a long-distance telephone call. Lidia is pleased to help whoever is there and to help them connect with each other.

Life runs smoothly. Everyone knows each other in Ravenna and knows all about them. But disaster falls on the Marchetti family just a few years after Fabrizio's birth. Giancarlo takes sick with testicular cancer, they operate, he recovers, but he's no longer the same person. Insecure, introverted, he becomes increasingly nervous and intractable. He's sure he is dying, and even though the doctors and Lidia try to reassure him, his life becomes an inferno. She tries to calm him, but her attempts are useless. Giancarlo swings from moments of euphoria to deep depression. He often shouts, grows angry, and has unforgettable outbursts that frighten everyone.

When Lidia becomes pregnant for the second time, there's a family revolt. Her mother, Maria, is opposed. She says two children are too much, it's already difficult looking after one, and isn't happy that Lidia wants that child at whatever cost. Fabrizio is almost nine. He's used to being the focus of attention in a complicated family situation and doesn't want brothers or sisters. When Lidia goes to hospital for the birth, her parents refuse to take her, Fabrizio has a fever (or says he has), and only Giancarlo wants that child as much as she does.

When Lidia returns home with the baby in her arms, Fabrizio sees him for the first time and decides his name should be Federico, after Barbarossa the Holy Roman Emperor, even though his hair isn't red but dark and curly.

I NOW APPEAR

It didn't take me long to realize I had ended up in a complicated family. We were living in a one-thousand-square-foot apartment in a 1960s block with a large inner courtyard. It had only two bedrooms, but my brother didn't want me in his, or at least he never offered to share it with me. So I ended up in my parents' room and remained there until I was thirteen, with a bedside table, and a poster that hung over my bed. My mother tried at some point to buy a larger house and gave the deposit to a realtor, but he gambled it away in the casino. He committed suicide, the deposit money disappeared, and we remained in the house where my mother still lives today, now in her eighties, living alone, surrounded by her keepsakes.

I've often wondered how I managed to live there for so many years without complaint. I could have developed some kind of complex, though fortunately it didn't go like that. I slept in a small bed in one corner of my parents' room while my brother had a space all to himself which I thought of as a kind of mythic Wonderland. One whole wall of his room was papered with a scene showing an American city with thousands of brightly lit skyscrapers. That panorama captured my imagination so strongly that when I arrived in the United States for the first time, it seemed as if I'd been there before, that I was returning to my childhood.

My father's state of health, in the meantime, continued to fluctuate. He was admitted to a psychiatric hospital, first in Modena and then in Verona, where he was given electroshock treatment. As a result, on his return home, he felt like an animal locked in a cage from which he couldn't escape.

I decided to protect myself so that, as a child, my mind had already begun to cancel out bad memories, retaining just the good ones. It works in much the same way even now. I store the files to be forgotten in a remote folder, and no longer open it. It disappears, I don't even know if it still exists. In this way, I wipe out the episode I have left far, far behind. I remember nothing about Christmas evenings, or my birthdays. I remember that I loved dressing up as Zorro or the pirate Sandokan but have no idea what I did when I was disguised like this. When I look back to my childhood, it seems a patchwork of memories. Some are clear and precise while others are vague and dim—it goes without saying that those are the more painful ones that I have put aside to make space for moments of joy and happiness.

I didn't like the claustrophobic feel of Ravenna, whose beauty I would discover much later. It was cramped, gossipy, everyone watched you, and nothing was secret, whereas I wanted to be invisible; I wanted my own privacy even then. My childhood friend Alex Majoli, the well-known photographer and member of Magnum Photos, once had this to say about Ravenna: "It's an island, it's not attached to the coast, it's a former swamp. If you want to see it, you must choose to go there. And we who are born there were brought up with a hidden beauty around us: the mosaics are invisible from outside, you need to go into the churches to discover them, they're a treasure you would never imagine. The same is true about the people of Ravenna: you need to get to know us to understand us."

The region of Emilia-Romagna where Ravenna is located also has its own distinct flavor and reputation. We Romagnoli are often playfully called the "southerners of the North." The stereotype of the people from the South of Italy are that they are short tempered, passionate; emotional and expressive, family oriented—in general, more focused on the enjoyment of life than achieving success. Northerners, the Milanese, in particular, are supposedly materialistic, formal, efficient, a bit cold—out for themselves, and to get ahead. So basically, we Romagnoli take the best of both and combine them. We are known to have a somewhat rebellious spirit—to be rather outspoken, and a little fierier than people from other regions. We too have a reputation for knowing how to enjoy life, and food plays a big part in that. Romagna has a renowned food culture, with dishes like the *piadina* (a flatbread) and handmade pasta like cappelletti achieving an almost sacred quality.

Ravenna was a prosperous town in the 1970s. Via Cavour was a succession of luxury shops, and my classmates were rich, or to me they seemed rich. Their fathers were architects, businessmen, lawyers. They drove around in smart cars and lived in tastefully decorated houses. They had everything I didn't have.

My family was different, problematic. My father, Giancarlo, was intelligent and bipolar. He smoked all the time. My mother, Lidia, was a rightwing Roman Catholic and the epitome of precision. Hell would often break loose in the house. He would start shouting, while she suffered in silence. I'd try to protect her, to help her, but the only advice I could give her was to leave him, which was something she'd never do. When he was well, my father was charming, even though I hardly knew him—he and I never went out together, the two of us never went out for dinner alone. I remember no signs of warmth—he seemed incapable of showing love. He made me think of flashing lights. Sometimes they're on, sometimes they're off. It was only on the day of his funeral that I found out all about him, and even discovered some characteristics that we had in common. His colleagues told me how he was a perfectionist and used to arrive at the warehouse at five in the morning, before the sound of the siren, to make sure everything was in order. He protected his team, was the chief warehouseman, wanted everything to function perfectly, but if anything went wrong, he would take responsibility for any mistakes. He was a Red Cross volunteer, and when he set off with them on long journeys—after an earthquake in India or China in the early 2000s, for example—he was filled with enthusiasm.

Relations with him were never easy. I feared for my mother, for myself, for Fabrizio, and even though his violence was only verbal, I was terrified by the idea that one day it might degenerate.

The family was the full responsibility of my mother. She was my heroine. She had to follow strict working hours, and often, when I finished school, I would spend the afternoon with her parents. My maternal grandmother, Maria, was beautiful, tough, and tenacious. Her husband, Leo, had one eye after he had lost the other in World War II. He had been a local librarian, a kind and gentle man. I enjoyed playing cards with him, and with my aunts from Ferrara, and each summer we would spend a couple of days at the Arena in Verona, since he loved opera. I couldn't understand, at first, what he saw in these performances. They seemed boring, and I just wanted to get back to the Gardaland amusement park, our first stopping point on the journey home. But after a few years I became more enthusiastic, and opera is still one of my passions.

I didn't see much of my paternal grandfather, Gaspare, and his second wife, Elisa, whom he had married after the death of his first wife. Gaspare was a teacher and had a reputation for being mean and scrupulously honest. He gave low marks to his son Paolo, my father's brother who attended his school, just to show everyone how rigid he was. But he had a wonderful blue parrot that I couldn't take my eyes off. The harshness and indifference of my father's parents frightened me.

I CONFESS THAT I HAVE A DREAM

My brother Fabrizio was my idol. He had long hair, was funky, high-spirited, and went to discotheques with a group of wild friends. He wasn't clever at school, didn't study, preferred a carefree life. I could see that he had managed, in his own way, to escape from our gloomy family existence, and I tried to do the same. I wanted him to take notice of me at whatever cost, so I tried to attract his attention. He was a fanatical modelmaker and built beautiful airplanes which I smashed into a thousand pieces even just to hear the words: "Federico, if you do that again, I'll kill you."

At school I was the opposite—always top of the class, ten out of ten, and the teachers would tell my mother that I was a bright, inventive child, that my essays were filled with imagination. They asked if I read very much, they wanted to know where I drew my inspiration, who my favorite authors were, but my mother would always reply: "I don't know, Federico was always like this. He has a lot of ideas, but he reads little." I shared my homework with my classmates but never copied theirs. Throughout my life I've been obsessed about doing things well, getting to the top, never following anyone. I've also realized, however, that those who arrive later, who keep an eye on other people and copy and reuse their ideas, often manage to improve them and maybe to promote them in a more engaging manner. But my absolute need to set goals and always to get there beforehand in everything has urged me toward constant and ceaseless innovation, never to stop.

In truth, I read very little. I prefer to imagine things, to dream, to create fictional worlds. I invented an alter ego, an avatar ahead of his time, a showman called Federaco Marcotti. He held an imaginary microphone and broadcast shows from Los Angeles. During my afternoons alone at home, I invented new worlds and let my imagination run free. I wanted to be someone else, to be talented, to find an audience that would applaud, that would follow me. I was an introverted child, unlike the others, but I had one friend, Gigi, with whom I shared a desk at primary school. We're still close, as I am with all my childhood friends who I'm still always pleased to see. At home I used to joke that maybe the hospital had mixed me up at birth, that my family was another, that my father was a prince and would come looking for me. Instead, when I was invited to my friends' houses, my father would come to collect me in his Fiat Bianchina or his methane gas-powered 127, and I felt ashamed. I never invited my friends home because I didn't have a room of my own whereas they did. They also had a father with a flash car.

Sadly, it was only later that I realized that instead of hiding myself I should have been proud and pleased with what I had! Today I have homes in London, New York, Ravenna, Venice, Milan, and on Lake Como, and I often think how my thirst for space is boundless and insatiable. Maybe I'm looking for some compensation that I'll never find. I have an endless appetite for square meters and have fun transforming them from ruins into magnificent living areas, resolving the most complicated problems.

And yet, thinking about it now, I realize my parents did all they could to ensure we didn't go without. I played tennis almost daily at the Centro Tre Laghi, swam in an incredible pool on the second floor of an apartment block, and played the piano. Even then I was organized and multitasking. I didn't want to lose out on anything; I wanted my day to include everything: sport, music, school, but also friends. My obsessive organization of time began early and has lasted. My diary has always been full and I'm punctual for every appointment, rather like the Japanese. But I had to cancel tennis from the list. One day, while preparing for a tournament, I felt a sharp pain in my back. The doctor told me I had a L5-S1 slipped disc and would have to stop playing. Along with tennis, surfing also disappeared. I felt sad and angry because tennis required brainwork, the match result could change up to the very last moment, and I loved reversing the score. I was highly competitive and used to enjoy challenging and beating my friend Lorenzo. Surfing, on the other hand, meant freedom, being far from the shoreline and from everything else, letting yourself be carried by the waves. I didn't want to abandon these two passions and felt a deep sense of injustice: they were two sports I loved and at which I even excelled.

My attempts at attracting girls were another story: my first experience was a failure. At primary school I had two girlfriends, both called Valentina, though they didn't last long and were obviously platonic. Then nothing. I realized fairly quickly that women prefer "lame ducks," those who do badly at school but have an air of mystery. So at the end of August I made my resolution for the coming year: I would do badly, scoring six out of ten in every subject. I wanted to attract the girls in my class, to make myself desirable. But it didn't work that way—I continued to get top marks, and they continued ignoring me.

Yet this taught me how important reputation was: if you start well, everything gets easier. I had the reputation for being top of the class and the teachers stopped bothering to question me at the end of the year: they were sure I knew everything. The first impression became my calling card: I knew that if I showed I was clever at the start, it would open many doors, and I've used that calling card plenty of times in my life.

The summer was my moment. When school was over, we would move to Punta Marina near Ravenna; this was Paradise for me. There was everything I wanted: the sea, a bigger house, freedom. I shared a bedroom with Fabrizio. He was happy to agree since he went out every night. He went off dancing, returned at dawn, enjoyed himself: I wished I'd been old enough to go with him a few times.

Water is my element. I began to learn this almost immediately. I love the open sea. My passion for sailing began later, but at that time, when I was still surfing and was carried along by the wind and the rising waves, I was happy.

I met my first real girlfriend, Anna, at the Bagno Vela beach bar. I was sixteen, she was eighteen. She was pretty, lively, and above all enterprising. I fell in love with her straightaway, she introduced me to sex, to pleasure, my heart raced like mad. I felt life was finally beginning to smile on me, but the summer came to an end. She went back to Brescia and found someone else. It was my first heartbreak.

At Punta Marina, however, I discovered my talent as a salesman. I'm like a Byzantine merchant, I love the souk, I love bargaining. It's the bargaining I enjoy most, the haggling, arriving at the price. I've sold many things in my life. In 2005 I sold a blue Mercedes Pagoda on e-Bay, the same as the one in *American Gigolo,* even making a profit. And most of all I then invented YOOX, the first digital megastore where millions of customers from five continents could buy clothing and accessories online.

But let's go one step at a time. When I was ten, I sold my brother's collection of *Mickey Mouse* comics on the beach. We had always been subscribers; I read them from cover to cover, but once they'd been read and re-read, I thought it was time to get rid of them. I set up a stall and, at one hundred lire per comic, by the end of the morning I'd made a tidy sum. Most of all, however, I had the intoxicating sensation that I could persuade others, that

I could do it, that I could one day be independent. I went home feeling satisfied.

Summer soon ended, however. Punta Marina was the light, Ravenna was the darkness—a grim, foggy, claustrophobic town, filled with gossip, from which I wanted only to escape. This was another reason why I loved traveling. One July, when I was thirteen, I remember a period spent studying English in London.

Fabrizio, meanwhile, went off to do military service in Forlì. He no longer came home at night but stayed in the barracks, so I had his room at last which became mine for all practical purposes.

I was still doing well at school but even so, after endless discussions over what to do after middle school, my mother made the decision for me: I would go to commercial school. I didn't want to be a bookkeeper, I wouldn't even consider it, but she was sure it would be useful and an easy option. Today I find it amusing to think that I am a bookkeeper—as well as graduating from Bocconi University, gaining my MBA from Columbia Business School, and receiving the title of *Cavaliere del Lavoro* in 2017—but at the time I complained bitterly about it.

My brother went to the *liceo classico* but without any great results. After military service he decided to enroll at Modena University to please my mother but took no exams and dropped out. She wanted to avoid any repetition of what Fabrizio had done and stood firm about it: "Federico, you'll do bookkeeping, whether you like it or not." I dreamed of going to the *liceo classico,* I wanted to be a doctor or a psychiatrist, and the idea of bookkeeping seemed out of the question. Even now, I jokingly criticize my mother for this choice I found so hateful.

I went to school unwillingly and continued to break every record, but the part of the day I longed for was when I could take my Piaggio Sì, the motor scooter I was so proud of—which I had chosen with spoke wheels to save money while all the others had alloy wheels—and drove off to hang about under the clock in Piazza del Popolo. We were the Clockers, a group of buddies who went around together in Ravenna. Everyone knew us and we had great fun. We dreamt about the United States—the American Dream.

We went to the coast, danced like crazy at someone's house, played cards, and dreamt about our futures. In the summer of 1987, I was now an adult and had a driving license. I went off for a month with Davide, Gigi, Fabio, and Cristiano—who are still my closest friends—on what I remember to be the best vacation of my life. We rented an old lobster-colored Mercedes van, filled it with bags and surf boards, drove through France as far as Biarritz, then down into Spain and through Basque country to Tarifa on the Strait of Gibraltar. It was a wonderful journey—camping, sport, fun, and everything that carefree eighteen-year-olds might get up to.

THEN THE FINAL YEAR AT SCHOOL

For my final essay I chose the subject of the Holocaust but decided to tread a dangerous path. While I recognized the horror and the uniqueness of the death camps, I wrote about the tens of millions of indigenous people in Amazonia slaughtered through forest exploitation. My idol was Marlon Brando, who sent a Native American to collect the Oscar on his behalf. I sided with the weakest and with the environment, establishing the basis for what would become one of the arguments about which I'm still involved. I scored sixty out of sixty and remember the final question of the chairman of the exam committee: "But you, Marchetti, being so clever…what are you going to do next?" And my answer: "I don't know, but I know what I won't be doing. I won't be doing economics or law."

And yet, like so many times in my life, chance made the choice for me. In that year, 1988, Bologna University changed the regulations for enrollment in medicine, accepting only a limited number of students and introducing an admission exam. I had studied commerce, had no basic qualifications, and it would have taken me months of study, or at least the whole summer, to prepare for the exam. My summer was sacrosanct: travel, girls, surfing, friends, our house by the sea. I wasn't prepared to abandon any of this, to make so large a sacrifice. So I threw everything away and went off with a school friend to the Black Forest. We drove by car around Germany, stopping at Trier and then as far as Stuttgart.

When I got back at the end of August, I still had to decide what to do. I was ambitious, wanted to get away from home, to move to another part of Italy. I would have liked a career as a diplomat but could imagine how difficult it would be without contacts. So when my former classmate Paolo told me he was going to Milan to take the admission exam for the prestigious Bocconi University, I thought: "Why not? I could go with him, spend the evening in Milan, and try taking the exam too." A friend of mine from Ravenna, Andrea, a student at the Bocconi, let me use his apartment, so we set off. Having reached the building where Andrea lived, we realized we didn't know which flight of stairs to take, so we climbed to the top floor of the last staircase and tried opening the door, but they weren't the right keys. It was midnight and a few moments later three police squads arrived. They'd been called by the owner of the apartment who thought we were burglars. We tried to explain why we were there, but after one thing and another it was already two o'clock. Paolo was desperate, tired, convinced he'd find it impossible to concentrate during the admission test, while I, who had no real interest in getting into the Bocconi, was trying to reassure him. Worries about performance, and stress, can sometimes have a nasty effect. I had scored the top mark in the school final exam—which at that time counted for half of the score in the admission test—but I was there more to take part than to win. I was calm and said to myself: "There's no harm trying." I still hadn't decided what to do, and economics certainly wasn't my first option. The result was that I was admitted while Paolo, who'd had an attack of nerves, failed the admission test and ended up at another university. Fate decided for me. This regularly happens in my life. I often think of the film *Sliding Doors,* where things happen in one way or in the opposite way according to where you find yourself. On several occasions I would follow paths that would decide my future, and I would realize that a fraction of a second or an extra moment of indecision might have changed the course of events. I've always basically followed my instinct, and in certain situations I've let chance decide. And most of the time it has worked out well!

But the admission test for the Bocconi wasn't the first time this had happened. On another occasion I realized just how unfair life could be. I used to take piano lessons with Signorina Mercuriali and would arrive there straight from the swimming pool with my eyes red from the chlorine. She had another pupil, a girl who wanted to study at the conservatory and adored music, who was always perfect and well behaved. Music was my mother's passion, not mine. I hated playing scales, found them boring, but once again my reputation for being clever went before me. Signorina

Mercuriali, who wore glasses with thick lenses, stopped following the music at a certain point, so that I began to improvise, to let my imagination take over. The teacher told my mother that I had talent, whereas she advised the girl to give up. In fact I stopped playing soon after, and I hope the girl found some more enthusiastic teachers who could channel her abilities and fulfill her ambition to study at the conservatory.

When I was accepted at the Bocconi, before turning it down, I thought carefully about what it would mean to study there, at one of the leading universities not just in Italy but in Europe. I could get away from Ravenna—the dream I'd had for many years was within my grasp. I had only to pack my bags. I needed to find the courage to say that the first stage of my life was over, that I could start another completely different one.

I was at a crossroads: should I stay, or should I go? Should I cultivate my roots or throw myself into the unknown? Ravenna is a place by the sea, a junction, a town of great beauty. Ravenna holds some of the most extraordinary mosaics in the history of art. Several years later, in 2009, when with a team from Armani I saw Karl Lagerfeld stretched out on the floor of the basilica of San Vitale looking with meticulous care at the mosaics that would inspire his Chanel Paris-Byzance collection, I became deeply aware of how amazing and invaluable they could be for a creative. Mosaics are also to be found in the Memorial Church at the center of Stanford University campus in California. Its Byzantine architecture is inspired by the churches of Ravenna and the mosaics are based on religious paintings that its builder Jane Stanford—who dedicated the building to her husband—had admired with him in Europe. Ravenna is an endless source of interest and cultural inspiration, with not only the tomb of Dante but eight UNESCO world heritage monuments too. It is a center of trade, of transit, of business. A special place. Interestingly Ravenna is also the place where Julius Caesar collected his troops in 49 BC to cross the Rubicon River, an overt act of war that led to a domino effect resulting in the downfall of the Empire. The Rubicon is actually more like a muddy stream than a river, located south of Ravenna but still in Romagna. Now we know "crossing the Rubicon" as a shorthand for making a decision that cannot be undone, for venturing forth into the unknown.

I am no Caesar, obviously, but in choosing to leave Ravenna, I had to overcome my fears, to leave my mother and my problematic family in order to discover my own worth, to see whether I could defy expectations, whether I could succeed beyond every reasonable probability. To cross my own Rubicon, essentially, and to not be held back by expectations. If you want to arrive at new places to develop your talent, then you need to venture beyond your comfort zone. Being afraid, giving up, stopping, is wrong and frustrating. At nineteen you have your whole life before you, and you can only grasp it with the force and energy you need to change your destiny. Never be afraid!

2

At the beginning of 1989 I've been at the Bocconi for just a few months. But 1989 is not a year like all the others, and not just because of the fall of the Berlin Wall. On March 12, an Oxford physics graduate working at CERN, Tim Berners-Lee, presents a document called "Information Management: A Proposal." In this paper, the young researcher looks at the communication between some of his colleagues who send information via telephone inside the institute, viewing it on a video screen. He wants to assist their work but in fact he is laying the basis for what will become hypertext, a sensational idea whose value is recognized at first by very few people. His supervisor, however, realizes its potential and encourages him to take it further. After two years of work, Tim Berners-Lee publishes his first website. It is August 6, 1991, the beginning of a revolution, even though it will take time for the first embryo to develop so exponentially as to reach even the remotest corners of the planet. He writes that it's an "information retrieval initiative aiming to give universal access to a large universe of documents." In fact, it will be much more. Seventeen days will go by before the web page is visited: the first user outside the research center connects on 23 August, thereby marking the birth of the World Wide Web. What will become the event of the century is taking shape: computers situated thousands of miles apart can communicate between each other. They can share files, documents, and link up to a network that will grow out of all proportion until it becomes a gigantic web on which over five billion people depend each day.

I, too, was ignorant of just how important the web would be for me, and for the whole of humanity, but years later, at the World Economic Forum at Davos, when I was asked to take part in a roundtable, I felt a flood of emotion when I saw Berners-Lee among the other names. Without him I would have been no one, or at least I certainly couldn't have created a company centered around digital technology and the internet. I couldn't have connected millions of customers spread across 180 countries or served them by offering a kaleidoscopic range of clothes and accessories each day that would be delivered directly to their homes without them needing to pass by a store to try them on. I was eternally grateful to Berners-Lee for what he had done for me but above all for humanity...even if, during our meeting, I asked him for a selfie to immortalize the moment, and he rather scornfully refused.

My university years were the beginning of my future identity, and my studies provided the foundations for its construction. First the Bocconi, then Columbia University, would help me understand not only who I was but, above all, what I wanted to achieve. They would be the springboard from which I could plan what my work might be. They would provide the basis for moving forward and understanding the complex dynamics that lay behind the creation of a startup.

At the end of the "fabulous 1980s" (which unfortunately I hadn't experienced since I was too young and living in Ravenna, though I'd always thought of them as legendary years and imagined them to be exciting times) I arrived in Milan, on the threshold of my new life, with all the misgivings of a young provincial kid determined to shed his old skin and try on something different.

During my university years, and then my Master of Business Administration (MBA) course in New York, a new version of me was being born. I discovered then what I wanted to do. How could I have imagined becoming a doctor or, still more, a psychiatrist? Did I really imagine I'd have helped my family in this way, that I'd have been of any use? Did I seriously think I was the right person to treat illnesses and heal minds? I realized almost immediately that I was on the wrong path. I remembered the excitement I felt when I was selling *Mickey Mouse* comics on the beach, when I was earning money and had a tiny business. What I really enjoyed and was good at doing was something else. It had nothing to do with medicine and had another name: entrepreneurship. That was my destiny, my real life-changing opportunity and my passion, the compass that would guide all my decisions. From that moment it became my mission and my obsession. It took me ten years to achieve my dream, but in the end I succeeded.

The first step is to look deep inside, to drop down into the abyss, to reach the core and examine our true nature, our demons, and the talents we each have. Passion produces ideas, projects. We discover how easily we commit ourselves to working hard for something we enjoy and for which we have a profound feeling. I used those university years to carry out this work of introspection and I rejected all the intuitions that didn't truly excite me. I realized that passion opens many doorways that would otherwise be closed or invisible. Follow your instinct and it will take you far.

But let's go back to early September 1988, when I had just passed my entrance exam for the Bocconi. After a few days I went off for a week's skiing on the glacier at Stelvio—which wasn't then in such a precarious and worrying condition as it is now. I came back with pneumonia, which kept me in bed for many days. I couldn't arrange my move to Milan, so my mother did it all for me. Her own dire memory of this city, of how she had suffered, how lonely she had felt, and her own deep Catholic conviction prompted her to find me a bed in a religious hostel close to the university. I made no complaint about it, at least at first: I was there only to study. I returned to Ravenna each Friday and went back with a chill bag filled with cappelletti and other Romagnolo dishes that my mother had prepared for me. Even now, when I visit, she makes cappelletti for my daughter Margherita (though Maggie is the name she prefers) who adores them.

The hostel was a cramped building run by a priest, Monsignor Cagna, who was very strict. It was a year of sacrifices. My head was always in my books since I had decided to apply the same technique that had worked so well during my school years: to get top marks in the exams from the very start so that I could establish a good, indeed an excellent reputation, and then reap the benefit. And that's what happened. I collected a series of top grades but also a large dose of stress which appeared in the form of a horrible facial dermatitis that I found untreatable. I ended up going to a Chinese doctor who told me to drink an herbal concoction heated in a pan. One evening, while I was studying civil law (in truth I prepared only two out of three books, passing the exam all the same—deep down, I'm not always as serious as I seem, and I sometimes enjoy chancing my luck and taking the consequences, for better or worse), I forgot that the stove was still alight. I burned a linoleum square in my room and was summarily evicted.

I can't remember ever feeling so happy: I hated Cagna, loathed the room I shared with two other students (though they were polite and accommodating all the same), and detested the strict hours and total lack of freedom. It was nothing like what I had wanted and expected during my stay in Milan.

FROM HOUSE TO HOUSE

I needed more space: it was a physical need and an obsession. In three years, I moved from the shared room to a bedsit in the Navigli district, then to a two-room apartment, and finally to an actual house which, many years later, I managed to buy, restructure, and even extend—it was completely rebuilt by Luca Guadagnino with his interior design studio. Luca, the Italian film-maker, internationally known for his visually rich and emotionally nuanced storytelling, furnished my house on Lake Como, worked on the apartment I have taken in Milan, and on Villa Jankovmir, a splendid 1930s residence on the Venice Lido designed by Rubens Corrado for Elsa Venier which then became a residence for artists and writers, and which I had the good fortune to acquire.

At the time when I bought a former silk mill on Lake Como in 2016, Luca was already a brilliant film director with a strong aesthetic sense but had never tried his hand at interior design. In 2021 he was included in *By Design: The World's Best Contemporary Designers*, an authoritative survey published by Phaidon, as one of the hundred best design studios. Today he is a star, one of the most influential, and I'm proud to say he started out thanks to me. I was the one who encouraged him, and he, a true perfectionist, chose everything, from the teacups—which he wanted in a particular shade of pink—to the wood paneling and side tables. In an interview for the *Financial Times* monthly magazine *How to*

Spend It, Luca explained: "Marchetti could see something in me I could not. I would never have dared to propose myself for such a big job in a family home. And yet he had this gorgeous attitude and wanted me to do it." Yes, and I'm happy he did it because, with his vision and his cinematographic sensibility—his sets are a model of beauty and precision—he managed to transform an industrial building into a home in which my wife Kerry, Maggie, and I spent the whole lockdown when the COVID-19 pandemic broke out. At the time I bought it, it was a ruin that stood on land heavily contaminated by chemicals from a car repair works. After an astonishing and unexpected decontamination operation—we had to get help from Swiss engineers for the drainage of water and toxic substances—the former silk mill, thanks to Luca, has become a home where the light enters through the windows from the lake and blends with the colors of the walls and furnishings, creating an effect of peace and tranquility.

With Luca we shared everything, and for months we exchanged emails with ideas and suggestions until the night of the Oscars. He was there as a candidate for the film *Call Me by Your Name* and was still bombarding me with pictures of choices of sofa. Crazy! Luca never stops. And nor do I. Maybe that's why we've been friends for so many years (as I'll explain later), because although in some ways we're very different, in others we're quite alike, and when I go to the set where he is filming and see his obsessive attention to detail, I recognize certain parts of myself.

Having rebuilt the former silk mill, I added a small house in front and another piece of garden, and I financed the work for a very fruitful public-private venture to redevelop the road and the small piazza in front, once a dilapidated carpark, where children now play happily. The same happened with YOOX, whose first office was a warehouse and then, like Lego bricks that keep growing and growing, it was enlarged to become a proper headquarters. I move little by little. I add, I expand. My method is to work gradually.

That's how it was from the start. Having left the hostel, I moved with a friend to a tiny apartment in a tenement block in the Navigli, the canal district. We had just one room with a sofa bed, but it was enough. I began to enjoy myself, at last, and to take full advantage of the metropolis. I went out every evening, went to discotheques, met new people and, though I studied only as much as I needed to, still got top marks. I savored the happiness and carefree existence that I had so lacked in Ravenna. Meanwhile my horizon had changed: I viewed the Bocconi and economics in a new light. Having decided what I would do when I'd grown up, I felt sure I was on the right track for achieving it, or at least for acquiring the basics that I needed.

IF YOU CAN FLY, THEN FLY

The first year was difficult, the second easier, the third began what I would call my social life. Once my objectives were clear, my studies also began to take off. I chose the subjects that would best help me to create my new identikit and enhance the fundamental skills to reach my objective. I left the bedsit for a two-room apartment, was eager to get to know people, thirsting for new experiences, friendships, love. I wanted to make up for all the years that had passed. I wanted to graduate, to enjoy myself, to live a full and satisfying existence. I wanted everything!

I enjoyed the lectures on political economy but also followed a course on Japanese language, culture, and economy—Japan is one of my favorite countries—and even won a scholarship to go to the University of Kyoto, though I turned it down because at last I was starting to feel at home in Milan. I was beginning to lose that anxiety about doing well that I had felt through the whole of the first year. My first serious girlfriends appeared. I started organizing parties and dinners in my apartment and no longer felt alone. I saw myself in all respects as a fledgling entrepreneur and drew up impracticable business projects, including socks that wouldn't develop holes, a headrest for sleeping comfortably on planes, and wildebeest mozzarella.

This last idea was developed at a particular moment. On July 13, 1985, at Wembley Stadium in London and John F. Kennedy Stadium in Philadelphia, Bob Geldof organized Live Aid, a memorable fundraising concert for the famine that had devastated Ethiopia. People talked about commitment, about doing something, and I, too, wanted to do something useful. I discovered that the wildebeest was a member of the buffalo family. And it's true that their milk can be used for making mozzarella, but the problem from the practical point of view is that the wildebeest cannot be domesticated! So the project sank before it had really begun.

My first successful attempt at starting up a business was during the Christmas of 1991. A group of friends and I from the Bocconi decided to poke fun at some of our snobbish Milanese fellow students by forming the Christian De Sica Fan Club.

Christian's father was the actor Vittorio De Sica, who as I mentioned earlier directed some of the greatest movies in cinema history. He won three Oscars for the best foreign-language film with *Shoeshine* (1948), *Bicycle Thieves* (1950), and *The Garden of the Finzi-Continis* (1972) and in 1958 was nominated as best supporting actor for his role in *A Farewell to Arms*. De Sica senior, with his black-and-white films, was one of the leading figures in

Italian neorealism, a phenomenon that influenced many directors throughout the world, with its portrayal of Italy's transformation after World War II. His son Christian, who is also an actor, had chosen a different path and in the 1980s had invented a kind of farcical and politically incorrect comedy known as *cinepanettoni*. There were four of us, very determined, and already with an entrepreneurial spirit. We printed a thousand T-shirts with quotes from some of Christian's films, then organized a launch party in which he took part, and we sold everything in just a few days, making a tidy sum of money. I invested my share in my first cell phone: it was enormous, heavy, and was kept in a black case. Some time later I was given a walk-on part in a movie in which I had to walk to the Milan Stock Exchange holding just such a phone.

Reality is always more powerful than fiction. Many years later, in 2009, when YOOX was listed, I remembered that scene and how much it resembled the moment I was living. YOOX entered the Stock-Exchange list, and I had staked everything on sales through the mobile phone one year before the iPhone had appeared. Sometimes destiny is signaled, and my real story is encapsulated in those few seconds more than anything else.

My cell phone, so large and heavy, made me think of another idea: Why not insert a camera into it so that you could talk and take photos at the same time? The idea turned out to be a good one, but I was no engineer and didn't know enough about technology to produce a prototype and patent it.

I missed my opportunity for this invention too, but my love of unlikely projects and the possibility of innovation was already there.

My interests in business, technology, and retail were clear by then; I simply had to find a way of bringing them together and making them productive.

In 1993 I graduated from the Bocconi with top marks and was ready to face the adult world. I sent my CV to every investment bank and while I was waiting for a reply I traveled to the United States with a good university friend, Gabriele, for a journey from coast to coast. We hired a convertible and drove from Texas to New Mexico, from Louisiana to San Francisco, ending up in New York, where we stayed with Alessio Lewithin, a friend of Gabriele who managed a restaurant. His roommate was French, a great-nephew of Antoine di Saint-Exupéry, author of *The Little Prince,* who happened by pure chance to work at Lehman Brothers. I'd been looking for a job with an investment bank, not because I was passionate about finance but because I thought that learning about mergers, acquisitions, and listings would be useful for a young entrepreneur. It would be a way of building practical experience. I'd been called to various interviews but no one in the end had taken me on.

AT THE HEART OF POWER

As so often in my life, chance—or perhaps good fortune—came to my assistance. Alessio, who was now a friend, called me and said: "Saint-Exupéry tells me they're looking for an intern at Lehman Brothers in Milan. If you want to send him your CV, he can pass it on to them." A few days later they invited me in. I had a couple of interviews with my future bosses, was chosen as an intern, and started my first real job. The salary was low, the prestige stratospheric, the "slaps in the face" terrible.

Lehman Brothers was one of the strategic hubs of world capitalism during the 1990s but went bankrupt in 2008. Their casual way of arranging debts and selling off derivatives just to charge commissions and earn bonuses is now notoriously widely known. The banking debacle and subsequent Wall Street crash marked the beginning of a grave financial crisis that affected the whole planet, especially America, but when I joined in 1994 Lehman was the Power. They decided which companies to finance, at what price, and how to make them grow. The Milan office, headed by Ruggero Magnoni, was among the most influential, run by a very keen group of people with enormous talents and intelligence. They were all highly determined and able to decide the fate of the companies with which they worked. The atmosphere was tough, the staff highly competent, the competition intense. When I began, I knew nothing. I learned quickly, also because the professional level of the office was so high that I couldn't lag. Magnoni became incandescent when he was angry—today it would be unthinkable, but at that time it was quite normal. He would rage at me if I took more than five seconds to download data from Bloomberg. Vittorio Pignatti-Morano and Patrizia Micucci were two other key figures.

After less than three months as an intern, almost nine months earlier than anticipated, I was told there was a vacancy for an analyst in London. "This is your only chance," my boss told me. "If it goes wrong now, you can't re-apply in nine months. You have one shot, if it works the place is yours, if not you're out. The alternative is to wait. You decide."

THOSE WHO DON'T RISK LOSE FROM THE START

As a child I learned the importance of risking, even at the cost of failure: Giving yourself a chance is infinitely better than giving up without trying. My English wasn't good; I studied French at school. What would I do? I had little time and a lot to learn. I asked for help from Giuliana, an analyst who worked with me at Lehman. We wrote down five hundred possible interview questions and the respective answers. Eleven interviewers, all bankers, had to be unanimous before you got the job, and the thousands of applications for that job were probably much stronger than mine. I studied the answers at night, I memorized them: We had guessed right on 70 percent of them. For the other 30 percent, I improvised—and got by.

They took me on as an analyst, at the age of twenty-five, with a mega-salary and the prospect of a training program at Lehman headquarters in New York, in the Twin Towers on Wall Street. I really was reaching for the stars. At New York I worked like crazy but I was in the city of my dreams, a realm of opportunities and surprises. I've always felt that I'm a child of Ravenna, Italian in my DNA, but American by choice. The American dream was just one step away, I had only to achieve it.

The metropolis was full of opportunities and incentives, it was just a matter of grasping them. One evening I ended up at Nello, a famous restaurant on Madison Avenue, where a Romanian friend who was a waiter there gatecrashed me into Donald Trump's birthday party and where I met a black popstar with red hair with whom I had a love affair that lasted a week. Many years later I would receive an official invitation from Ivanka Trump, whom I had met at lunch with Wendi Murdoch, to a New Year party at her father's home at Mar-a-Lago in Florida. More *Sliding Doors* than this…!

I spent some unforgettable months in New York but sadly, once the training period was over, they said: "Your office is London." I was so hoping to remain there, but they sent me back to the City where the pace of work was even more grueling: ninety-hour weeks, Saturdays and Sundays abolished.

I didn't like London, I found it cold and distant, I didn't know anyone. So I was happy when the Milan office asked to have me back. There, as interns, I had two guys my own age, Diego di San Giuliano (who would become one of my best friends) and Giorgio Psacharopulo, with whom I'd leave the office at midnight and go looking for fun. We slept four hours at night but didn't miss out on discotheques, sushi bars, and the good times.

During those years, in return, I learned everything: the stages of a startup, who venture capitalists are, what a business plan is, how a company is valued, how it is listed. When it's a good idea to merge with another and how best to sell it off. I learned a method which I then put into practice when I launched YOOX and on every stage of my journey. But that wasn't all. Many of the people I knew at Lehman Brothers played a fundamental part in my life, in my business and in my career. I arrived there by chance but—as if by magic—that became the right place and the right moment to be there and to work.

At Lehman I also discovered the benefit of the internet. I was one of the first to do online research—the internet enabled me to work faster and finish sooner. Sometimes an hour a day was enough, and I worked eighty-five instead of ninety hours a week. On the other hand, I discovered my aesthetic side. I'm aware of it in the most absurd situations. I loathed the banality, the anonymity of PowerPoint presentations that lacked personality. I was convinced that you needed to capture the attention of your audience. Always. You needed to keep them fixed on what you were saying. Care and aesthetics are powerful magnets. Beauty is never too much. I remember a project for the weapons manufacturer OTO Melara where I searched for pictures of missiles made by artists. It was an unconventional presentation with drawings that astonished everyone. This form of creativity would become increasingly apparent, and I would use it as my hallmark.

A few years later, when I began to have more money, I started investing in art and bought my first picture. I am now a collector and have quite a few works, but at that time I was excited by a painting by Mark Kostabi, an American composer and artist who wasn't well known at the time. Its title was *Against the Odds*, a slogan that perfectly described my life.

An aesthetic sense meant many things—I loved graphics, photography, fashion. I had my own style and, when I was young, I used to dig out American jackets from A.N.G.E.L.O., a secondhand clothes stores at Lugo di Romagna. I liked vintage clothing and had a fashion awareness. Many years earlier, in one of the shabbier parts of Ealing, in London, I found a tall pair of orange shoes, by all accounts ugly but which I found really beautiful. They were being sold off at a knockdown price but would later become the Iconic '80s Timberland boots that my generation went mad over, becoming a cult object.

Returning to my career—after three years at Lehman I had the chance to become an associate. It would certainly have meant more money and prestige, but I wasn't sure. I wasn't wild about finance. I was tempted to remain in that gilded cage, but at the same time I felt my time there had come to an end. Fate decided for me once more. I'm not saying that I put my trust entirely in chance, but often—maybe unconsciously—I trigger events that cause me to change direction. On that occasion it was my indignant response to a top boss who was on a visit from London to Milan.

It was nine in the evening and my secretary, Annalisa, had kindly stopped to help me finish a presentation, when he flung a sheet of paper at her, telling her to transcribe it in Word for him. "No," I replied, "Annalisa is about to leave, she's unable to do it." He was furious but the matter ended there. I had almost forgotten about it until the time when my bosses had to fill out my performance review prior to my becoming a partner. They all wrote positive comments, whereas the boss from London, who had nothing to do with it—we had never worked together—made some terrible comments about me. I protested, we ended up in a kind of Lehman tribunal in London that made decisions on compliance, conformity with company regulations, and where each of us had to explain their position. I argued my grounds, but he was more important, so they ended up finding in his favor.

I felt the decision to be deeply unfair and dictated by the logic of power. I was expecting they would find for me, that they would even approve of my stopping an abuse, that they would accuse him of bullying, but instead it seemed exactly the opposite—that the law always favored the person with more money. It was the last straw. I realized it wasn't the right place for me.

In any event, my career there was finished, so I sent several applications for MBA postgraduate degree courses in business administration. I was accepted at INSEAD, the Institut Européen d'Administration des Affaires at Fontainebleau, in France, and at Columbia University in New York. Stanford and Harvard turned me down. I was in no doubt. Between the French countryside and the Big Apple, I chose the second. Above all, the master's degree in New York lasted eight more months. I'd put money aside from my earnings over these three years, I was independent, and was determined to leave.

It was October, the courses began in January, and I had three months free. Fabio Canè, a friend of mine and the husband of Patrizia Micucci with whom I had worked at Lehman, asked me to handle a project for Bain, an American consultancy company with branches around the world. The Italian office was run by Gianfilippo Cuneo and Giovanni Cagnoli, and the client was Rizzoli-Corriere della Sera. I presented a project proposal which went particularly well, Cagnoli was impressed by this alchemy that had been created between me and the client, and he offered to pay for my master's course on the understanding that, on my return, I would work with them for two years.

I accepted the money straight away, which served to cover my back in America—it would enable me to lead a less austere life, to allow myself a few extra comforts. But I also knew that consultancy companies weren't the place for me. My colleagues weren't as talented as those I had found at Lehman Brothers and I wasn't as enthusiastic about the type of work, but I took the money without thinking too much about it and thought: "I'll sort it out when I get back. Maybe I'll find another job to repay the debt."

I felt I was at a turning point. Four years at the Bocconi and three years' employment had shaped me. I was no longer the innocent kid from Ravenna arriving in the big city without the means to understand and deal with it. At university I had learned all the basics, absorbed as much as I could, chosen the most useful courses to work out who an entrepreneur really is and what he needs to do, how he needs to move, what instruments he needs to use to create his own company. At Lehman I was thrown into practical matters: business plans, acquisitions, listings. My thoughts were now clearer; I knew what path to follow. All that was missing was the idea—the right, bold, unexpected but practicable idea. I needed to find my own field, my own area, but I couldn't do it without discovering what my real passion was. I realized I had little time.

If you decide to do a startup, you must do it as soon as possible, while you have all the energy and determination to get there, to succeed. It's better if you're under thirty since you're more ready to take risks. But there was one part missing, a desire that I had always had: to experience the American dream from close at hand. I wanted to try entering that ocean of infinite possibilities, where all leap off the same trampoline and hurl themselves into a deep ocean from which those who are smart, motivated, and capable reemerge and succeed in reaching their goal. I had many questions: What is it that makes that place so special and so intense? What is the magic? Why is what you're doing more important there than who you are, and why can everyone do it? I was sure I would return from America and from Columbia University with a successful idea. And in January 1998 I left flush with enthusiasm.

3

From the moment I landed in New York I felt I was in the right place. For anyone involved in technology, 1998 was an important year. On September 4, in the garage of a house at no. 232 Santa Margarita Avenue, Menlo Park, in the heart of Silicon Valley, two Stanford University students, Larry Page and Sergey Brin, set up Google Inc. It all started from a thesis project by Page, who wanted to study how the World Wide Web operated. Brin joined in on this idea and the two kids set to work on BackRub, their first search engine. They had guessed that an engine based on mathematical analysis of relationships between websites would produce better results than the methods used up to then. They were convinced it was important to concentrate on pages that had the greatest number of connections from other relevant web pages. This led to the creation of Google, one of the most brilliant ideas in the field of technology. By 2000, Google could respond to 18 million queries a day. Twenty-three years later—it's reckoned to process around 99,000 search queries per second, which means approximately 8.5 billion searches per day and over 3 trillion global searches a year.

Internet was taking off and I was in the United States, the place where I wanted to be and where I would gain a real understanding of the value and potential of digital technology. I spent the most carefree two years of my life there. Ilaria, the cousin of my friend

Diego whom I had known at Lehman Brothers, wanted to return to Florence. She had a wonderful loft in Soho at a fixed rent with three bedrooms where I went to stay with two roommates: Leonardo Casalini, a guy from Florence who was studying at New York University, and Christian Auer, from Bolzano in northern Italy, who was at Pace University. We became an inseparable and rowdy trio. When Christian returned to Italy, we were joined for one semester by Nasser Kabbaj, who had come from Morocco to study at Columbia.

As excited as I was to be in the United States, which truly felt like the beating heart of the new modern world, I still had Italian blood in my veins. And Italian tastebuds, too. As soon as I settled into my Soho life, I managed to sniff out the nearest Italian grocery, a shop around the corner on Lafayatte Street run by a man named Domenico from the south of Italy, somewhere near Naples. I and my Italian roommates used to go every weekend to buy prosciutto, mozzarella, pasta, and it truly was a taste of home. Visiting Dom's shop also made me stop to consider the deep ties to their heritage felt by so many Italian Americans—new immigrants as well as those who had arrived before or during the peak period of 1880–1920, when over four million Italians made America their new home. They weren't exactly welcomed with open arms at first; as we know, this was a period of discrimination and hostility toward many newcomers to America, encountered by many Irish and Asians too. In fact, though millions stayed and millions more arrived later, as many as 50 percent of the Italians who first came to the United States during that period of what was called "The Great Arrival" returned home within five years—a group called the *ritornati*. Those who stayed brought foods, traditions, cultural elements—and some less savory things too—that became woven into the complex tapestry of America. They were also able to pursue a degree of economic prosperity and security many had never dreamed of before—yes, the American dream.

Meanwhile my own dream was turning into reality: the kid from Ravenna who had managed to get to Milan had now made his way to America. He had woken from his torpor, had worked at Lehman, and knew what he wanted to do. I no longer had to be top of the class, to get top marks: I could study the subjects I enjoyed, those that I would need in future, aware that top marks are useful only for those who want to work in consultancy companies, in investment banks, for those who want to join Goldman Sachs or McKinsey. I, though, wanted to be an entrepreneur, and while everyone in Italy imagined I was busily studying, in reality I spent the whole of my MBA searching for an idea which, to my mind, would "change" the world. They were eighteen interesting, intense, enjoyable and non-competitive months. A unique opportunity in my life to think, to reason, to broaden my mind, to become an adult, and become more aware of what my interests were.

I left finance classes to those who wanted to deal with economics and listings, and instead I chose those classes on entrepreneurship. I was nearly twenty-nine, the ideal moment for launching myself, for creating my own business. Professor Alan Kane's course on retailing was one of those from which I learned a great deal. This helped to turn my attention toward the customer, and I understood how important it is to put yourself in the position of those who are buying, to anticipate what they want, to follow them, to accompany them through the buying process. Kane was practical, effective, he taught you the tricks of the profession, and invited a number of well-known figures to the lectures. This was a technique that I followed in 2021 when I spent a semester at the Bocconi teaching a course to which I gave the title Creating a Startup in the Digital and Sustainable Economy, and involved various entrepreneurs, venture capitalists, and experts on sustainability.

One of the people Kane invited one day was Mickey Drexler, CEO of Gap Inc. and a legend in American retailing: a very powerful man who had run many companies and was regarded as a true guru. That day he gave a mesmerizing lecture that particularly inspired me. I wanted to meet him. I stopped him on the stairs but, instead of congratulating him, I decided to do the opposite and say something negative: "Don't come to Italy. You're going to fail," I said. He continued a few steps down, came back up and asked: "Why?" He then asked his assistant to give me his email address and I gave him mine. I wrote him explaining why, in my view, there was no space at that time for Gap in Italy, telling him about the difficulties foreign brands had in finding interesting locations in Milan. I had begun an exchange of emails with him. It was a real boost to my self-esteem—I had managed to open a dialogue with one of the greatest international CEOs! But it was also a fundamental lesson that has remained with me over the years: Don't be afraid of important people, find the courage to engage with them, to interest them. Don't say well done to them, or something they expect. Surprise them. If nothing happens, if they don't stop on the stairs, too bad, but at least you'll have tried.

During the entrepreneurship course I developed a business plan for an activity that I called *Slow Food in a Fast Food Environment*. The name was *Mediterranea*. We eat very well in my home region of Emilia-Romagna, and as I mentioned earlier, one of our specialties is a type of thin flatbread called *piadina*. I knew that it went well when accompanied by many other ingredients and thought of extending the business to include all quality Italian food. I knew that a taste of Italy gave a competitive advantage and was easily exportable: for a successful formula it was enough to add speed, rapidity not just in delivery but also in the possibility of eating it quickly, even in the street. Time had become a mantra: you had to make the most of it. People are in a hurry. My plan was to produce luxury quality street food made with the finest ingredients, chosen from among the top producers. The project went well, the professors liked it, and for a moment I thought I might really go ahead with it. Then I thought about having to spend at least ten years in front of a food counter, supervising the choice of products, their preparation, their delivery, and realized that food wasn't my passion. I said to myself: "You can't commit yourself to a business you don't love, you can't work twenty hours a day on Piadina & Co. when you don't even have a passion for food!" I felt that the idea was right—the success almost ten years later of Eataly, which is now found in many parts of the world, shows there was space for the quality and excellence of certain small ventures—but it wasn't right for me. It was the embryo of many notions that helped me when I founded YOOX—Italian spirit, speed, care for the customer—and, even if many startup companies that later worked on food have been a success, I decided to wait. I needed to find the inspiration that was right for me.

IN SEARCH OF THE LOST IDEA

There's no point sticking with a project unless you really believe in it. You need to be honest with yourself and decide just how far that idea is right for you personally. Starting up a company means committing to it, living 365 days a year with it. It means knowing it, discovering all its opportunities, its defects, the possibilities that emerge. There's no point doing it unless you feel a single and overwhelming passion, unless you feel prepared to fight tooth and nail to make it work. In this case I didn't, so I decided to let it pass, not even to try it. It was better to continue with my studies and my research.

In addition to useful courses, I took some time away to follow some fascinating lectures. Uma Thurman's father, Bob, a tall giant with a large and varied collection of Texan ties, taught oriental philosophy—he now lectures in Indo-Tibetan Buddhist studies. I attended his course, which was so far removed from what you might expect from an MBA. I also enrolled in Media & Cinema, where they teach you how to do an elevator pitch. What is that? Imagine you're in an elevator with the biggest Hollywood producer, and you have sixty seconds—the time it takes to reach your destination—to tell him your idea for a great movie. I had written two storylines which turned out to be somewhat prophetic. This was 1998, and the first script still sends shivers down my spine. It's called *Conflict of Interest* and it's an action movie, a financial spy story, halfway between *Casino Royale* (2006) and the September 11 attacks. It starts off with a CNN report on an air disaster, the third in six months. The finger of blame points to Iraqi terrorists who are striking America with various terrorist attacks in retaliation for the Gulf War. The US president has already ordered the army to invade Baghdad and then to remove Saddam Hussein. Hilary, a talented thirty-seven-year-old FBI agent, a Harvard graduate, has just fifteen days to solve the case. She remembers her professor telling her that air company shares drop 20–30 percent on the day after a crash, enabling some investors to speculate on the fall in the market. Hilary has a feeling that this could be the key to solve the investigation but has only four days before the president gives the go-ahead for the attack on Baghdad. She asks the SEC (Securities and Exchange Commission) for all the data on investors in American airline companies and discovers in this way that one of the funds was not only among the short sellers of shares but was also one of the firms that would be appointed to rebuild Iraq. The fund belongs to one of her friends, the billionaire Gavin Hodrick, who has paid mercenaries to blow up the airplanes and to pretend to be Islamic terrorists in order to trigger the war. Hilary has twenty-four hours in which to arrest Gavin and convince Washington, the FBI, and the president that Iraq is not responsible, thereby preventing the war. The marketing pitch that I attached to my script explained that the movie brought together terrorism and Wall Street corruption and might attract Hollywood stars interested in playing lead roles in the story.

The attack on the Twin Towers took place three years later and would shock the world. I was terrified when it happened and thought the FBI and the CIA might suspect me: I had imagined everything three years beforehand, except that the planes really were in the hands of Islamic terrorists and the United States did topple Saddam Hussein.

On rereading the second pitch of the course, this now seems prophetic too. The story is philosophical and fantastical, a kind of precursor of *The Matrix*, and very different from the first. It's called *2099 Paradise* and is divided into two parts. Part one: in a hundred years' time we'll be able to recreate Paradise, and someone will be behind this creation. New York will be bathed in bright blue, scientists will be able to create an ideal climate, automobiles will be electric, there will be neither smog nor sound pollution. People will be happy, clothing minimalist, technology will have triumphed. Everyone will have a microchip planted into their brains at birth (what Elon Musk is doing with his Neuralink) thus simplifying communication. We will also have a small portable computer that will choose what we eat, how we shop, what we do. Sex will be virtual, and abuse will disappear. Babies will be born through virgin birth. Part two: the screen goes dark while a baby comes into the world, and the creator, a mega computer, Maestro, appears and directs the orchestra of life. Each beep is a person who is born or dies. It's rather like what will happen with artificial intelligence....

I've always loved science fiction: *2001: Space Odyssey* and *Blade Runner* are two of my favorite movies. They're philosophical, Orwellian, and they predict what will happen, exactly what I most like: to bring together imagination and fantasy so that we can dream and project ourselves into tomorrow. I'm so drawn toward the future. I think about it so often that I sometimes seem to see it even before it arrives.

I don't remember a happier period in my life. Everything in New York seemed to fit together perfectly. Columbia was providing me with all the tools to become a good entrepreneur; the United States was encouraging me to believe in my own potential, giving me the hope that I too would be a part of the American dream, that everyone has a chance to make it. I seemed to be breathing a new air—and air of opportunity, ideas, merit and intuition. I wanted to capitalize on all this.

At the end of the 1990s, the city was at its best: stimulating, fast, intriguing, adrenaline-charged. And I was much changed. I was no longer shy—I loved this sweet-tasting and exciting metropolis. I wanted to experience it all.

JUST LET YOURSELF GO

The house where I lived was the other side of Manhattan from the university, I had to take a long subway journey to get there, so I concentrated my courses from Monday to Wednesday, so that I had Thursdays, Fridays, and weekends Downtown all to myself. At Columbia I had three close friends: Kristen Mustad, a Norwegian; Nasser Kabbaj, a Moroccan; and Michele Ridolfo, a fellow Italian. We were a fun and close-knit international quartet.

With Leonardo and Christian, on the other hand, I organized Italian dinners: my specialty was risotto, which I still do at Christmas with mushrooms—a traditional dish that's ideal for those like me who absolutely can't cook. Preparing it requires a certain expressiveness, almost a sensuality, that used to fascinate American girls. Leonardo was great with roast meats while Christian was the god of the tiramisu. Guests were surprised by these hosts who worked so well together that they could rustle up a three-course meal in no time, and they were always happy to return. We organized parties and celebrations. The most memorable was my thirtieth birthday. The house was in darkness, all the shutters closed, I'd found some disco lights and a DJ who often played in Ibiza. The dress code was everyone in black. I alone wore a white suit with white twisted devil horns—that's right, I wanted to be the center of attention because with those lights the whiteness became dazzling. I'd been to a Chinese shop in Canal Street and had bought phosphorescent plates and glasses that lit up with me. It was a dinner based on sushi, a discotheque, and a special party. At two in the morning, two policemen turned up. I promised we would turn the volume down and told them it was my birthday party, that friends had come from all over: from Milan, London, Paris, Los Angeles. At which point one of them said "Enjoy!" and they left. Our cleaner did the same thing the next morning when she opened the door and found us half asleep on the sofa with everything in disorder, as in *The Hangover* (and in effect, everything imaginable had happened, as in the film). She refused to clean up, slammed the door, and was never seen again.

I really had changed, was no longer introverted, and had become indeed more enterprising. I had several girlfriends: the latest was Hilary Bowers. She was the assistant to Edward Pressman, a famous movie producer, and worked particularly with Abel Ferrara, a genial and capricious director who drove her mad. Hilary would follow me when I returned to Italy.

Let's take a leap forward. It was May 1999, the moment of my graduation. My parents couldn't come because my father wasn't well. I understood, tried not to get upset about it, and focused on after, on what to do from there on. There were two roads in front of me: I could either remain in the States or I could do like *haigui*, like Chinese students who return home after attending foreign universities, like sea turtles (the word is actually a Chinese pun) that return to their native beach.

I tried the United States. I sent my curriculum to Disney, but they didn't even consider me—I wasn't even called for an interview. There again, in America, it's hard to employ anyone from abroad who doesn't have a green card. And I wasn't interested in working from Italy: I wanted to be there, where the decisions are made. I had read *Mickey Mouse* since I was a child; Walt Disney for me was the brand that conjures dreams, that creates and fosters imagination. It's a magnetic universe, and a company I've always loved. Many years later, in October 2019, when I was invited to Laguna Beach, on the West Coast, to talk at the annual conference of *Wall Street Journal Tech Live*, I found myself at a table with Demi Moore, Naomi Campbell, Lachlan Murdoch (Rupert's son) and above all with Bob Iger, the legendary CEO of Walt Disney, who was launching Disney+. I was thrilled because he was my idol, and I told him his company was where I would have liked to have worked more than anywhere else.

After being turned down by Disney in 1999, I tried other broadcasters but with no success: apart from one offer, from a small producer. Everyone else ignored me. I went to see the producer; his office was in a cramped dark basement in which I too would have to work, dealing with accounts. I was disappointed, I didn't like the place at all, and asked myself: "You've worked so hard, are you going to put up with this measly offer just for the sake of living in America?" Maybe the American Dream was elsewhere.

"NOTHING IS KNOWN, EVERYTHING IS IMAGINED"

I love cinema, entertainment and the media in general, it's a sector that interests me, but not under these conditions. I refused the job, even if movies and science fiction are two things I've always followed. I'm a great admirer of Federico Fellini, who has inspired me in many things. He had twelve Oscar nominations and received four statuettes, plus one as a special lifetime award. He was a world movie giant, a visionary, born in Rimini, in the heart of Romagna, and used imagination like nobody else. He used to say "nothing is known, everything is imagined," and I have tried to follow this precept, in my work and in my life. I started from imagination, from dreams I had with my eyes open. I didn't know whether I'd manage to achieve them, but it was important to continue letting the imagination wander. My mind is regenerated in this way, with the unknown that can become reality, with digressions that follow their own fascinating course. I watch Fellini movies time and again, and know some scenes from memory, so when YOOX and the Bologna Cineteca digitally restored one of his masterpieces, *Amarcord*, we put it on CD and gave it to various personalities of the tech galaxy, drawing a very mixed response.

Bill Gates was happy to receive it. It was 2016 and I was one of the very few Italians invited to the tech summit organized by Microsoft at Redmond. Every CEO from the major American corporations was at the meeting, and no one knew YOOX. I felt like a fish out of water. Gates was sitting a few meters from me, highly focused as he took notes on his computer, and it seemed impossible even to approach him. Reed Hastings, co-founder of Netflix, was there too: I suggested a TV series to him on fashion, which I'm still thinking about. "When the storyline is ready, let me have it," he said. And maybe one day I'll write it.

A dinner was held in the evening at the Gates villa, Xanadu 2.0, a magnificent and endless building with a surprising and highly original architecture. It is built on a hill overlooking Lake Washington, an enchanting place: design and technology have found their Eden. Feeling rather like Peter Sellers in *The Party* (in which an Indian film extra ends up by accident at the party of a Hollywood mega-producer), I started wandering around the rooms and came across the wonderful Leonardo da Vinci codex in a display cabinet. I was spellbound and admired many other priceless works of art hanging on the walls. I even nosed around the refrigerator to see what someone like Bill eats, and found it in robotic order, rather like he is. The fridge was full of jars with labels and the name of the person who was to eat it: Melinda, Bill and their children Jennifer, Rory, and Phoebe. As

I continue roaming the house, I see Bill alone, holding a plate of sushi. I approach and ask him for a selfie—how could I resist the idea of a selfie with Bill Gates!—and I tell him I've brought him a CD with a restored copy of *Amarcord* (I had checked what format could be watched in the States but later discovered he had a projection room that could show any resolution). He knew everything about Fellini, was well-informed and knowledgeable, told me about his films and awards, and I think he appreciated that unexpected gesture.

I couldn't say the same for Kevin Systrom, co-founder of Instagram, who I'd met a couple of days before, and who had declared with much satisfaction that Roberto Benigni was the director of *Amarcord,* whereas Gates, as well as being a fan of European cinema, remembered even the year, 1975, in which Fellini had received the Oscar for that film.

STAY OR RETURN?

My studies in New York had come to an end, as well as my disastrous attempts to find work in America. Now I had just two options: to carry on trying, or to leave the United States for good and go back to Italy. This, I realized, was the only true prospect, and my dream in reality was to create a company in my own country. I was convinced an Italian product would provide enormous advantages and I wanted to link it to technology, but my idea was still not complete. I had all the tesserae but couldn't yet piece together the mosaic. I knew that I needed to combine my attention to the customer with a digital method and an Italian product. But what? For the moment I had no answer.

It was mid-May 1999, and I decided to take a long vacation before resuming work.

My friend Diego, whom I'd met at Lehman, was sailing round the world in a yacht. His family, the Paternò Castello di San Giuliano family, is one of the oldest and most noble in Sicily. His father, Giuseppe, was a charming and elegant man who seemed to have come straight out of *The Leopard*: a dandy with an endless and eclectic wardrobe. Giuseppe was a globe-trotter and was returning from Brazil, where his father had moved after World War II, and had known Fiamma Ferragamo, the daughter of the shoe designer Salvatore. She had taken over running the company with her mother and brothers, and she and Giuseppe had married in 1969. When she died in 1998, I returned to Italy for her funeral. Giuseppe lived in a wonderful house in Florence, frescoed throughout and with a thousand objects of exquisite beauty. He would be an important figure in my life.

So I called Diego, who was in Polynesia, and he suggested I join him for a couple of months. He told me to meet him on a specific day at the end of May at a remote bay, several hours' drive from the airport on the Marquesas Islands, in the middle of the Pacific. I arrived punctually as usual. But unfortunately there was no sign of Diego that afternoon, nor that evening, nor throughout the night. I couldn't call him: my cell phone had no signal. So I lay on the beach in the moonlight.

At a certain point, like in a horror film, a whole army of crabs arrived. I jumped onto a parapet wall, which was covered with blood suckers, and there were large fishes in the water with which I didn't fancy my chances. So I spent the whole night standing up, and at dawn the boat appeared. Diego and the rest of the crew had been sailing for several months. They had a very relaxed approach to time and decided to stay in port for several weeks. The days went by. They still had a long voyage in front of them, and I had just a few weeks when at last we decided to sail toward Tuamotu, one of the Polynesian archipelagoes. We arrived at an almost deserted island which, until a month before, had been in the hands of the French foreign legion that guarded the nuclear testing site at Mururoa. It had always been out of bounds to tourists. We docked in the port flying the Italian flag, and a legionary ran up to greet us, waving his arms. He was Italian and treated us with great kindness, bringing us fresh milk from the base and introducing us to the captain. To return the favor we invited him to spend a weekend sailing with us. He accepted immediately and reappeared the following morning with a T-shirt, toothbrush, and a bag with a gigantic fishhook. We had been trawl-fishing and had just caught a large tuna. He gutted it and put the entrails onto the hook.

After a few seconds, an enormous shark took the bait; he hauled it onto the boat and immobilized it with a single finger pressed onto its back. We were terrified. Spielberg's *Jaws* is the most frighting movie I've ever seen and sharks for me were a taboo, but he reassured us. Next day I followed him into the water, and we swam within three meters of these marvelous fishes. I felt as if I were in front of a vast TV screen. Since that day I developed a fascination for oceans and became an avid viewer of documentaries and Instagram accounts that show images of the sea and explain that sharks aren't so nasty.

Once the vacation was over, it was time to start. I seemed to have a clock chasing after me, telling me I had to hurry, that I had to move on from this long surge of American optimism. It was time to stop talking and start doing something about my future. I took the plane and flew home. It was my destiny, it seemed, to be another of the *ritornati*.

4

I arrived in Milan and started my job at Bain on September 1, 1999. We were at the end of the millennium, a moment of transition and change. The world as we knew it would soon be gone. According to the economic and social theorist Jeremy Rifkin, "The great economic revolutions in history occur when new communication revolutions merge with new energy regimes."

In his book *The Third Industrial Revolution,* he traces the steps from the early farming societies of Mesopotamia, Egypt, and India, which had to invent writing to manage the complexity of cultivation, warehousing, and seed distribution, up to the beginning of the modern age, where the convergence between the invention of coal-powered steam technology and the printing press gave rise to the industrial revolution. He continues:

> *In the late Nineteenth century and throughout the first two thirds of the Twentieth century, first generation electrical forms of communication—the telegraph, telephone, radio, television, electric typewriters, calculators, etc.—converged with the introduction of oil and the internal combustion engine, becoming the communications command and control mechanism for organizing and marketing the second industrial revolution. A great communications revolution occurred in the 1990s. Second generation*

> *electrical forms of communication—personal computers, the internet, the World Wide Web, and wireless communication technologies—connected the central nervous system of more than a billion people on Earth at the speed of light. And, although the new software and communication revolutions have begun to increase productivity in every industry, their true potential is yet to be fully realized.*

At the end of the twentieth century, the Third Industrial Revolution was at a turning point. And while technological innovation, the birth of the robot, space shuttles, and above all the central role of information, have opened the road toward new frontiers, in the dawning years of the 2000s everything was in place for a new era, for a leap into the future. A form of interconnection was being created that would change our way of working, of producing, and of communicating.

The world didn't yet know it—though it already had its doubts—but it would soon have a change of heart. On the night of December 31, 1999, millions of people throughout the world went to sleep terrified. Various gurus of digital technology had forecast that the Millennium Bug would crash their computers. They would wake on January 1—some hadn't slept the whole night, waiting for hour X—to discover that nothing had happened, but the notion that technology was still fragile and unreliable was widely felt.

At the end of the 1990s people were still communicating by landline telephone. Cell phones—mostly Nokia—were still rare and had none of the functions that smartphones have today. Cell phones were used simply for calling or sending text messages. Connection to the internet was made through extremely slow modems at 56 Kbps. Apple, created in 1976 from a brilliant idea of its founder, Steve Jobs, was fighting to establish its identity and was still waiting for Jobs's brainwave, in 2007, which would be the iPhone. Facebook didn't exist—it was still only in the imagination of Zuckerberg who would launch it in 2004, while Twitter and Instagram weren't even on the horizon. Amazon had been created by Jeff Bezos just a few years before but was still far from reaching the shores of Italy, where it arrived in 2010.

In 1999, just 3.6 million Italians were connected to the internet, rising to 10.8 million in November 2000. In 2000, only 6.8 percent of the world population used the net—today there are 8 billion of us, of which 5.5 billion have access. If we think of what has happened in just twenty years, we see how the acceleration has been supersonic, so fast and deep-rooted.

Could it all have been foreseen? Maybe yes, maybe no. In order to glimpse what could happen, everything needs to be viewed with fresh eyes, with curiosity and, as always in such cases, with a good dose of audacity. Not everything was clear, betting on the future can be risky, but it's the greatest adrenaline-rush imaginable. It needs to be tried.

I made my appearance in this new era with no technological background, I had no digital experience, I wasn't a computer scientist, I didn't know any programming language, but I had the feeling that we'd reached a frontier, a moment of transition from an old to a new paradigm. I wanted to be there. I wanted to be one of the protagonists in this revolution that the internet was bringing like a storm in a clear sky. I wanted to get there first. I wanted to try out the potential of this medium that had fascinated me from the first day I used it at Lehman Brothers. I wanted to be a pioneer in this still unexplored terrain.

I wasn't happy at Bain. I had asked the head of human resources to move me to the area that follows retail projects—I've always had an interest in customers and sales—and to use me in their fashion sector, since it attracted me from the aesthetic point of view. They had agreed to this before I accepted the job. But instead, the first project they put me on was Plasmon baby foods, and then, if that weren't enough, I was moved to BTicino electrical switches.

I was frustrated, dissatisfied, didn't like the work, and didn't get on with my bosses, who I respected less than those at Lehman Brothers. There was just one thought in my mind: to get out as soon as I could.

That summer was now a distant memory, America was far away, and the October days in Milan were turning ever gloomier, reflecting my mood—I felt depressed and kept saying: "What a dead end! You wanted to start your own company and now you're caught in a routine you don't like." Maybe this was the fuse, the spark that made me erupt. When you're happy, you delay decisions, you avoid throwing yourself into new projects because, after all, what you're doing is fine, you're satisfied. But when your life seems to be falling apart, when you can't see the way ahead, then you're more willing to take a risk, to throw yourself into some new experiment, since anything is better than what you have.

That was exactly my situation—I didn't like the direction that my work was taking—so I decided to go for it. At first, I could see no way through. I spent my evenings at home trying to create an idea for a business that might work. "Federico," I told myself, "that's enough, stop whining, do something, it's time to think about your startup."

I knew the internet was becoming a real revolution in America, and that many young people were finding easy funding to create their own businesses. Banks had never been so ready to finance those with no capital to offer as a guarantee. I had none, my parents certainly couldn't help me, but I was convinced the timing was perfect.

I began to link up some of the points I'd been focusing on and regarded as essential: digital technology, Italian quality, attention to the customer, and speed. I thought about the areas where Italy is strong, in which Italian products provided a guarantee, synonymous with quality and beauty, and I chose fashion. My competitive advantage was that I'm Italian, I live in the country which creates the fashion that's sought throughout the world. I wasn't in Silicon Valley, but I was a few steps away from the top artisans, designers, brands. The right place is where your future partners are, because it's from there that you need to start, and since a market didn't yet exist, to create one you need to start from supply and then attract demand. I just needed to find a way of merging fashion with the immense flow of digital technology which, I was sure, would overwhelm our lives in a few years. The project began to form in my mind.

As a good son of Ravenna, I thought once again about those wonderful ancient mosaics in my city, made with tiny fragments, never perfectly equal because they are of different sizes, placed beside each other to create a fixed image. The Ravenna mosaics are like puzzles. Their wonderful workmanship is carried out by fragmentation and reassembly of the material from which they are made—tiny squares of marble, shells, glass and mother-of-pearl which, together, go to form the decorated surfaces and figurative elements that everyone admires. YOOX was also a mosaic, an assembly of ideas. I had no flash of inspiration; I didn't wake up one morning with a sudden brainwave. Instead, I spent evening after evening, sitting and trying to build an outline into which, little by little, I fitted the pieces that I had in mind. Mine was a plan thought up at the drawing board, with a thousand lines of reasoning and intuitions that lined up, like planets, forming a simple, interesting project that didn't yet exist. YOOX was the product of reason and awareness.

AGAINST ALL REASONABLE LIKELIHOOD

The genius often creates alone, has an idea that might be feasible in the future but isn't always possible to achieve. This is why many geniuses are not understood, because they are so far ahead of their times and so highly imaginative that many of the things they propose at first remain enigmas. When creating a startup, on the other hand, it's important to follow your own intuition, especially if you're aiming toward unexplored areas where no one has ventured before. You need courage and mustn't listen to those voices that say: it's impossible, out of the question, you'll fail.

Let's go back to early November 1999. I was now sure there was only one way to merge fashion and technology: by selling clothing online. No one had ever done it, but if Amazon was becoming America's e-commerce leader in books, I asked myself: "Why not try it with clothing?"

In the early 2000s, fashion was a closed, elitist enclave, and shops themselves were the temple of this microcosm to such an extent that fashion houses thought of their "customers" as the shops and not the people. Fashion shows were reserved for insiders, the collections were kept secret for six months, and items of clothing had a short life, which became even shorter with the expansion, at the other extreme, of fast fashion. But fashion was also an extraordinary market that was destined to grow.

My project seemed simple but, in truth, to be successful it required a complicated architecture and engineering that would prove above all to be a sound investment for the future. I wasn't a fashion expert but had a strong aesthetic sense and a notion of beauty that I always followed in YOOX. I wanted to sell fashion and luxury online. I wasn't even an IT expert, but I was the "end user" of the technology. I saw it from my point of view and realized it had all the potential for becoming highly useful and, above all, user-friendly.

I then imagined being the very first customer in an imaginary, virtual store, the first person to go through its doorway via their computer, to find themself in a wonderland. I could choose clothes in different colors and forms, in different styles, from different collections and different periods. I just had to choose, using my imagination, match them together, buy them with my credit card, and wait in the comfort of my own home for someone to deliver them. And I also thought, once I had decided what to keep and what not, that I could then return those items I didn't want to this techno-store.

The idea struck me immediately as strong and persuasive, but to achieve this would mean bringing together two worlds—those of luxury and technology—that had never met, that seemed far apart and suspicious of each other. Luxury is warm. Technology is cold. Luxury is exciting, elite, mysterious, slow, sensual, and unpredictable. Technology is rational, exact, rapid, repetitive, and democratic. How could two such mutually different entities find a way of working together? Which of the two should predominate? Was there a right proportion for the mix to work? The answer was yes; putting together two different entities can create a unique phenomenon and, as for the proportions, the choice to be made was an impartial fifty-fifty.

At the dawn of 2000, the two sectors—the internet and fashion—had never worked together and were not yet aware of the close but potentially explosive connection they would have in the coming years. Jeff Bezos, in his book *Invent & Wander,* tells how he directed his attention toward e-commerce because he had read that the internet had grown by 2,300 percent. I too was convinced that the margins of increase were enormous but, above all, I was convinced that I could be the first person in the world to embrace the idea of bringing together these two entities that were so different and yet so much in need of the other. Since I was a child, I had always been attracted by opposites.

At the end of the 1980s Italy achieved a miracle: Half a dozen fashion designers focused the spotlight on glamour—first in Florence, then in Milan and Rome. Giorgio Armani, Valentino, Gianni Versace, the Fendi sisters, the Missoni family, had invented "Made in Italy," had made their models universally desirable and saleable. It was 1980, the year of *American Gigolo,* when Richard Gere's wardrobe, created by Giorgio Armani, burst into the collective imagination as well as into Hollywood productions and the star system. From that day, Richard Gere's image was that of unstructured suits in tones of grey, lightweight shirts, and matching ties that the stylist had designed for him. In this way, the new sensual, chic, smooth uniform of modern man was born, and Italy became the Eldorado of glamour, "the place to be," and above all "the place to shop."

The story had started not in the 1980s but with Salvatore Ferragamo, the first Italian stylist to arrive in the United States, when he moved to Santa Barbara and opened a small repair shop, and in just a few years had become the "Shoemaker of Dreams." Salvatore was the eleventh of fourteen children, born in a poor village in Campania, southern Italy, who went to join three of his brothers in America, became famous for the cowboy boots he made for western movies, and worked for some of the leading directors of the time, from D. W. Griffith to Cecil B. DeMille. The American press went mad over him, calling him "The Shoemaker," and when the film industry became synonymous with Hollywood, he moved with it, opening a shop in Hollywood Boulevard. Salvatore's adventure would later become a magnificent documentary directed by my friend Luca Guadagnino.

The stories of all the major figures in "Made in Italy" have become fairy-tale legends. They each believed in themselves, they each made it alone, and customers around the world started dreaming just at the mention of their names.

I was mesmerized by what they had managed to achieve, by their incredible, powerful approach that began from nothing and reached the stars. I felt that Italian fashion was the best sector with which to work, with which to create an association of names.

I began work in October and started to put down a business plan, to think about how to make this idea as smart as possible, about how to persuade people to buy clothing online, even if they've never done it before. Those friends to whom I described it thought I was crazy; they told me nobody would buy clothing without trying it on, that it would be a flop because women love shopping in main street stores on Saturday afternoons. Everyone tried to dissuade me: They kept telling me we weren't in America where some cities had very few stores and the leading brands were impossible to find. Here in Italy, they said, even the smaller towns had marvelous shops that sold many brands and where customers loved receiving advice and assistance. I tried not to listen to these doomsters—it's sometimes important to remain impervious and to ignore the advice of those who stand against change. You need to find a way of getting round obstacles.

I knew customers as yet had no experience, that they would need to be helped, encouraged, almost educated in the online experience. I then decided that the simplest and most sensible thing was to start with surplus stock, with unsold clothing from the previous season, which had the advantage of costing less. My idea was to overcome customer resistance to distance buying by offering them products that are beautiful but less expensive than those available in the stores. I wanted to play on creativity, quality, and saving.

In my business plan the objective was very clear: to become world e-commerce leader in fashion and luxury, which is what effectively happened. I decided that my project would be international from the very start and, in fact, the first order to arrive would be from Holland, for a Versace dress that cost around L.80,000 (about €40).

I had clear ideas and a definite plan. It was now time to put them into action. I wrote to my friend Diego, who was still on his yacht in the Indian Ocean, suggesting that we do this project together. His father Giuseppe, the marquis, owned among other things a stock wholesale business in Florence—managed by a keen and intelligent Neapolitan, Gennaro Grosso, who knew this world extremely well—and a small shop at Casalecchio di Reno, just outside Bologna, run by Alberto Giuliani, who bought stock for some of the finest stores in Italy. Gennaro and Alberto, with whom I later worked for years, taught me all the tricks of the trade, such as how, where, and from whom to buy the previous year's collections. I explained to Diego that we could take products from his companies and resell them online on a specially built website, that we could create a highly innovative company, and could divide the shares fifty-fifty. I would later realize that I could have offered a lower percentage, but it's also true that I couldn't have started up so quickly without them. Finally, after several days, Diego gave his answer: he agreed!

I wanted to find the right name. I wanted it to be short, pronounceable in any language—as I've already said, I never intended to stop at Italy, I'm after the whole world—and would prefer it to have very few letters. I tried putting together a few letters that I liked, that had some meaning: an *X*, a *Y*, and two *O*s. *YOOX* came out. I really liked it; I found it musical, harmonious, modern, sufficiently mysterious to make people want to know more. And above all, it's a brand. YOOX is a name that includes the chromosomes of man and woman, *Y* and *X*, and mixes in two *O*s which can also be the zeros of binary code. The DNA of technology is held inside that of man and woman: a philosophical manifesto that well described the identity of the project and would remain perfectly valid and relevant through the years to come. The two *O*s together reminded me at first only of technology—Google, Yahoo!—but in fact they've been almost prophetic because they refer to all the projects on sustainability and circularity that we have done. When seen together, side by side, they are the sign of the infinite, and Infinity is the very name we gave to a vast initiative—the last that I endorsed as CEO of the YOOX Net-a-Porter Group—on respecting the environment, that I'll mention later.

I tried to register the domain name and found it miraculously free. It cost me a handful of dollars, and www.yoox.com was mine!

The idea had taken concrete form, it belonged to me: there were all the elements that excited me, that could make the difference.

DIGITAL PIONEER

The idea of having a digital company in Italy wasn't straightforward. Indeed, it required much courage and a great deal of madness and vision. The sector was in its infancy, and few were betting on how it would develop. I didn't come from that sphere, I knew little about it, and yet I had very clear ideas about what I wanted to do.

But first I had to leave my job, and then I had to find investors. This is where I began. I contacted various people in November and December, meeting them in the evening or on a Saturday when I wasn't working. This is how I got to know Paolo Ainio, who had created Virgilio.it, the first web portal and search engine in Italy, and Carlo Gualandri, with whom he had founded Matrix. Two Italian startup gurus, two personalities who, along with Marco Benatti, breathed life into the Italian digital sector. Ainio liked my project but then disappeared, stopped answering my telephone calls. Almost everyone asked me the same question: "Who else will be putting up the money, apart from us?" And my answer was always: "No one, yet." At that point they vanished. I'm convinced that the real venture capitalists are those who have an instinct, those who sense before everyone else when it's worth investing in a startup, those who risk and often score. But everyone in Italy at that time was too cautious and too reluctant to take a chance.

My former boss at Lehman Brothers, Ruggero Magnoni, introduced me to the industrialist Carlo De Benedetti, who received me at his offices in Milan and invited me to work for CDB Web Tech, but I was no longer interested in finance. When I told him I was planning a startup, he sent me to his son Rodolfo who, with great intuition and before anyone else, offered me L.500 million (around €250,000) in return for a 50 percent share in the company. But I had already offered a 50 percent share to Diego and, in any event, I knew that such an amount wouldn't be enough to achieve the ambitious undertaking I had in mind. On the first page of my business plan I wrote: "YOOX is the global e-commerce partner for the leading fashion brands." I didn't just want to start a little techno-store for selling stock, I wanted to start a revolution.

Unfortunately, it wasn't so easy because I had a debt with Bain. They had paid my fees for my master's degree, but the sum I needed to repay was much higher than what I had received because there was tax on top; I had received the net figure, but I had to return the gross, which was more or less double. Result: a load of money. I didn't know what to do; my future seemed bleaker and bleaker: I saw myself spending many years at Bain to repay the loan.

One day, however, my life suddenly changed, taking an unexpected path. I went for lunch with Fabio Canè, who asked me what was wrong—I was now finding it increasingly difficult to conceal my depression. I explained that I had an idea for a business but had no money and didn't want to work another two years for Bain. At that point Fabio said: "I'll lend you the money,

I'm sure you'll pay it back," and he wrote out a personal check in the restaurant at the end of the meal and did so without getting me to sign any undertaking or asking the advice of any lawyer.

I couldn't believe it. Instantly, I felt a different person, I could hardly control myself and, without even finding an investor, I decided to leave my job.

I talked to Giovanni Cagnoli, the CEO of Bain, and explained my idea but, instead of encouraging me, he told me I had until Christmas to return the money. I was happy to have Canè's check in my pocket and proudly replied: "Here it is!" and I left, slamming the door behind me.

We're at the end of 1999: I was unemployed, with no money, and now in debt to Canè. I left Bain instinctively, without considering the consequences, with no alternative plan. "Federico, what will you do?" my mother said. "I know you couldn't cope any longer, but now..." before then adding: "I'm sure you'll manage!"

In a further act of recklessness, I decided to go to Brazil for the Christmas holidays. If YOOX was really going to take off, I knew I would need to immerse myself body and soul 24/7 in my work. So I flew off to Rio de Janeiro with a group of friends, and on to Trancoso. I left everything behind, with the sole commitment to return on January 6, as I had to start on the seventh, with no further excuses, and work full-time to find an investor. If I didn't find the money, I really did risk ending up in Brazil—though not on vacation this time but making *piadine*—and yet I was still convinced in my heart of hearts that I would succeed, that my idea was at last the right one, and that someone, when I got back, would be sure to understand it. That I would find someone who would help me.

In recent years, when I meet young people, they often ask: "If I don't like my job, should I leave it? Should I risk it, take a gamble, maybe take a leap in the dark?" My answer is always: "The answer lies with you. Are you really fed up? Do you think you can create a startup of your own? Do you have an idea that you really believe in? If your answer is yes, then you know what you must do. Take a risk, choose the right moment, and make a change in your life." As Jeff Bezos writes in his autobiography: "I knew that if I failed I wouldn't regret that, but I knew the one thing I might regret is not trying." Finding a job is extremely difficult, leaving it with nothing to fall back on might seem absurd, but I invite them to see things the other way round. Creating a startup means creating jobs. With their microbusinesses they can turn the situation round, and instead of going looking for work, they themselves can offer work to other young people who are desperate to satisfy their hunger for commitment, creativity, and devotion to a new initiative that makes them feel useful and appreciated.

Courage and madness often seem to go hand in hand, but if the courage involves a practicable project, the madness is pushed aside and leaves room only for boldness and intuition.

Returning to my story, I flew back from Brazil and was in Milan again by January 6. Time was running out, I needed to find money, I could wait no longer. In a moment of desperation, not knowing who to turn to, I picked up the Yellow Pages—those were the days of fat telephone directories that listed people's numbers—and I looked up Elserino Piol. Who was Piol? A remarkable person who sadly died in 2023. He grew up at Olivetti, where he started off as a programmer of punch-card machines, rising to vice president. He left in 1996 to concentrate on venture capital and financing startups. It was Piol who introduced Steve Jobs to Mario Bellini, the chief design consultant at Olivetti and the designer of Programma 101, the world's first personal computer. It was he who inspired Steve Jobs to bring together design and technology, form and function—whoever would have imagined that there's a touch of Italy even in Apple!

It was also Piol, together with Oliver Novick, who was responsible for the birth and success of Tiscali, the first Italian telecoms company to offer free access to internet. It was thanks to them that the web spread throughout Italy.

Elserino Piol was extremely fast and clear-thinking, his decisions were instant and had immediate effect. With his red braces he looked like the star of a movie about Wall Street, but in fact he was the founder of venture capital in Italy and responsible for the growth of the internet in our country.

In short, I dialed the number, asked for an appointment, and went with Fabio Canè to meet Piol and his right-hand man, Andrea Di Camillo. In two weeks they drafted an agreement. At the end of February, Elserino said: "Okay, I'll give you L.3 billion [around €1.5 million] in exchange for thirty-three percent of the company. But you have three months to get going. I'll give you the next slice only if in that space of time you've set up all the logistics, the technological platform, the team, and have generated the first orders."

Piol had immediately sensed the novelty and realized that selling collections from past years could be an innovative and successful resource. He gave me the money and laid down the timescale. I had some very tight deadlines but a clear objective: in ninety days I had to set up the whole company, the technological side, the sales platform, the software, and the clothing warehouse. At this point I rented a small building next to the shop at

Casalecchio di Reno, near Bologna, owned by Giuseppe di San Giuliano: The idea was to transfer a part of their products so that we could digitize and try to sell them on yoox.com.

I called Diego and told him: "It's done, we have the money. I'll deal with the company, it's your job to persuade your father and the two people who work with him to make their whole stock available to us for the startup's first seasons." I suggested having the products on consignment, so that, if a customer came in and bought an item at the shop in Casalecchio, I would remove that item from my availability, whereas if the customer buys on YOOX, he would remove it from the shop's availability. This operation, known as omnichannel—which I'll describe later—is used today by all brands, but I realized almost immediately that it was an impracticable nightmare. Computers were not yet able to synchronize operations and update in real time. It was a superb idea, but too complicated and too advanced for the time. We therefore decided to give YOOX its own inventory. I told Diego that his 50 percent of the capital would be translated into a certain number of products that I would choose and put up for sale in my techno-store, and that if I had sold nothing by the end of the summer, I'd return all the clothes.

I was absorbed twenty-four hours a day in the construction of my business. I decided not to do any market research since it's impossible to ask people if they're satisfied or if they trust a thing that doesn't exist—there was no such thing as an online market for clothing and accessories, so that no one could have a view—negative or positive—about it. Better not to waste time and to think instead about who to employ, about the website, about the opening date for the company.

THE MAGIC OF DATES

Let's start with the date. Piol's money—L.3 billion—arrived on March 21, the day of the spring equinox. I've already said that dates fascinate me: I think they hold a magic that I want to grasp. Timing is crucial, not just because our destiny is written in numbers, but also because it can be fatal to arrive late, the whole operation may be compromised. And later I'll explain why. It therefore seemed a good omen that the beginning of spring coincided with the beginning of my business. I signed the company's articles of association a couple of days before: The appointment was at midday at the office of a public notary in Bologna. I took the early train and sat opposite, almost in front of, a beautiful young woman. As you will have understood, I'm more of a nerd than a Romagnolo Latin lover, I don't have the killer looks that attract women, and it often takes me quite a while and a long period of acquaintance before a relationship gets going. This time, however, I was aware the girl was looking at me. I turned to see whether anyone else was behind and, since there wasn't, I assumed that I was the object of her attentions. I couldn't believe it! I moved seats and we started talking. She's a model and in Italy for a photo shoot, but most of all she tells me she's Miss Venezuela. She invited me to go with her to Rome, not to stop at Bologna. I didn't know what to do: on the one hand there was the notary and YOOX waiting to be born; on the other there was this sweet and irresistible young woman to whom I already feel attracted. What do I do? Continue? No. I got off at Bologna. I went to the notary's office and established YOOX SpA.

After the deed of agreement, I had an enormous clock hanging round my neck. Piol was clear: I had precise objectives to reach and ninety days to reach them.

5

On March 21, 2000, my great adventure begins for real. My dream of becoming an entrepreneur is so close that I feel I can touch it: I have just three months to create YOOX, to transform an idea into reality.

Some ten days before I started, on March 10, shares on Nasdaq had reached an overall value exceeding $6,700 billion. From 1995 to 2000 the growth of tech companies had been vertiginous, and this had also been swept along by share speculation. There were hundreds of new startups every day, especially in America, and any company with ".com" in its name was sure to obtain finance. The quotation of internet companies at the beginning of 2000 took the Nasdaq index to 5,100 points—in 1995 it had reached over 1,000 points for the first time. Excitement was sky-high. Everyone wanted to finance these young Silicon Valley neo-entrepreneurs who were pervading American customs and lifestyles with their clever new ideas: producers of computers, e-commerce, search engines but also small startups that were using digital systems and technology to manage their businesses. Enthusiasm for a new sector fueled expectations: internet mania and the New Economy spread fast.

March 11, 2000, was the beginning of the end. The market began to fall. In the United States several important mergers were canceled, and capital was soon flying elsewhere. Banks were no longer lending money to tech pioneers: they wanted companies with solid foundations, companies that were making profits.

The parable of the tech bubble was very similar to that of the tulip bubble that burst in mid-seventeenth-century Holland, as described in 1841 by the Scottish journalist Charles Mackay:

> *Symptoms of gambling now became, for the first time, apparent. The tulip-jobbers speculated in the rise and fall of the tulip stocks, and made large profits by buying when prices fell, and selling out when they rose. Many individuals grew suddenly rich. A golden bait hung temptingly out before the people, and one after the other, they rushed to the tulip-marts, like flies around a honey-pot. Every one imagined that the passion for tulips would last for ever, and that the wealthy from every part of the world would send to Holland, and pay whatever prices were asked for them.* [...] *People of all grades converted their property into cash, and invested it in flowers. Houses and lands were offered for sale at ruinously low prices, or assigned in payment of bargains made at the tulip-mart. Foreigners became smitten with the same frenzy, and money poured into Holland from all directions.*

The prices of bulbs reached crazy, stratospheric figures but there was always someone prepared to pay them. They reached their peak, according to Mackay, in 1636 when the price of one bulb was ten times higher than the average wage of an artisan. At this point the euphoria dissolved and turned to panic. In 1637, no one wanted bulbs anymore, the precipice was near, and the market vanished.

The same happened with dot-coms which, from being highly sought-after, very soon turned into junk assets. It took several years to reverse the trend and for tech companies to return to the top of the share markets, before dropping once again.

On March 21, when the first installment of Piol's money arrived, I had the feeling of having slinked out just before the gates of Paradise had closed. The digital castle in the United States was teetering and here in Italy everyone was warning me not to continue, forecasting disasters and catastrophes, and telling me I was crazy to risk it with a tech company, while the Nasdaq index was dropping, and the web seemed on the brink of extinction. The sky was looking bleak but I, who am a dreamer and was now passionate about innovation, decided not to look at the sky but to go ahead with determination, following my own path, because I was convinced the internet was the real future and, as soon as the bubble had passed, that it would take off again with a bang. Events were to prove me right: That's exactly what happened.

A QUESTION OF TIMING

If you're in the right place at the right time, then choosing the toughest road and following your own instinct with determination really can change the course of events. Timing can also be a matter of coincidence, and behind every success there's also a touch of magic, or at least many sliding doors. It's called synchronicity. According to this theory of Carl Gustav Jung, no event is a question of coincidence, but our life is studded with a series of coincidences. Or rather, those events we tend to regard as coincidences are not in fact coincidences. Most synchronous events that occur in our lives represent a message, a signal that points us to the road to take, the best one to follow.

Being a tech guy, I know I ought to be algebraic, algorithmic, statistical, purely rational, but a part of me firmly believes in destiny, in fortune, and in human talent. Only by putting passion and determination into the things you do can you make the most of the fortuitous coincidences that aren't always due to fate but are sometimes due to the predisposition that makes you seize them and take the risk. There are two Latin proverbs: *Audentes fortuna iuvat* (Fortune favors the bold) and *Faber est suae quisque fortunae* (Each person is the author of their own destiny). Success is probably a magic formula that has many elements.

I seized the opportunity and took the money at the last possible moment; if I had waited just fifteen days, I wouldn't have seen it again. When I said that I consider time to be crucial, this is what I meant: I was referring to coincidences but also to listening to your sixth sense which tells you: "Go, this is the moment." If there's one thing I have learned, it's this: never delay, never postpone, never think you have your whole life ahead. There are certain appointments at which it's good to arrive in perfect time.

I was at a turning point: Everything I learned at the Bocconi, at Lehman Brothers and at Columbia, all the theories I had studied, the business models I had examined, had to now become real and be translated into a solid, operational, and profitable business. I could at last use the kit I'd prepared for myself over all these years to set it up. The Lego pieces I had as a child, or those pieces of Ravenna mosaic I admired in the churches, must fit together to create a new structure. It seemed an impossible task, and I had so little time to achieve it. I felt as if I was under a thousand spotlights: I was convinced that everyone was watching me, and I didn't want to disappoint anyone.

Since my return from vacation in Brazil on January 7, I'd used every free moment of my time to perfect my project and imagine it in the tiniest detail. Diego would help me out with the business plan after he left the office. I was clear about certain things: I wanted to create a company that was new, modern, forward-looking, that focused on the customer, that was exciting and had never been seen before and was about to be launched.

So many times I had heard people say that going into a luxury store was intimidating. Snooty sales assistants looked you up and down to figure out whether you had enough money and interest to buy, or if you were just there for curiosity. *Pretty Woman* and Julia Roberts were the example that everyone had in mind. A prostitute on Hollywood Boulevard can't also go shopping at high-class shops on Rodeo Drive.

In my imaginary store, all this would miraculously disappear. Anyone who had a computer could come in and nose around for as long as they wanted. No one would ever pass judgment. All they needed was confidence: confidence in their ability to choose, and confidence in us for everything relating to delivery, payment, and any returns.

I wanted my customers to experience something they had never felt before, to experience fashion in a way they had never imagined it before, and above all I wanted them to feel free—free to enter the site; free to match clothing by simply following their own imagination; free to put aside ten items and buy just one, or none; free also, once they had received them and tried them on, to send them back if they didn't like them, or if they weren't right, without any feeling of guilt.

I had an endless list of things to do—the company office, staff to employ, the website, contracts with shipping agents—but I also firmly believed that I had to turn the rules upside down, I had to be as disruptive as possible, I had to leave space for my innovative spirit, for my urge to anticipate the future.

At the lawyer's office I settled my debt with Fabio Canè, who became a shareholder of the newly formed company. Fabio trusted me, he took the risk of lending me money, and would become invaluable from that day on because he would help me through every stage of the launch and would also be president of YOOX for a number of years.

At this point, before hurtling on, I had to list our priorities: at the beginning, it's important not to waste time, to concentrate on what is essential.

WHY DO STARTUPS BEGIN IN GARAGES?

I didn't yet have an office. Have you ever wondered why so many successful startups begin in garages and basements? The answer could be simple: because they have affordable rents. Sure, but that's not the only reason. These are places that encourage freedom, experimentation, the smooth circulation of ideas. There are no hierarchies, everyone lives in a single space, they talk to each other, help each other out, work, and have fun. A pioneering spirit is one of the components of success. Exploring new territories (physical spaces too), forgetting the old rules, overcoming taboos, attempting the unthinkable. This is the way to innovate. The same thing happened for YOOX which started off at Casalecchio di Reno, on the outskirts of Bologna (a perfect crossroads between north and south and a strategic position for logistics and deliveries) in a warehouse—the same concept as a garage, but here we were dealing with physical products that wouldn't be right in a garage—next to the store selling retail clothing stock that belonged to Diego's father. I rented it, together with the clothes that I had chosen, and we painted the walls in pastel colors. The offices were on the floor above, and we photographed and digitized the clothes and prepared the consignments in the warehouse.

I had chosen the office but there was still no team. How do you put together a good team? That was the first question that came to mind—I've given it much thought over the course of my career. Is it better to choose top managers with solid experience, at the risk of hearing them say "you do it this way, you don't do it that way" and playing safe? Or is it better to go for those who are young and less experienced, hungry and foolish as Steve Jobs put it, at the risk of going wrong but leaving space for innovation? I've always chosen the second option, from the very first day—long live youth and its capacity to challenge conventions!

The team is crucial: With the wrong people you're at risk of not achieving your aims, but with the right ones you can go beyond your expectations and can even resolve the difficulties that are bound to arise from time to time. At the beginning, when I first set up YOOX, the team was very diverse: a graduate in econometrics, an American girl, a store assistant, the girlfriend of a famous photographer with Magnum Photos, a hacker living in a squat who started laying the network in the office, all held together with eager enthusiasm. There were no working hours or days of the week. The idea was that the life was there inside, in that warehouse where all of us together were determined to make everything work. Many of us lived in a large house that YOOX had rented in Bologna, but none of us remember exactly how many we were: eight, ten? It depended on the moment. Thinking about roles and priorities in an anti-conventional manner attracts a diversity of talents and skills.

In the original group there was also an anthropologist, a philosopher, people who dealt with statistics, experts in calligraphy, artists, and designers. Why? Because much of Apple's success—beyond technology—is due to its design; because philosophers add vision, and electronic engineers and statisticians transform it into usable and predictive data.

We need to bring together a great mixture of creativity and rationality. Only in this way can there be experimentation as well as fulfillment. And then there's the vital importance of happiness, enjoyment, passion, feeling part of a project. Diversity, creativity, cross-fertilization and rationality. YOOX was all this from the very beginning.

In early April of 2000, however, I was still cautious: I chose very few people, I avoided risk, either for myself or for them. "If things go wrong," I thought, "how will I find the courage to lay them off, to tell them it's all over?" Nicola and Alessia were among the first to join me. Nicola was a childhood friend and quickly turned his hand to anything: he rented the office, organized telephone contracts, got the whole warehouse operational. Alessia, also from Ravenna, did the photography and needed to work fast on pictures of the clothes we had to digitize and publish on the website. Hilary arrived from New York and looked after marketing and PR; Tiziana I took on as web master; Andrea, a guy with long hair and an organized manner, I soon appointed as head of logistics; Alice, also from Ravenna, brought Tony from the Marche, and they worked in the warehouse with some other guys, including Erika, who had blue hair and was responsible for parceling. Finally, I put two buyers under contract: Gennaro and Alberto, the first of whom worked at Scandicci, near Florence, the second at Casalecchio.

This was the launch group: no McKinsey-style manager, no one with pre-formed professional skills. I start from the bottom and then gradually expand. This is the logic I've adopted through every stage of development. It's not true that you must always rely on specialists or people with lots of noughts to their salaries. In a startup you need to roll up your sleeves and involve everyone to some extent in everything. This serves not only to cement the group, to give it cohesion, but also to understand what the real needs are, at least in the initial stage.

On rereading my long list of things to do, I found other entries—agree on a contract with UPS for deliveries; create a barcode for digitizing products; work out how to introduce credit cards for digital payments and prepare forms for any returned goods. But what kept me busiest was creating the website. My company was digital—it based its whole operation on the internet and technology. Without these two elements it had no reason to exist, but in 2000 we were still at the very beginning.

INVENTING AN IMAGINATIVE SITE

I wondered what the YOOX site must look like, what requirements it must meet. I had several essential starting points: it must be attractive, flexible, user-friendly, must encourage customers to navigate, must allow them to move easily from one product to another, but it must also be fun and, above all, different. Those who arrive on yoox.com don't just want to go shopping—they want to be entertained, they want to dream. I also needed to create a system for credit cards, for payments and returns. Behind its captivating appearance I must construct a very complicated architecture that provided many functions and was above all simple and fast for customers. I looked around and started investigating the best existing sites. The first that came to mind was obviously Virgilio, the Italian success story of those years. I looked for the web agency that made it and discovered it was called Matrix and that one of the directors was Paolo Ainio, one of the investors I had contacted without success. They seemed impressive, bright, competent at first, but I failed to realize that Virgilio was a portal, like Yahoo!, whereas I wanted to make an e-commerce site. The functions were completely different and, even if they had smart and skillful programmers and developers, none of them had real expertise in online selling.

I had undertaken with Piol not only to be online by June 21 but also to generate a hundred orders before the end of the month. What was more, the contract required me to appoint certain key figures by that date, including the heads of logistics and technology.

I lay awake at night, listened to the ticking of the clock, and wondered: "Am I going to make it?" I knew perfectly well that if I didn't keep to the timescales, I'd have to shut up shop. The internet bubble had burst a month before my deadline, and no one would listen to me any longer.

There had been some sensational disasters such as boo.com, an e-commerce site for streetwear founded in 1998 by three young Swedes. They had announced that they wanted to create an "avantgarde, ultra-sophisticated" site, planning to spend $20 million, to have thirty employees, and to launch in just three months. In a year and a half they had spent $135 million, which they had managed to obtain from a first round of funding—part of these investments came from Bernard Arnault and from Benetton—and had gone bankrupt on 18 May 2000. They had made many tactical errors which also helped me to understand what not to repeat, such as squandering millions as though they had already earned them, using Flash technology that was too slow and bandwidth-heavy, and investing immediately in an excessive warehouse inventory without yet having a firm hand on demand.

After the collapse of boo.com, investors were no longer interested in e-commerce—they all took to their heels.

I had no means of escape. Piol and his group were my last chance. He had promised me another L.6 billion (€3 million) if I achieved the objectives he had set. I could not and must not fail.

A grueling battle began with Matrix—I remember my atrocious fits of anger: It wasn't just my idea that was in jeopardy but the fate of the young people who had followed me from the very beginning of this adventure. Looking back, it was maybe one of the most difficult moments of my career. The site was the pivot around which the whole project turned, and in mid-May we still had a long way to go.

Meanwhile, we had to install the whole office network when my friend Alex Majoli told me about Gabriele Tazzari: "He's a tech genius! Federico, you must meet him. He knows how to fix any problem." I met him, I could see straightway that he was brilliant, it was rumored he was part of a group of hackers (I never found out whether it was true or not), and I felt sure he was the right person for YOOX. I asked him to set up the office network and after a few days I invited him to become the head of technology. I had no choice: Matrix seemed likely to end in mayhem, or to put it more politely, as a waste of time. I had no way of finding anyone else. Gabriele said yes. I don't know which of us was the more courageous, but from that day he was the Chief Technology Officer. We tried, so far as possible, to straighten out the Matrix proposal and get to June 21 with a publishable website. It was a battle for survival, and I still think that without Gabriele I wouldn't have managed to launch yoox.com in time for the second installment, and therefore to ensure its survival.

There were two more points on my list of wants and needs that could not be delayed—I had to find a lawyer and decide on a market strategy. I needed legal expertise. Contracts with venture capitalists are complex. I had complete faith in Elserino Piol because he was a true gentleman but, meanwhile, other somewhat sharkish figures had stepped in and would be involved in the second installment. I could not arrive unprepared. At that time I would play poker in the evening with friends. One of these, from Puglia, often invited Stefano Valerio, a childhood friend, who was a lawyer. Stefano was always winning, he seemed bright, and I asked myself: "What shall I do? Hire him?" I relied on instinct, didn't ask for references, didn't take him on trial, rather as with Gabriele who had become head of technology in a week. Stefano already worked for an important law firm, and I asked him to be my lawyer and assist me in all the contracts I needed to negotiate.

You'd be quite right in thinking that I was in a bad situation, that I was desperate, making wholly irresponsible decisions; that being a poker player, I knew I could have lost everything in a single hand; that I enjoyed the risk and wanted to run it.

That's all true. I knew that a wrong move could be fatal, but sometimes the force of despair carries you to the root, to the nub of a problem. You're free from all the circumspection, caution, foresight of those who have time to ponder their choices. I was in a hurry, I was hungry, I wanted to reach my objective. Later I'd have time to readjust things, but for now I could only follow my instinct and complete this first phase as quickly as possible. I often explain this to young start-uppers who feel overwhelmed by problems, who would like to begin with everything in order, everything in place. If you wait until all is perfect, you'll never get going. Accept the chaos, the uncertainty, because from chaos comes order. It happened in the cosmos and will happen in your business too. If there hadn't been the Big Bang, we wouldn't even be here.

The pieces were beginning to fit together, but there was still no branding project which, along with marketing, is my passion. My ideas for YOOX were clear: I wanted something unique, something that had never been seen before.

I didn't have much money for branding, so I asked Alberto Biagetti, a friend from Ravenna, a designer with a studio called Radiosity—and by now you'll have realized we're a group of genuine *romagnoli*!—to have a go at designing the logo and image of YOOX, including the site graphics. I had known Alberto for a while. He had done the page layout for my graduation thesis at the Bocconi, and worked with Alessandro Guerriero, an architect who had been one of the founders of Studio Alchimia, along with Ettore Sottsass.

From Matrix I had received a graphic proposal that didn't convince me at all: It seemed like Amazon. White pages with small product images with background removed. The effect was banal, totally unexciting. I was looking for something different.

Alberto and Alessandro were an unusual and very creative couple: they suggested I devoted the home page to imaginary clothes. The idea was to strike customers' imagination without necessarily getting them to buy. Home pages were very important at that time, rather like magazine covers. They were calling cards that encouraged users to go in, to navigate the site. Alberto and Alessandro had thought of an architectural construction and an artistic message: Their idea was to invent fantastical, digital clothes, and to wrap them around a real model. Today the metaverse revolves around this concept, of avatars that resemble us and who wear digital clothes that don't really exist. But we were then in prehistory.

When I first spoke to Alberto about YOOX, he felt confused. As a designer, he was used to a physical universe but was immediately fascinated by the prospect of putting real and virtual together, of constructing an identity from nothing. I was very taken by the idea of digital clothes, I found it original, attractive, and decided to work with them to improve it.

A few weeks later I left for New York with Alberto and Nicola. We'd been invited to an event. We took the first presentation of the graphic project with us and worked on it during the flight. Alberto started designing the site with a Greek temple in mind, with a goddess, an icon dressed with desire, who welcomes you into her surroundings. The goddess was in the central part, the pillars on either side supported the building, and they contained all its essential functions. Ancient communicated with modern. Together we thought about a series of buttons and displays as if they were the keyboard of a remote control which, instead of changing channel, passed from one brand to another, from one product category to another. The virtual image would change every month and would resemble the cover of a magazine: The result would be vivid, lively, and active. No one had yet made a site like this: Its effect was completely new and powerful. I, though, was trying to reach out to people who had never bought online. I had to invent a friendly environment for them, something to which the user could relate, something useful, innovative, and creative at the same time. I wanted to emphasize the user experience, now much in vogue: for me it meant putting myself in the position of the customer, sharing their imagination, and stirring their dreams.

I like to think of this analogy, without claiming any comparison: Steve Jobs is to Jony Ive (the design wizard whom I met many years later—I'll explain later in what circumstances) as Federico Marchetti is to Alberto Biagetti. Form and function together, in a radical uniqueness.

By the time we landed in New York, the project was finished. I had two proposals: that of Matrix, the highly rated web design agency of the moment, and that of Alberto and Alessandro. I was at a crossroads: One way was a familiar road, one already taken by Amazon, while the other way was a road completely unexplored, never tried nor traveled before. I needed advice. During these months I'd taken too many decisions alone, but now I didn't feel up to it. I went back to Casalecchio and arranged a meeting with Diego, Hilary, Fabio, Michele (my friend from Columbia and BCG consultant who had given me a hand with the business plan), and other professionals from a whole variety of backgrounds. There were ten of us. I presented the two proposals and asked everyone to vote. Matrix won, of course. Everyone chose the familiar road. They were unanimous, and I didn't really want to criticize them—the easiest answer, the less arduous route. My vote was not yet cast, but my head was full of conflicting thoughts. On the one hand I heard the voices of those who said: "don't take a risk"; but on the other I wanted to focus on service, on putting the customer at the center of every decision—I wanted to attract, seduce, amuse, surprise. I then realized that the only way to hit the right results is by wrong-footing our viewers, by creating a screen presence, being different, being provocative. After all, these were the years of Apple's "Think different." I therefore decided that, although the overwhelming majority had expressed a preference for the one that's familiar, I needed to be more courageous. The moment had come to take a risk and choose the other path, the one that pointed toward the new, the unknown, the unexplored. And so in the end I chose the less obvious direction.

THE POWER OF THE GRAPEVINE

We are told there are nearly two billion websites in the world today, and that we live in an algocracy, a society governed by algorithms. In early 2000 there were not many websites (even fewer in Italy), broadband didn't exist, there was no social media, and above all there was no mention of algorithms. What does this mean? Essentially, that you had to go searching for sites, they weren't indexed, you had to listen to the advice of friends, or find recommendations. The few resources at that time relied on word of mouth. Search engines were slow and often ended up taking you where you didn't want to go, they rarely hit the target, and you had to make numerous attempts before you found what you were looking for.

I had a budget that was too meager for an advertising campaign; I could rely only on word of mouth, on customers who talked about it with friends, and friends of friends, but I was determined not to become invisible. Once again, I needed to stand out, surprise, be different.

I was selling end-of-season clothing, I didn't have the money to photograph them worn by models; they were static, I didn't have 3D or any of the technology that will arrive later; if I put them on a white background I would "kill" them, I would take away all their inherent personality and poetry. I refused to produce an ugly catalogue like those used in the 1960s.

In my mind I pictured something dreamlike and spatial that no one had ever seen before; I was determined to revalue these end-of-season products and make them look cool, beautiful, and enduring. And give them a second life. I resolved to let imagination predominate. I wanted a site that resembled Walt Disney more than Amazon; I steered clear of anything commonplace, traditional.

Matrix, of course, were not happy—not at all. But I was now working with Gabriele and Alberto, and my objective was to do everything in-house until the launch, until I'd received the second installment of money, so I accepted criticisms and complaints but stuck to my idea.

Alberto would become creative director of the group and remain there until 2013. From the beginning, we were a laboratory, a breeding ground for ideas. We moved ahead by trial and error, through intuition, we had no models to inspire us but were bold, free, irreverent. Many would later follow the same route.

I'd reached the last mile: I needed to invent some form of marketing before emerging online. I had one urgent question: "How can I get people to buy my products? Apart from word of mouth, how do I reach customers in Europe?" Yes, because among other things, though I only had three months, I hadn't abandoned internationality, in fact I was working on a site in two languages—Italian and English—and was preparing to deliver throughout Europe: I was aware that Italy is an important market for supplies but certainly not for the number of customers. Going abroad was a question of survival: If I could reach a vaster audience, I'd be able to expand, otherwise no—I'd remain tiny and then probably disappear. Looking back, that's exactly what happened. Strangely, the first order arrived from Holland, and Europe gradually became our first market.

Through a friend of mine from Columbia, I contacted a group of guys who had worked for Procter & Gamble and had now created a small marketing agency. I entrusted the launch of YOOX to them. They proposed an action plan, obviously with numbers for and against, and decided to focus on Holland—something which at the time I didn't properly understand—and England. They had an interesting work method because they were analytical and were efficient in the way they spent the little money available, but on content I held my ground and insisted on following my own ideas. They suggested "Top designers at fifty percent off" as a payoff for the campaign: they wanted to emphasize the discounts, the low prices. I said no: I explained that the price was one of the attractions but not the main one. I had chosen to follow Biagetti and Guerriero, and I put the emphasis on imagination, on beauty, on the fact that if a dress was beautiful, it would always be beautiful, even after the season for which it had been designed. We felt certain that our customers were ready for a new world, that they would think about clothing first as dreams and then as real objects. And for the launch campaign, in fact, we adopted a payoff that made no mention of saving or prices cut: "Fashion victims, welcome home."

On the morning of June 21, 2000, everything was ready. It was the summer solstice, a bright warm day, when without thinking too much about it, we started the countdown. It goes without saying that the first attempt failed. We panicked and started wondering: "And if it doesn't work? If we can't get the site online?" We tried a second countdown but again it wouldn't take off. It was no good. On the third attempt we were all having heart attacks when suddenly, at last, the site went online: visible, accessible, operational. YOOX was born.

Our happiness was boundless. We were excited, exhausted, extremely happy. We had believed in a project, and we'd achieved it. It was a moment of change in our lives—and particularly my life. I will always be thankful to the fantastic group that worked with me from the first day, and which managed, despite everything and everyone, to create one of the world's first e-commerce fashion sites. Energy, enthusiasm and determination transformed ideas, feelings, thoughts, and intuitions into an innovative digital company. A prototype that many would try to repeat.

A tinpot army had achieved a miracle: the first order arrived an hour later from Holland, for a Versace dress (as I've already mentioned). In nine days, by the end of June, we had received many other orders. The machine had started. Now it was just a question of getting it to move faster.

6

In the nine days from June 21 to the end of the month, some hundred orders had reached the site. I had completed most of the jobs on my list: some of the YOOX team and I had manually created the interface, shaping it to meet the needs of fashion, and with it we could control content and functionality. It was homemade but brought together the objectives I had set for the operational effectiveness we needed to support a structure that combined technology, dynamic human resources, and approach methods that would allow continual improvement.

I had now met the demands of my financial backer: I had an office, had appointed the key figures, and had succeeded miraculously in launching the company.

So I went to Elserino's partner, Oliver Novick, for the second installment of the capital, as promised. Oliver, a plain-speaking American, went straight to the crux of the problem. "For us, e-commerce has become like AIDS," he said. "Best to keep away from it." I froze, but I knew that Piol would never go back on his word, and he didn't. Three billion lire arrived from them, and another three came from Net Partners, a company created by Fausto Boni and Michele Appendino.

The machine now had enough fuel to continue its journey.

"At the end of the twentieth century, however, the whole system of consumption and textile manufacture was radically changing once more," explains Enrica Morini, a fashion historian. "A new model of large-scale distribution, sustained by decentralized production in countries with low labor costs, began to offer attractive ready-to-wear of acceptable quality, and at low prices. The success of chains like Gap, Zara or H&M grew out of the fact that consumers were less and less attracted by status symbol or high-quality clothing that would last a whole season: buying was linked more and more to the pleasure of modifying personal appearance with things always new and different, following short and passing fashions. A new era had dawned for fashion: that of bulk garment-making for the mass global market."

The phenomenon described by Morini had already started in 1989. On December 31, *The New York Times* used the expression "fast fashion" for the first time when the Spanish brand Zara opened a store in Manhattan. The meaning was simple: it took just fifteen days for a fashion idea to be transformed into a dress delivered to the store. Zara now produces twenty-four collections a year, and that intuition has become a worldwide success. And while it is true that this system of production means that anyone can dress following the latest trends and spending little, it is also true that it carries with it certain disastrous consequences: Some consumers treat cheaper clothes as if they were "disposable" and discard them—when all goes well—after they've been worn seven or eight times. But in 40 percent of cases they throw them away without even taking them out of the packaging! Only 1 percent is recycled.

The fast-fashion phenomenon also affected the luxury end of the market. Over that same period, the number of fashion shows began to multiply with the addition of cruise collections (clothing for those who spend the winter on cruises or in hot climates), pre-collections (simpler garments to preview to buyers), and capsule collections (themed collections in a limited edition), on top of the principal lines. In this way, the number reached seven or eight key events every year, rising to around ten if menswear shows were included.

Quantities of clothing grew out of all proportion, along with the problem of what to do with the leftover stock that lay idle in warehouses after the sales.

In early 2000, brands would send the season's unsold stock to outlets or give them to wholesalers who exported them to countries far from their traditional distribution area, such as Russia, Saudi Arabia, China, or Africa. Sadly, one part was incinerated, as still happens. It was not until 2023 that the European Commission finally introduced regulations and charges that brands had to meet for the end-of-life management of their products, to reduce the overall environmental impact.

My idea was to transform somebody's mistake into an interesting surprise. YOOX was resolving a problem for the sector, as well as providing an opportunity for customers: for twenty years it would be a world lifestyle leader on the internet, never replicated by any other online player. Buying all the leftover stock of a cult store like Colette in Paris at that time—one of the first that we contacted—meant acquiring garments that had been wrong for them: They hadn't managed to sell them, so they were clogging up in their warehouses. But when they were mixed together with a thousand others from the surplus stock of other stores, they created a kaleidoscope, an extraordinarily curious and stimulating mix and match for customers. People today talk about sustainability, about extending the life of clothes. They talk about viewing them from another point of view that no longer follows the latest fashion but opts for quality, for use, that emphasizes sentiment, the attachment to a garment which makes us feel good, and from which we are inseparable. YOOX grew from an intuition that would prove successful, and would show the way ahead: who is it that establishes the use-by date of a garment? Who determines its uselessness and its death? It's we customers, we consumers, who do it, who can use our imagination to create interesting looks, beautiful stylish outfits as we face a market v.2.0 that leaves us free to choose and to invent new combinations. Sustainability is already incorporated. Added to the original idea, there would later be other projects for protecting the environment, which I'll describe later.

ONE, TEN, A HUNDRED BRANDS

After a couple of seasons I realized the goods that arrived from Diego were no longer enough; I needed to broaden my horizon, to go directly to stores and companies, to develop new contacts and new relationships. People liked what the site offered, customers started to arrive, and we reached the year end on budget, as I had hoped, with sales of almost L.2 billion (€1 million).

I didn't find it easy at first; I was looked upon as an outsider, many requests for meetings come to nothing, but I was determined from the beginning that I must find a new balance between an "old" world and a new one that hadn't yet arrived. I knew that fashion had enormous potential, but it lacked any technological and digital approach. No one could yet imagine that one day we'd be talking about information highways and would be living in the "onlife" era. What is it? The Italian philosopher Luciano Floridi describes it like this: "It's like mangrove societies. They live in salt water where rivers and the sea meet. It's an incomprehensible environment if we think of it in terms of fresh water or salt water. Onlife is this: the new existence in which the barrier between real and virtual has dropped away, there's no longer any difference between 'online' and 'offline,' but there's an 'onlife,' which is our existence, a hybrid like the mangrove habitat."

I, a tech entrepreneur, write letters by hand. That's because I think emails end up in the spam folder, whereas nobody writes letters anymore and someone has to open them. I wrote to heads of fashion houses, asking to meet them. After the first noes, I received a few yeses. They began to show interest. They were surprised to see garments bearing their label coming from the leftover stock of multibrand stores onto the yoox.com site, and while they wondered who had sold them, they also began to realize that their styles might have a longer life than they had imagined, without however disrupting their traditional physical distribution outlet, that of the stores.

During the 2000s, the fashion industry was healthy and constantly expanding, and Italian style was celebrated everywhere. All seemed to be going well: stylists had magnificent luxury stores on five continents and customers were accustomed to making their purchases in these "temples." Fashion had never thought of the internet as a sales outlet. The luxury experience revolved around the emotions: it seemed an essential experience to see, to touch, and to try on a garment. My stroke of fortune was that, at that time, almost no one fully understood the potential of the online experience, leaving me a free hand. Maybe, as the great French chemist and biologist Louis Pasteur said, "Fortune favors the prepared mind": the fact remains that I felt ready at that time to embark on this undertaking.

I realized straightaway that the idea wasn't so weird, that there was a market to be conquered.

During my meetings, I would talk about this internet planet, still uncontaminated, that could be theirs. It was the ideal place to put all the leftover stock they didn't know what to do with, but above all it was a new distribution channel that had nothing to do with stores, because it didn't interfere with physical distribution. It was the right answer for the brands, and maybe it was also the obvious solution for an industry that was producing much more than it could sell.

The brands were selling us goods at a large discount in comparison to their price to the public. We always sold them with a margin that could amply absorb all fixed and variable costs. This margin is essential because e-commerce has very high costs and, at the end of the process, the profit is small indeed. The model was clear: If we wanted to reach sales of €1 million, we had to buy products for €500,000: in this way our growth was guided by us.

FIRST ENCOUNTERS WITH RENZO ROSSO AND GIORGIO ARMANI

Renzo Rosso was one of the first to call me, even before the launch of the site. He invited me to his farm at Marostica, near Vicenza, a kind of "estate" on which he had created the Diesel Farm. Renzo is a genius because he managed to export his Diesel jeans even to the United States, making everyone—including Italians—believe they were made in the USA.

That day, he was there with all his managers. He was curious, he wanted to know how e-commerce worked; he even asked if he could invest in YOOX, though his director of finance at the time advised against it. He agreed however to let his end-of-season Diesel products be sold directly to us.

My real work for the first few years was exactly this: to contact the leading brands one by one, and ask them firstly to sell us the leftover stock from their past collections, then at a later stage to offer to create their web sites.

Armani was also with us from the start, along with Marni, and it was the trust I gained from such important fashion houses that gave me the final momentum. I had decided to ferry a whole universe online.

My relationship with Giorgio Armani had begun a long way back. In 1995, I organized a party on the balcony of my apartment in Milan: I was single and liked to enjoy myself when I left the office. That evening my old university friend Gabriele, who I'd gone to America with after my degree, turned up with a girl I really fell for. Warm, genuine, amusing, we spent the whole night talking. It was Roberta Armani, Giorgio's niece. For two years we had a passionate relationship, I moved into her place, then in 1997 she left me, and soon after married Angelo Moratti. In the meantime, we spent a couple of vacations with her uncle—once, I went to his villa on the island of Pantelleria but I was working for Lehman and could only stay for twenty-four hours. All the same, I got to know Giorgio, I admired him, but absolutely didn't want my work to interfere with my relationship with Roberta. All the same, Giorgio asked advice from time to time, knowing I worked for an investment bank, and I tried to answer. Even after Roberta had left me, I would think of some present he might appreciate. His birthday is on July 11, the same day as my father and my daughter Maggie. A friend at Lehman told me about the Scottish Fold, a placid breed of cats with a magnetic gaze, "very docile, very good, very appealing." I went to collect the kitten and discovered it was the last of the litter, and as black as night. Help! How could I give a black cat in Italy when everyone thinks it brings bad luck? But the cat was truly irresistible, it was called Angel (I smile because I'm "devilish" and jealous: Roberta has just married Angelo) and I took it as a gift for Armani, who developed such an affection for Angel that he posed for a publicity shot with him in his arms.

My friendship with Giorgio Armani has continued over the years, but always on one condition: I prefer never to ask anything of him. I've offered only advice and assistance when the opportunity has arisen. Ruggero Magnoni, one of the top bosses at Lehman and coordinator of some important financial transactions during that period, tried many times to get me to persuade Giorgio Armani to enter the stock market when he discovered my relationship with Roberta, but I always told him I didn't want to mix my personal life and business. "Signor Armani trusts me precisely because he knows I wouldn't use our acquaintance for other purposes."

We remained in contact over the years. He invited me to events that signaled moments of expansion for Giorgio Armani SpA, I gave him guidance when the company was digitized, and in 2021, during COVID, he telephoned to invite me to join his board of directors as the only member who wasn't part of his family. I told him I had signed a non-competition agreement and needed to get permission from Johann Rupert, Chairman di Richemont. I remember emailing Rupert on June 2, 2021, the day after his birthday, thinking he'd be in a good mood after the celebrations, and indeed he replied straightaway: "What an honor!" So I've been a member of his board since then.

But to return to my first contact with Giorgio Armani SpA, it was not through Roberta, and I didn't ask anything of Giorgio. In fact, it was through Gerbotto, his general manager, who called me at the request of his commercial director, Roberta Colombo, to "take me to task" because she had seen some Armani models on yoox.com and he wanted to find out where they came from. After a stormy beginning with Gerbotto, who came from the catalogue business before arriving at Armani and therefore spoke my "language" because he knew the dynamics of this sector, we immediately reached an understanding. I then did a test—it's a request I get from everyone, even from Dolce & Gabbana—because they wanted to see how it worked and, soon after, we were off: They sold us their garments directly.

Many brands were curious, they could see the potential of e-commerce, but some were hesitant; others, like Giorgio Armani, were more innovative and immediately accepted my proposal.

I knew I had two sets of customers, not one. First, I had the final customers who buy on yoox.com, but the second and even more important customers were those in charge of the brands. I was sure that the more I managed to involve this second group of customers, the more YOOX could grow. Everything I did in terms of marketing, packaging, and image was also designed to avoid treading on the toes of the fashion houses. I didn't want to frighten them—I've never pulled out a placard with the words: "Valentino 50% off." We used imagination: our slogans were: "Dress as you wish," or "The Never-ending Store." We would say to our customers: "Come into this fantastic space and choose what you like." We emphasized mystery and imagination. The garments cost less than they did in the stores, but this wasn't the main attraction; indeed we never displayed the original price crossed out, even though every successive marketing director at YOOX would always make the same proposal of explicitly showing the discount (something which, in fact, they did as soon as I left YNAP in 2021). We wanted customers to fall in love with the clothes, to buy them because they liked them, experimenting and—why not?—also saving money.

From the very first day, from the organizational point of view, I was inspired by America, by its speed, by the internet, by the thousand opportunities I had found on the other side of the Atlantic. But from the point of view of ingenuity and creativity I'm 100 percent Italian. I believe in intuition, in our innate capacity to bring good taste and creativity together and, above all, I was customer Number One. I tried everything for myself that the site offered in terms of performance, delivery, entertainment.

OBSESSION ABOUT THE CUSTOMER

"This is the most amazing experience in the world" is what companies would like customers to say every time they make contact with them.

From the first moment I thought of YOOX, the customer was my personal obsession. Being obsessive can be useful because you focus on one aspect, and you examine it so thoroughly that it becomes part of you. I was, am, and will always be a customer. If you run a business, you need to know your customer is your point of reference. Those who go to a company expect to be listened to and get what they want. Those who connect specifically to an e-commerce site don't just want to buy a garment: they want an experience, to enjoy themselves, to feel confident, relaxed, to discover new things. The sensation must be much more like going to a movie theater than one of completing a transaction after having mechanically chosen an object. Navigation must be simple, fast, intuitive. Users won't imagine there's a complex structure behind it, because all they see is the tip of an iceberg, designed to make them feel at ease. I'm convinced that if you know how to entertain your customers, they'll remain loyal. Otherwise, you'll lose them. There is no purchase without excitement, especially in luxury products: the two things are closely connected.

In 2000 the great tech companies that transformed this slogan into their mantra didn't yet exist. Now that they are world economic giants, we find this common trait in every one of them: put customers at the center, give them an unforgettable experience, entertain them, inform them...in short, make them the protagonist. This is the basic principle that enables a company to call itself truly digital. All employees must focus on this objective, must work to achieve it, and must never forget that this is why the company exists. If you think of Netflix, Apple, or Amazon, you'll understand that what they do is give you the impression that everything revolves around you, that you are the pivot, you are their mission.

I feel sure that the ability to bring together shopping and entertainment was one of the keys to YOOX's success, to the point that I invented the neologism "entertailer," crossing "entertainer" with "etailer" (online retailer), which I registered as a brand name.

The nuclear fusion had begun—what seemed an impossibly revolutionary project was becoming reality. Fashion—which had lived until now in its soft, gilded, luxury rooms, which had always lived in fear of contamination and novelty—began its long courtship with the frenetic, open, anti-elitist internet. Suspicions began to fade, and in my mind's eye I saw these two worlds happily and inseparably married. Innovation is the driving force of this titanic work. Technology is a work in progress, there is never a point of arrival, only a point of departure, yet we must be first to get there, always with an urge for novelty, and so obsessed about focusing 100 percent on our own objectives, at the risk of turning our personal lives—and those of others—upside down. In twenty years at YOOX, and then at YNAP, it was always my absolute imperative to get there first. To experiment, make mistakes, adjust our aim, but always be pioneers. To look ahead, never back.

Gradually the fashion labels agreed and swam like little fish into the net, and by the end I can say that I won them all over, including Hermès and Marinella, to mention the most reluctant and the last to arrive in our substantial portfolio. I was now part of this "inner circle," I knew the leading players that I'd managed to link to YOOX, offering them a place in the new world. Welcome to the future!

People were hearing about YOOX even farther afield. Buying on our site had now become a trend, an alternative approach to the collections of stylists, to such an extent that even *The New York Times* wrote about me, describing me as "the man who put fashion on the net." *The New Yorker* writes: "No one has had more to do with bringing e-commerce to fashion than Federico Marchetti." I like to think of myself as being like Dante's Virgil, the figure who helped fashion to navigate the uncharted waters of the internet, steering it toward modernity.

THE TEAM IS EVERYTHING BECAUSE GETTING IT RIGHT IS EVERYTHING

Let's return to the creation of YOOX. As soon as I'd received the next L.6 billion (€3 million) of finance, in July 2000, I could strengthen the team. I recruited another two key figures: Max

Benedetti and Alberto Grignolo who, along with Gabriele, the head of technology, would remain with the company for twenty years.

In April, I put an advert in *la Repubblica* newspaper through a company called Praxi which said: "YOOX: young team, office in Bologna. You like working in fashion? You like the internet? Send your curriculum to Praxi." I was looking at that time for a head of logistics. Max Benedetti, an engineer from Rimini, another Romagnolo, meticulous and reliable, who was involved in change management and worked in Rome for Andersen Consulting, had a girlfriend in Bologna and wanted to move closer to her after various ups and downs. He had an interview with Praxi and several weeks later received a telephone call from Filippo Ridolfo, a friend with whom he had done military service. Who is Filippo Ridolfo? Coincidences, happenstances, minor strokes of luck. Filippo, who had done a summer internship with us in 2000, is the brother of Michele, the friend I had known when I was at Columbia University in New York and who had helped me out at the start. Filippo telephoned him, but Max thought it was for the reunion dinner they regularly organized. He started talking about soldiers and veterans when Filippo stopped him and told him he was here with me, that we'd looked at his curriculum and thought he was the best candidate for the position we were trying to fill. The following Friday, Max set off from Rome "dressed like a penguin," as he puts it, "in a dark blue suit, waistcoat, white shirt and tie," and arrived at Casalecchio.

Max often tells an amusing anecdote at this point. He arrived at the office warehouse perfectly dressed in his suit and polished shoes, and outside the entrance he saw a man dressed all in white with long hair, whom he assumed to be a decorator.

He told him he had an appointment with signor Marchetti and didn't know where to go; the "decorator" pointed the way, but once inside the warehouse, Max found himself in a kind of circus. He saw a young woman with blue hair (very common now, but not then), tattooed all over, holding an enormous parcel. He saw Gabriele Tazzari with his head completely shaved, his trousers tied with a piece of chain, and a router on his head. He saw a couple of guys glued to their PCs who gave him sideway glances, but above all he saw his friend Filippo, with whom he had done his military service, dressed in sandals, Bermuda shorts, and undershirt. He could not believe his eyes. Filippo gave him a worried look and suggested he might put a T-shirt on instead of his formal get-up, and asked him to reread the FAQs of the site they're designing. After a while he came into my office, and there he was even more amazed to find that the "decorator" was me, the founder of the company.

It's true that this was a technique I would use to watch and get to know people before an interview. I wanted to see how they moved in a particular situation and how they interacted with humbler folk: in this way I could work out how they might behave with colleagues and above all with their subordinates. My grandfather always used to say: Watch how a man treats his staff, and you'll know whether he's a true gentleman or a cad.

At the end of the interview we both agreed he was not the right person for head of logistics, but I had the feeling he might be perfect as the Customer Relations Manager. At that time, none of us was an expert in anything. If you knew how to hold a camera you were our photographer; if you were a computer geek you became head of technology; and if you spoke English, like Hilary, you were in charge of English content and overseas PR.

At the end of the interview, just as he was about to leave, Max saw a woman cyclist in immaculate sports gear enter a room with a bicycle under her arm; ten minutes later he saw her emerge with full makeup and wearing a pantsuit. He later discovered it was a tiny bathroom where Hilary had hooked her bicycle to the ceiling and changed her clothes. Max was convinced we were mad, but felt a deep fascination for this likeable, completely unconventional group. He felt the magic of the place and wanted to be a part of it.

But he couldn't leave without giving his employers two months' notice, and I couldn't wait. I wanted him there the next day, but he, being serious and professional, said no, and that was it. I chose another candidate but realized my mistake after two months and called Max again. We met at a party in Ravenna and, while music was playing and everyone was talking and laughing, we discussed the terms of his contract, lying on the grass in a park, gazing at the stars. So Max came on board and became head of a team of which he was the only member!

ETHICS AND DATA

One important aspect of digital and e-commerce companies is data. In 2000, no one spoke about artificial intelligence, no one mentioned robots, and no one was yet raising the problem of privacy and the way certain tech companies, set up later, would avidly collect our personal information. This is one of the most controversial questions of today, and positions are very polarized. There are some, on the one hand, who think that those who collect data are "stealing" from their customers, and others who are resigned and believe we have given so much of our data to Facebook and other social media that it's now too late to talk about protection of privacy.

A former Google employee, Tristan Harris, described as "the conscience of Silicon Valley," has written an article in *Thrive Global* in which he asks:

> *Where does technology exploit our minds' weaknesses?*
>
> *I learned to think this way when I was a magician. Magicians start by looking for blind spots, edges, vulnerabilities and limits of people's perception, so they can influence what people do without them even realizing it. Once you know how to push people's buttons, you can play them like a piano.*
>
> *And this is exactly what product designers do to your mind. They play your psychological vulnerabilities (consciously and unconsciously) against you in the race to grab your attention....*
>
> *The more choices technology gives us in nearly every domain of our lives (information, events, places to go, friends, dating, jobs)—the more we assume that our phone is always the most empowering and useful menu to pick from. Is it?...*
>
> *We're all vulnerable to social approval. The need to belong, to be approved or appreciated by our peers is among the highest human motivations. But now our social approval is in the hands of tech companies.*

The question is very complex, and the success of social media raises many questions, some very pressing, that need to be resolved. I'm convinced, however, that an "ethical" path exists in the use of data—and it's one I have always followed. I have never "stolen" data. I have used it from day one to improve the experience of customers, to help them choose, without ever reselling any information to anyone else. A journalist from Forbes described me as a "dataphile" because of my passion for numbers, and I'm firmly convinced that one of the keys to YOOX's success is that we have known how to collect and use data ethically. We managed to become the group leader of online luxury, we reached 5 million customers and over 1.2 billion visits per year and gained a thorough understanding of our customers' tastes. We gave them advice, helped them find what they were looking for, and collected important information in order to provide a state-of-the-art service. We have photographed everything we put up for sale since YOOX was first created, even when we had only one article of that kind. It was extremely expensive at the start but an invaluable asset after a few years.

The information tells us what our customers like, what sizes are most popular, their favorite models, colors, shapes, lengths. They provide information for our buyers about products to purchase, they give exact profiles of the tastes of those who are buying and have enabled us to create 8 by YOOX and Mr P., two proprietary YNAP lines based exclusively on the indications of customers and brought up to date by the group of stylists that work on the two collections. The capacity to produce collections based on data, as we will see later, is one of the key factors that creatives should consider if they really want to promote sustainability, because these lines, since they are customer-led, produce more accurate purchases, fewer returns, and therefore less wastage.

Since I was conscious from the start about the importance of data in my business, in the summer of 2000 I set about looking for an expert. I interviewed a young guy from a consultancy company and told him I wanted *A Beautiful Mind*, someone who was brilliant with numbers. I could then concentrate on the creative part for the simple reason that it was more fun. And he very honestly replied: "I'm not the one, I'm not *A Beautiful Mind*, but the guy who shares my apartment is exactly what you're looking for—a graduate in Economics and Econometry, and a real wizard with numbers." He introduced me to Alberto Grignolo and I could see straightaway that he was a genius. He started with the role of data miner, the one who sifts all the data. And then, gradually, we discovered that through numbers we could understand consumer tastes, the clothes that work, and those that nobody wants. We learned how to reduce logistical costs, how to rationalize activities. Alberto became something of the pole star of the whole organization, which was still only maybe fifteen or sixteen people, and at the end of 2001 would become fifty. Everyone looked to him, and I therefore created this structure that was called "data analysis for decisional support."

At meetings with brands I turned up with Alberto who tried to charm them with numbers while I presented them with a future in which the internet would become essential.

Alberto and I were a strange couple: the entrepreneur outsider constructing a path of innovation, and the mathematician obsessed by calculations and percentages. We told them about our store and its wonders, where there was space for everyone, from Dsquared to Issey Miyake, and invited them to take part.

Alberto arrived badly dressed and wasn't particularly bothered about it since he worked from dawn to dusk. He intrigued them; they could see we inhabited a faraway place that they had never explored. They listened in awe to analyses, numbers, and figures, and thanks to Alberto we passed all the tests they set us: Little by little they gave us more products and showed more interest in working with us. I've always said that without Alberto, YOOX would have been only half as great.

We were a group who worked well together, with some extraordinary talents—and we worked like mad, with an energy I rarely saw in other companies. The enthusiasm for a new project unleashed energy and creativity. I had rented a two-bedroom apartment in Bologna, in Galleria Cavour, where I often let anyone stay who hadn't yet found somewhere to live. The others were in what we called "the commune." We went to eat at the Drogheria della Rosa in via Cartoleria, under the *portici*, a typical Bologna trattoria where the owner, Emanuele, gives a rose to all the women who come to dine. He's a real Don Juan who entertains his customers holding a glass of wine. It became our regular eating-place, the menu is always the same, but the stracchino and squacquerone tortellini are unforgettable. He now has loads of YOOX memorabilia on his walls and likes to say this had been our real office for many years.

I smile when I think back to those early days. They were complicated, nail-biting times, yet they were fun, lively, exciting. And I was lucky enough, in all that pandemonium, to meet some unique and remarkable people. We gave the best of ourselves: we had little experience, and people were expecting me to provide answers, suggestions, advice. I improvised, used plenty of logic and good sense.

O CAPTAIN! MY CAPTAIN!

What kind of leader was I at that time? Alberto Grignolo always described me like this: "Marchetti was to the fashion world what privateers were to the English navy in the Sixteenth century." I wondered in what way I could be regarded as a "privateer." Sir Francis Drake, the famous buccaneer, was an explorer, sea captain, trader who, with other Sea Dogs, attacked the Spanish fleet many times, plundering their ships to bring riches and treasures back to England. Queen Elizabeth rewarded him with a knighthood when he returned with a vast cargo of spices and treasures.

Maybe the answer is this: I entered that world as an outsider to bring about a fundamental change and to demonstrate that people were not just ready to invent a new way of choosing and buying clothes without trying them on, but that technology allowed us to have experiences that were unthinkable until then. And in the end I brought added value to the fashion sector. Think of 2020, the year of COVID, when every store was shut. How would certain brands have survived if they hadn't had their online stores with sales that rocketed? I have a Japanese friend, Mihara Yasuhiro, a brilliant designer of shoes and sneakers (he was among the very first to launch designer sneakers with Puma many years ago); he always says he thought at first that I'd destroyed fashion with my revolutionary idea, but then changed his mind and admits that I have saved it.

When you create a startup and want to innovate, however, you must forget the classic rules of business—you need to free the mind and accept new ways of organizing work. I started out with a team that was totally inexperienced, like me. I followed my intuition in choosing people to employ, and focused on courage, personality, ambition, motivation. More than their work record, I felt that enthusiasm and a sense of belonging would compensate for any initial shortcomings. And that's how it was. The original members of the group told how for several years, though they knew that YOOX was my company, they all felt owners in some small way, and were ready to defend it, because the creative act in which they were involved was all-absorbing. They often said: "YOOX is a successful project designed to revolutionize an era." They wanted to be there and to beat the challenge. "We're sure we're on the right track," they would say, and recognized that my leadership gave them motivation.

I never asked more of others than I asked of myself, seeking always to set an example and working on quality and results. I've never been interested in how much time a person has spent in the office; I've never been bothered about working hours. I introduced remote working well before the pandemic, so that in 2019 we were already working remotely two days a week, and moving to five days was simple and natural for us. All I did was simply to encourage everyone—but first of all myself—to push ourselves beyond our limits.

I always trusted my team, I delegated much, and followed no pre-established course in making innovation. For years we navigated as we went along, changed course, accelerated, slowed down, played for time when necessary. And I know that leading by example is fundamental. Everything that happened to the rest of the company happened to me: if procedures were imposed, I obeyed them too; if everyone had to have a hybrid car, I had one too; if everyone had a 40 percent discount on YNAP group sites, then I had one too (even though my contract allowed me 50 percent). From the smallest things, like these, to the distribution of shares, I always respected this principle: to share equally. More than two hundred people have earned cumulatively over €300 million along the history of YOOX, through shares and stock options, creating a true American-style story. This is YOOX: an American Dream, Italian Style.

Disruption, empathy, and a strong desire to transmit a concept of collective participation: I tried in every way to encourage the others to reach a specific objective; I always explained the company mission with employees in such a way as to create a kind of group epiphany. When I identified a clear direction, I tried also to get my team to visualize it. I was seen as a successful outsider surrounded by a passionate, crazy, enterprising group; together we achieved an objective we never expected to reach.

But things didn't always go smoothly. For years, for example, there was the nightmare of secretaries. Yes, because at a certain point I was convinced that I needed an assistant. Max used to poke fun at me, exaggerating: "For Federico, there's no such thing as the perfect secretary, not even if you were to build them with artificial intelligence."

And I'll explain why. When we left the warehouse at Casalecchio in 2001—which was now too small—and moved to a cube-shaped building at Zola Predosa, near Bologna, I made various attempts to look for a secretary. The dilemma was always the same: Do I take them young, ambitious, highly motivated, but at the price of them having little experience? Or do I choose someone already trained, who has maybe worked with some captain of industry and is therefore highly regarded?

First of all, I looked for someone young and ambitious, but after several minor mishaps I realized it wasn't working, so I moved to the second option: I tried an experienced secretary who had worked in the office of a top manager, and on paper she seemed perfect. The only problem that we discovered fairly soon was that she drank during office hours. She had a stock of liquor hidden in a niche beside her desk, so that she sometimes seemed rather distracted whereas in fact she was half sloshed. I'd have liked to give her some help and support, but one day she fell on the office steps, sprained her foot, and left the next day. At this point it was time to play my third card: a psychologist-seer who was full of advice. "Never wear anything purple at an important meeting. Put this lucky charm on your table and the meeting will go well." She helped me furnish the house in Bologna, chose cushions which she told me had positive energy, and Zen furnishings. Half psychologist, half sorceress, always dressed in black, in the end she didn't last long and handed in her resignation.

The final solution was to take someone from the sales office. I found a young woman with plenty of experience in that area. She was very good, but one day took one of my jokes too seriously (we *romagnoli* like making jokes). There was a black cat wandering around outside the office—not the one I'd given to Armani as a present years before!—and pretending to be superstitious I told her that it was bringing us bad luck and we must make it disappear…but instead it was she who disappeared, as fast as she could.

The cycle of four secretaries came to an end before the year was out, but it led me to try an experiment—no more personal assistants, but a group of people to whom I could give different responsibilities. I wanted them to follow the business logic of what I was doing, I didn't want them merely to carry out orders but to be colleagues who shared strategies and decisions. I therefore created the CEO's Office, not just a center of operations but also a sort of thinktank. And so, after the failures of the first few years, I had some exceptional people in this office whom I nurtured and who then moved to managerial positions in other departments.

7

With a startup company, especially if you're involved in a sector that doesn't exist, you can only learn by yourself. There's no past to look back on, there's no literature to help you, nor even just an experience to follow. You take your first steps as if you were a spaceman who had just landed on the Moon in 1969. You don't know how firm the ground is, what it's made of, whether your feet will sink in or whether you'll leap about from one rock to another. You must simply try it and see. And sometimes you'll get it wrong.

And that's what happened to us, like on a roller coaster when one moment you're up, then down, then back up again. The first experience of this goes back to August 2000. For us it was a successful month: We received a flood of orders from England. It was exactly what we expected; we were delighted. Max had just joined us as head of Customer Relations; his absolute priority was to take care of these "fantastic" London customers. They ordered a load of stuff. Who knows, maybe they would resell it, but we were so naïve that we had no idea, or rather we weren't even interested. All that mattered was that they didn't stop buying. We thought of them as our best customers. We asked Max to handle them well, with kid gloves, so he started to keep an eye on them.

"In those days," Max recalls, "our systems were so basic that we used an Excel spreadsheet and extrapolated the data manually from the site. I often went to sleep at five in the morning, on the floor in the office, but I wasn't the only one: If I sent Federico an email at four thirty a.m., he would reply at four thirty-five. Anyway, one night as I'm transcribing the data of the top ten customers, I notice the orders are all coming from the same London address: 33 Blackfriars Road. I start wondering why, but we assume it was thanks to a strong marketing campaign that had papered two London underground stations with YOOX virtual covers."

Do you remember the virtual clothes designed on models by Alberto Biagetti and Alessandro Guerriero? These had a great impact on the London underground. At the same time, we had sponsored a tennis tournament at London's Royal Albert Hall between two stars from a former era (I always preferred McEnroe to Borg, even if I had the Fila Björn Borg outfit which I've now passed on to my daughter, a tennis enthusiast). In short, Great Britain was in our sights and the orders from those customers were coming from a district not far from that underground station. So nobody was suspicious—in fact we were convinced that our marketing action planned by ex-Procter guys had been a great success.

While Max was studying our customers, an email arrived from Banca Sella, which managed the YOOX payment systems, telling us that a transaction had not been accepted. We were in 2000—when credit cards were first being used on the internet—so no one knew what to do. Max called the person dealing with e-commerce at Banca Sella, who explained either that we'd sent the wrong product, and the person was not accepting it and wanted their money back, or it was a fraud and a stolen card number had been used. And he added that, if the credit card was stolen, we would be responsible and would have to pay the money back: it's a rule that governs e-commerce sites and distance selling. When Max asked: "But is this an error or a fraud?" Banca Sella told him it was certainly a fraud and suggested we pay up. Max was seriously worried because a third of the orders came from this address, and many had been made by someone called Koji Adom, third on the list of best customers. Looking again at the names of the first ten, he discovered they were anagrams of each other. "Basically," Max continues, "I realize after being in YOOX for just ten days that a third of the business we are generating are frauds. Most of all, I wonder how to go about telling Federico. I'm the last to arrive, everyone here is convinced the English are big fans of theirs, so how do I tell him it's not like that?"

Max knocked on my door. "I have something I need to tell you," he said. He came in and explained what had happened. I believed him, I had not the slightest doubt about what he was telling me, but I looked at him and asked: "Couldn't you have realized earlier?!" I was terrified. We didn't have much money, we needed to generate orders, to sell our goods, we couldn't let anyone steal them.

WITH THE HELP OF SCOTLAND YARD...

We decided to set up a task force in the hope of catching the thieves. We became internet policemen and started to keep a check on orders arriving from England. It was a Friday, and that weekend the group made the largest number of purchases ever made on YOOX. It was a full-scale attack. We contacted an insurance company to cover ourselves for the future, but above all we went looking for a lawyer with experience in these matters. In 2000, finding a lawyer experienced in internet crime was like looking for someone who had flown into space, but Fausto Boni, one of the investors in Net Partners, suggested a lawyer in Bologna who dealt with cases like this. We called her.

"On one evening of torrential rain, my doorbell rang," Max recalls. "I don't know whether you've seen *The Exorcist* and whether you remember the scene where the priest arrives at the house during a downpour wearing a hat and carrying a bag. Well, in the middle of a storm, I find a woman at my door wearing a hat that's half-cowboy and half-exorcist. She has a black bag and an overcoat down to her feet. I think to myself: I'm finished! Who is this person? All the same, we start discussing what has happened and she explains that there are, in fact, sufficient grounds for having these people arrested."

But to catch them and charge them with all that had happened so far, we needed evidence. We needed to arrange for them to "steal" something else from the website, then we had to deliver it without raising suspicion. At that point the police must arrive at the very moment they receive the pack. They'd have used the same stolen credit card so it would be easy to prosecute them.

This all sounds simple, but we were in Casalecchio, on the outskirts of Bologna, they were in London, and between us were the British police. Hilary went to talk to Scotland Yard, taking all the evidence. That's how we discovered they were especially interested in online fraud and were happy to give us a hand. We sent some of the orders made that weekend and came to an agreement with UPS, explaining that the delivery would be tailed by a Scotland Yard patrol.

The packages were due to be delivered on the following Tuesday. We were all there in the vast hall where we worked.

Then, over the link with London, we heard Hilary shout: "We got them!"

We all went crazy. They told us they'd caught five or six teenagers and that most of the stolen goods were still in their storeroom. We retrieved some of them, which were taken away by the police.

We learned at our own expense about the existence of internet crime, and we immediately introduced a system that allowed us to quickly identify suspicious cases. But unfortunately at that time we had no protection networks. We were naïve. Every additional order was a source of satisfaction rather than suspicion.

Cybersecurity today is a major worry, not just for tech companies but for any computer user. Attacks are happening more frequently and it's essential to act fast, not just in dealing with them but also in damage limitation. Criminals are now using highly sophisticated and up-to-date systems based on artificial intelligence, but those of us who need to defend ourselves have learned to rely on the same weapons. Once again, technology can create problems, but it can also help us tackle and resolve them.

FASHION'S BEST KEPT SECRET

It's true that large numbers of young entrepreneurs have thrown themselves into the internet believing that it was all simple, that success was easily obtained, but the reality for all of us was far more complex.

I worked extremely hard with my team to achieve success, often with much more sophisticated marketing than we would have used in "the real world." If I think back to the early years of YOOX, I see a succession of problems that arose one by one. To resolve them we sometimes used traditional approaches, while at other times we had to be completely innovative. Everything ran along a razor edge, with the precipice on one side and salvation on the other. YOOX wasn't born in a day. It was a project conceived and remodeled over years of experimentation.

We had to stand out, be noticed, we had to put together a personality: many pressing needs had to be faced. A touch of daring helped.

Lina Sotis, one of the most experienced fashion journalists of the time, wrote an article in the *Corriere della Sera* describing YOOX as "Europe's largest and most visited e-concept store. In other words, an internet seller of clothing and accessories by great designers, hard to find in stores." Rhys Blakely, who worked for *The Times* from Asia and is now their science correspondent, wrote that YOOX "likes to be known as 'fashion's best kept secret,'" and continued: "Signor Marchetti has chosen to avoid normal marketing strategies, preferring to rely on satisfied fashion victims who spread the word."

One of the reasons behind these declarations is that YOOX from its inception has always had a strong identity and an unmistakable style, and this thanks to the brand marketing strategy I devised for my company. We were different from other sites: we were careful in choosing to present our products in a way that did not conflict with the fashion houses, or with our rival, Amazon. We wanted to become known, to expand, to be seen as more "intelligent," because we had always thought of our customers as being smarter than others; we offered clothing that was not sold in shops, and our prospective market was as large as the net. Potentially, it covered the whole planet.

A JOURNEY INTO BEAUTY

I've always been against the total look which in those years was almost a diktat among designers: to dress from head to foot in Armani, Prada, or Valentino was normal for those who followed luxury. We, on the other hand, encouraged our customers to mix and match, to pick their own style through our virtual wardrobe looking for the piece that was "just right" for them and to combine it with absolute freedom in such a way as to create a personal look. We were a breeding ground for trends, a storm in the panorama of glamour. The result was a journey into the beauty and into the dream that makes you want to own those objects. I've always felt that we have transformed our customers into bricoleurs, into people who play at composing lines of fashion phrases that depend on their sensibility, their culture, and their patience. The website was like a colored spray in a static environment. On the home page there was originally an area where customers could leave comments, The Voice of the Customer, a kind a social forum ahead of its time.

Over the years we became a major research center for the study of customer tastes and the evolution of fashions. We were considered important from the point of view of information on the changes in social behavior and style trends, as well as on the identification of development programs for many products.

YOOX was always on the move, in continual evolution. I was often dissatisfied with the results; I felt I could do something more or better. I had an absolute urge for perfection that forced me to question everything. YOOX may not have changed so much when seen from the outside but, in fact, there were continual and gradual variations.

The pursuit of freedom, of difference, has always been the lifeblood of YOOX: each person finds their own clothing and their own personality. This was its heart—a young experimental heart.

Most of its customers were aged between twenty-four and thirty-four, lived outside the great urban centers, and had a fair spending power. They went online from their office. Instead of going out for a cigarette or a coffee, they'd allow themselves something they might not otherwise have bought, behind the boss's back—after a while we started using a plain cardboard box rather than the original colored packaging so as not to make it too conspicuous when delivered to their workplace.

Over 70 percent were return customers: they started with a casual visit, then came back to buy, returning many times over the years.

Moreover, right from the start, I chose young people to work with in the company. Our customers were young, so was I. We knew what they wanted because we wanted the same. There was a generational understanding. Much of YOOX's success was generated by word of mouth. We decided never to push too far with marketing to the detriment of other forces. We simply did what we had to do; we invested in service rather than in advertising and, as an indirect effect of our creativity and reliability, many people encouraged others to get to know us.

Word began to spread almost immediately; people were talking about this crazy colorful, free and democratic site, in which you could match and purchase clothes online, you could try them at home, return them easily, and save money. The YOOX experience was like choosing the best garments from a large basket of designer labels which, for some unknown reason, had gone unnoticed until that moment.

YOOX was fun, it was a meta-brand where fashion multiplied and spread, re-emerging in a multiplicity of forms. It had an essence and left space for those who had the curiosity to follow it.

In all the cultural projects we have created, and which I will describe, the logo was intentionally hidden. It never appeared as it does in the traditional commercial initiatives—it was discreet and had to be searched out.

CIAO, ROBOT

In January 2001 we decided it was time to give YOOX a proper launch, in full splendor—we had the money, we'd had a good financial year and knew the market existed. We just needed to display ourselves at our best.

I met Raffaello Napoleone, CEO of Pitti Immagine, a company in Florence that organized one of the most important international fashion fairs. I suggested a highly innovative installation that embodied us but would catch the eye. After all, to put up a stand with end-of-season products is unthinkable and pointless. Producing a video would be a traditional but tedious way of promoting ourselves—the big names had more money and better skills to do that. So we devised something more artistic and unusual: With Alberto Biagetti, we opted for a robot. The idea was triggered by a specific brief: I told Alberto that when people ask me what YOOX is, I'd like a robot to give the answer in my place.... There again, the cover models on our site were conceived as muses, as goddesses that shifted between the sacred and science fiction, so we decided that our transposition from virtual reality to an open space in the center of Florence would occur in exactly this way, through science fiction. We didn't want our fascination to be lost—we didn't want to look normal. We preferred to arrive in physical space through a "person" and a guise that this time was no longer virtual, as on our site, but was tangible. We therefore did exactly the opposite of what we were doing with the virtual covers: We created a rigid, architectural piece that was also a design object.

Alberto was working at that time with Studio Azzurro, a group of artists that created installations using technology. They had just created software for autistic children who had relational difficulties and yet opened up to a 3D interface operated with a glove by a human behind the scenes. We decided to use it to construct an imaginary creature. The result was an androgynous robot, half-man, half-woman, a celestial figure with different-colored eyes, like those of David Bowie. It had a monitor on which an artificial face appeared, and a body built on a frame. The face was created in 3D by a videogame designer and, thanks to a mass of computers, came to life in real time. It had an incredible voice because we built it with sound modulators, and the effect was truly impressive.

An installation with a gender-fluid flavor—we were already working on concepts that are now taken for granted. A graceful figure, no hair, indeterminate sex, a magnificent creature wearing a garment that resembled a spacecraft.

The result was magical because hidden behind the structure was Massimiliano Foà, a brilliant Neapolitan actor who made the robot interact with the public. People asked him all kinds of questions, and he gave his answers using poetical, almost philosophical phrases. Everyone knew it wasn't just a robot, but no one could work out the trick behind it. The effect was fabulous. Massimiliano never said: "Buy Armani or Diesel end-of-season clothing at 50 percent," but would talk about other things like: "I don't know what scent your flowers have, for I have never sniffed them."

It was arranged so that you could sit in front of the monitor with alluring images: there was a camera that saw you, a microphone that heard you, and a loudspeaker through which you heard Massimiliano's voice.

The result produced a surreal effect that drew so much interest that at one point our robot in the main Pitti pavilion was surrounded by hundreds of people who wanted to talk to it.

This was YOOX's first real marketing venture to launch itself in the fashion world. The next step, a few months later, was to put the robot in the window of the Fiorucci store in Piazza San Babila, in Milan. Elio Fiorucci was a brilliant designer and businessman, adored by Bianca Jagger, Grace Jones, and Andy Warhol. In 1984 he had invited the US artist Keith Haring to design the walls of his store, giving him a free hand. Armed with spray cans, Haring created wonderful graffiti formed around his unique stylized human figures. Fiorucci was a great inspiration when it came to the playful aspect of YOOX. His shop in Milan was a kind of Mecca where fashion journalists went to look around, and always came away enthralled.

Eager for novelty and passionate about art, Elio fell in love with our robot. He wasn't the only one. Some people came back every day: a kind of magnetism had been created around the mystery of how it managed to talk, and around Massimiliano's rhetorical gifts.

The inauguration in the store took place one evening. We invited Elserino Piol too, who had great fun. Massimiliano had been given photos of the more important people who would be there, and he called out in the darkness: "Ciao, Elserinoooo." It was like something from a Fellini movie with the robot repeating: "Elserinoooo, where are you? Elserinoooo, Elserinoooo," like *Amarcord.*

Massimiliano's words were romantic, never commercial. He was hidden away and had a camera screen to show him what was going on, but you looked around and couldn't figure it out, because behind the robot there was nothing. All the same, you would hear: "My name is Yoox. I live in a world where there are only clothes, but I like meeting people, I like talking to them."

It wasn't so obvious then as it might seem now. Robots weren't so common then, and the combination of a digital monitor and a genuine old-fashioned voice created a modern-day Pulcinella, a carnival mask, which cast a spell over its audience.

The robot then ended up as an exhibit at the Triennale Design Museum in Milan. It was there, in 2005, that we organized a memorable exhibition called *Dressing Ourselves,* curated by Alessandro Guerriero. It was a remarkable project with models designed by great creatives—names like Gaetano Pesce, Devendra Banhart, Ettore Sottsass, Enzo Cucchi, Andrea Branzi, Nathalie Du Pasquier, Alessandro Mendini, Mimmo Paladino—as if they were self-portraits.

It was an incredible, absurd, crazy project: an end-of-season fashion site was putting on an exhibition that could easily have been devised by Fondazione Prada, in terms of investment as well as creativity. No other site of our size would ever have done it. Guerriero's idea was that clothing was a contemporary way of immersing ourselves in a reality that was becoming more inclusive. They were dresses created not by designers but by artists, who transformed their ideas into a collective experience.

Today we see many projects that go in this direction, but at that time it was futuristic.

YOOX's marketing and communication was centered on creativity and imagination. Our platform has hosted various artistic collaborations. From a virtual emporium we have become a center of culture: these two things have always gone hand in hand. The content was important, whereas the sales came from the involvement of our potential customers who entered a room with a feeling of anticipation, surprise, excitement.

YOOX in its early years was a training ground. We were getting ready to play at national level, to be smart, to get to the top, but we still wanted to be ourselves. The true challenge lies in tackling real problems that will take us farther than we expect to go. We were dreamers who stimulated the desires of our customers.

Our goal was to transform the brand into a combination of emotions that promoted its success. What emotions were our customers looking for? YOOX has never used sound bytes or catchphrases (it has never, for example, had a slogan such as Nike's "Just do it"), but has always remained true to its core values: great usability, a tendency toward fun and working on the playful side of fashion, content that is different though never banal, presented with lightness, though at the same time we wanted to be totally serious in our dealings with customers.

PASSIONS & COLLABORATIONS

I tried to bring my own passions, to make them penetrate by osmosis into the company philosophy. Innovation, reliability, honesty—every time I left the house my mother would remind me to be honest!—but also art, music, and a very contemporary feeling toward nature and sustainability.

We wanted to astonish our customers, to be one step ahead, to excite their curiosity, so we chose to launch collections designed by artists, architects, and designers created especially for us. There were so many projects, but I want to recall some of them because they were also the result of my insistence on asking people to do out-of-the-ordinary things which not even they imagined they could do.

In 2002, with the American journalist Holly Brubach, staff writer for *The Atlantic* and *The New Yorker* and style editor of *The New York Times,* we created a vintage clothes section with various selections, including one centered around the creations of Emilio Pucci. Holly, much quoted in the fashion world, devised a project with the slogan, "Good fashion never dies." Everyone today talks about vintage. We internet pioneers put it online in 2002. We placed the emphasis on beauty, on the fact that if a garment is fabulous, it will always be fabulous. We gave our customers the opportunity to buy masterpieces of top fashion designed by legendary designers and couturiers—blending vintage with all the rest created a short-circuit whose date of birth was no longer important; its beauty was all that mattered.

Holly, with great intelligence, was able to perfectly interpret the character and personality of YOOX. Our vintage collection didn't meet a market demand, it mirrored our obsession for the unexplored, which in this case meant recouping capital otherwise lost in the fashion romance.

All these concepts at the beginning of the 2000s drew a younger, technological audience to glamour. It was an audience that had no interest in the rules of the system, one that was prepared to experiment in a new way, and to match garments that had their own life regardless of market deadlines. Today these are highly topical concepts. Sites have been created in which you can buy just vintage and items from past seasons, and where you can buy and sell wardrobes that belonged to other people. But at that time we were the only ones doing it and mixing everything together.

THE ONE AND ONLY MALCOLM MCLAREN

Another collaboration I will never forget was with the great Malcolm McLaren, the legendary manager of the Sex Pistols, who created a children's collection exclusively for YOOX.

I met Malcolm at Holly's birthday party in 2003. She had invited twenty friends to dinner at a lodge in Connecticut when it started snowing madly. We were incarcerated; no one could get away for three days. Among the guests was McLaren, a great friend of hers. I started talking to him and was fascinated by his stories, by his personal history and his whole past. Malcolm was a visionary and I decided to throw out a challenge. I've done this many times in my life: with Luca Guadagnino, inviting him to become an interior designer, with Stefano Accorsi, urging him to direct his first film, and with Malcolm McLaren, suggesting he became a fashion designer. He had been married to Vivienne Westwood, the famous English fashion designer who died in 2022. She had played a significant role in the creation of the punk image as well as revolutionizing the British spirit of irony, but he himself had never designed a collection. I suggested an experiment. He was struck by the fact that I hadn't asked him to prove himself on his own territory but to invent something entirely new. The most obvious thought would have been a punk collection, but Malcolm decided instead to do a line for children inspired by video games, and particularly by retro gaming and the vintage Pac-Man fantasies.

Malcolm felt that the two cultural phenomena of that moment were karaoke and video games, and he worked on the latter. He was creative, demanding, and perfectionist. I tried to support him in every way, like any patron who loved the work of his favorite artist. Over certain details he really drove us crazy, but the results were extraordinary. He was convinced that children were the real subjects to focus on because they were still untainted, not targeted by official diktats. In his view, they were perfectly able to interpret the playful spirit that stops fashion from taking itself too seriously, a concept that I embraced from the very start with YOOX, and to which McLaren gave a highly personal look.

We began to study the collection, produced in Italy, in the Marche region, therefore all Made in Italy, working with his partner at that time, Young Kim, whose memoirs about sex published in 2020 caused quite a stir in the United States. The project lasted a year: He and Young would fly from London to the Marche to follow the whole production aspect. The end product was a fantastic and amusing line, connected also musically to the whole of retro gaming. And to launch it we printed a vinyl with some of Malcolm's unpublished pieces. I can't say that we became friends, but we saw a great deal of each other. I remember going one evening to his house in Paris. I expected to find an infinity of punk-rock memorabilia but instead the apartment was white, ascetic, minimalist, with no picture, nothing. Maybe her taste had prevailed or—I don't know—maybe they both hated knickknacks and had turned against the past. Then, at dinner, two unlikely things happened: at one point he asked me to follow him behind a window and to keep him covered so that he could smoke a cigarette without Young seeing (the inventor of the Sex Pistols frightened of being caught with a cigarette!), then, since he much enjoyed his drink, he fell asleep rather drunk at the table just like that. He was funny and unconventional. When he came to Milan we took him to visit a student squat and what I remember most was the discussion about our society which, according to him, would become "no sex"—he would certainly laugh now if he read Young's racy book *A Year on Earth with Mr. Hell.*

The collection went well and, most of all, we had great fun.

BUT LEONARDO HAD PREDICTED EVERYTHING

Another project I'm proud of is the support we gave in 2014 to Milan's Biblioteca Ambrosiana which houses Leonardo da Vinci's *Codex Atlanticus,* one of the most important Italian treasures of humanity, a voyage into the artist's imagination and into his brilliant intuitions. I like to think of Leonardo as the precursor, in his own way, of the internet. In fact he imagined the invention of a means by which people could connect and communicate across boundaries in a shared language: "Men of distant countries speaking to one another and answering and speaking and touching and embracing each other, being in opposite hemispheres, and understanding each other's languages." Today we call it the internet, or even Zoom!

Codex Atlanticus comprises 1,119 sheets of designs, projects, and sketches which illustrate his extraordinary studies. If it were in New York, I'm sure there would be a queue stretching at least three blocks to see it, whereas we hardly know it's there.

After McLaren, there were many more collections and special collaborations: Jeremy Scott in 2006, Antony and the Johnsons in 2007, Hedi Slimane in 2010, Takashi Murakami in 2014, Vanessa Beecroft in 2015, JW Anderson in 2020, and in 2019 we sold the whole wardrobe of Franca Sozzani's private collection after her death in 2016. With her son, Francesco Carrozzini, we selected 397 garments and 190 accessories she had owned and treasured, trying to respect her social commitment and her ability to deal with important topics even in the glossiest glamour magazines. The proceeds went to support the Franca Sozzani Fund for Preventive Genomics at Harvard's Brigham and Women's Hospital.

An encounter with the extraordinary Rosamond Bernier sat midway between fashion, art, and culture. Who was she? One of the most enchanting women I've ever met. An extraordinary storybook life: a highly cultured art expert, journalist, and glamour icon. She married three times, and had lived between Acapulco, Paris, and New York. After World War II, *Vogue America* sent her to Paris to write about the artistic and cultural renaissance of the French capital. She knew the artists most in vogue such as Jean Cocteau, Pablo Picasso, Henri Matisse, Georges Braque, Joan Miró, and later David Hockney. She was a friend of Frida Kahlo, with whom she flew to Mexico piloting airplanes and hunting wild animals, and knew Diego Rivera. She created and directed the art magazine *L'ŒIL*. On her return to New York after her second divorce, Rosamond lectured on Matisse, Picasso, Léger, and Max Ernst at the Metropolitan Museum of Art. When I was introduced to her by her granddaughter Chloe Grimshaw, an English friend of my then-girlfriend Kerry, I was besotted by her. She was ninety-seven years old but discerning, chic, and had a unique charm. When she came to New York it was customary to invite her to dinner at Four Seasons, her favorite restaurant.

It was my special date: She would tell me a thousand stories and was enthusiastic about what I was doing, about this new internet, which moreover she used freely, writing emails and browsing websites. She woke each morning at eleven, drank a glass of champagne, then worked from bed, never rising before midday.

To mark the publication of her second book, *Some of My Lives: A Scrapbook Memoir* (her first had been *Matisse, Picasso, Miró: As I Knew Them*), we prepared a presentation box for it, signed by her and sold on yoox.com. It was something special that blended art and fashion—exactly what I loved. For the occasion we organized an event at Four Seasons with the whole American fashion elite, including such names as Holly Brubach and Anna Wintour, editor-in-chief of *Vogue USA*, whom Rosamond had mentored.

The last time I saw Rosamond was on her hundredth birthday. We celebrated at New York's Colony Club. She was still going out—just five years before, she had been on a long journey through India—and though physically weak and now in a wheelchair, she was splendidly lucid.

When I think back over these events, I realize how lucky I've been, and often ask myself: How did I get from Ravenna to the very heart of the New York elite and its glamour? I've tried many times to answer this question: the first answer is that it was chance, but then I add that it was a mixture of audacity and having no feeling of inferiority. In fact I've never done much in the way of networking, as they teach you in college, but over the years I've come to know a load of people almost by accident. And then I'm a great believer in the magic of coincidence; you'll certainly know the theory of the six degrees of separation by which each of us is connected to another person through a chain of acquaintances in which there are no more than six intermediaries. Well, Rosamond is also the inspiration for Wes Anderson's film *The French Dispatch*. Her character is played by Tilda Swinton, the actress who is the muse for my friend Luca Guadagnino. She and Luca both came to spend a day at my house in Como. Coincidences seem to play a large part in my life; I have a long list of them!

As I was saying, we were a breeding ground of ideas, and every year we invented crazy schemes. Some, I must admit, were too far ahead of their time and didn't bring the anticipated results in publicity terms because not many people understood them.

In 2010 we launched a perfume in a bottle shaped like a stiletto-heeled shoe and named after the fashion journalist Anna Dello Russo. She now has 2.7 million followers on Instagram and is one of the most popular influencers. At that time she was creative director of *Vogue Japan* and had the idea of becoming a personality. Years later, on Net-a-Porter, she auctioned off her bottomless wardrobe collected over thirty years. She organized a mega-party during Milan Fashion Week and announced that she wanted to lighten up her life, get rid of all her clothing, and donate the proceeds to young people with talent.

In 2008 we decided to produce signed calendars. We thought of Chiho Aoshima, a Japanese artist and member of Takashi Murakami's Kaikai Kiki collective. She was unknown at that time but later collaborated with many fashion houses, including Louis Vuitton.

YOOX was a talent scout and launched stylists who would become famous—names such as JW Anderson or Giovanna Battaglia, now the global creative director of the Swarovski Group who in 2013 designed a mobile phone cover for YOOX, as well as the model Bianca Balti, who made her debut on our site with her extremely successful first collection of beachwear.

We also succeeded in getting Antony and the Johnsons, an American music ensemble on the crest of the wave in the early 2000s. Antony (now Anohni) is a transgender singer with a special sensibility and voice. We enjoyed experimenting and asked her to design a garment that we could then put up for sale on eBay with the proceeds donated to a charity working for transgender people.

We produced the garment and when the moment arrived for her to sign it, Kerry and I went to her home in New York. Her apartment was pure white with a wonderful grand piano at the far end. I had been given two garments: one to leave with her as a memento and the other for her to sign, which I would take back to Milan to sell. And there, as I often do, I got into a real mess—I gave her the wrong one, then took it from her to replace it with the right one. She stared at me and wondered who this Italian was who first handed her a dress, then snatched it away. I didn't know where to hide myself and, having sorted it all out, I scampered off with Kerry telling me: "You're the real master of disasters!"

GET IT WRONG, TRY AGAIN, LEARN

Not every project worked. Some barely got off the ground, or they flopped shortly after.

We tried selling sex toys shortly before our stock exchange listing in December 2009. We organized a "Quirky Christmas," introducing a section of luxury sex toys on the website. We called it Good Vibration and sold a line of underwear called Agent Provocateur and several vibrators. This was 2006, and such items weren't often found outside sex shops. Years later they would be on display in concept stores, but at the time it was a taboo. Some customers were pleased to see them on the site, others gave us a hard time. Our chief financial officer, who had to guide us through the listing process, was an old-school practicing Catholic. He called Max and told him: "If you put vibrators on yoox.com then I'm not quoting you." Max tried to explain, to remind him that ours was a young, fun site, but he wouldn't listen. At that point I suggested he call Jimmy Jane, the Los Angeles supplier who made these designer vibrators studded with Swarovski, asking him not to send any more to us.

"Okay, don't worry," Jimmy replied. "But what's the name of your CFO? Let's play a trick on him: I'll have a vibrator made with his name and telephone number engraved on it, then I'll send it to him." We arranged everything with the courier so that it arrived as an urgent delivery during an important meeting with all the managers around the table. I pretended to get angry and told him: "Okay, if it's so urgent that it has to be delivered during a meeting, then open it, let's see what it is!"

He swore he had no idea what was inside and, when he opened the pack, shouted: "It's not mine!"

But I looked at the name and telephone number engraved on it and said: "It's obviously yours!"

We fell about laughing, but from then on vibrators vanished from the site. Max, in a fit of guilt, bought the remaining stock of a hundred at fifteen euros each and gave them as Christmas presents to his women friends.

The sex-toy debacle was followed by disappointment with the Pet-A-Porter line of collars and other accessories for dogs and cats. It had been created to irritate those in Net-a-Porter, my fiercest rival at the time. Pets are found on every site today, but I could persuade only Dsquared to work with us—all the other brands held back. It was too early: They weren't yet ready.

The idea of including music in the site and launching Radio YOOX died before it was born—in fact, I was the one who killed it after my initial enthusiasm. I thought that since customers could neither touch nor smell the clothing, they deserved at least some sound to accompany their purchases. But our information showed that most orders in Europe and the United States came from offices, nearly always made during the lunch break, except for the Japanese who connected late at night, and I realized it might backfire. When you're at work it's not a good idea to listen to music and be caught by your boss while you're on YOOX instead of doing your job. It's better if there's silence and if the package that arrives on your desk looks anonymous.

Another project that never got off the ground was our decision to invite several magazines to manage their own e-commerce. Only *Harper's Bazaar America* accepted, but the results were disappointing.

Being far ahead of the times can offer an extraordinary opportunity or be a catastrophic disaster. In these cases it was the latter and when in 2022 I saw that *W*, the famous American monthly fashion magazine, was launching its e-commerce store, I had the feeling it's sometimes better to arrive a little later. I could carry on listing project failures: the magazine *The New Yooxer*, ecological bicycles inspired by the iconic Graziella bike I had as a child, sportswear, the Strambo bags that you could personalize in a hundred ways, but most of all I remember the Billie Eilish collection. I was sure she would become a star and it seemed she wanted to design a line of her own. We would have sold it exclusively on YOOX—it would have been a real coup—but the marketing director at that time (we're talking about 2018) was someone interested in numbers, data, processes, therefore level-headed, unconscious of this creative aspect, and it took him many, too many months to complete the contract, substantially wrecking the project. Billie Eilish shot to fame a year later, becoming one of the greatest female singer-songwriters of all time, with over sixty-five million album units sold, a worldwide success, with countless awards and accolades. We could have had sole rights to sell creations designed by her. Instead, through the fault of a technocrat, it came to nothing. You will ask: Why put everything in the hands of a marketing director? Why not push him to clinch the deal? Good question. Up to two years before then, I was the person responsible for communication and creativity, but after the merger with Net-a-Porter my thoughts were elsewhere; I'd left YOOX to my team. The marketing director was a genius when it came to figures, and the largest part of e-commerce company investment is technical. He was insensitive to content and therefore failed to understand Billie Eilish's potential, which unfortunately in the end never traveled through our site. Never mind!

DREAM THE IMPOSSIBLE AND MAKE IT POSSIBLE

We wanted to break the sound barrier, to go beyond, to see something that had never been seen before, something unimaginable. This is rather the opposite of influencers today who create publicity at the same time for lots of companies who, in turn, are oblivious to the fact that the same influencer has maybe spent a year on Instagram promoting handbags sold by their number-one rival. Well, I've never copied or followed anyone. I wanted to do something entirely new every time. It was thrilling because you never knew what the end result would be; there was an overriding sense of uncertainty. I never knew whether something good would come of it, but I've always felt that experimentation sometimes needs to end in failure, that there would be no surprise or success without error and defeat.

My "alternative and nonsense" marketing didn't stop at the capsule collections. I wanted everything to be special. I asked Luca Guadagnino one Christmas to design a panettone container to give to friends of YOOX. He created a magnificent object in a wonderful glossy blue, a real collector's piece, as was the presentation box for André Aciman's book *Call Me by Your Name*, on which he had based his film. We asked the author to sign copies which we sold online.

We had a spirit of adventure. We headed into unexplored and alien territory. There was a creative exuberance and an urge to communicate our diversity. We wanted to surprise. Everything was worthy of intricate care, and even our brightly colored workspaces were created to stand on the very edge, to fluctuate between real and virtual.

It's generally known that the more recent premises of Google, Facebook, and many tech companies have their own play spaces. The theory that an inspiring and creative environment can have a positive influence on work quality is equally well known. In 1999 the digital companies and Silicon Valley weren't yet models copied everywhere, but while I hadn't installed hammocks, or slides to get from one floor to another, I always chose "offices with a view" and created a work setting in which enjoyment and commitment went together.

Shawn Achor, American author and Harvard graduate, considered to be the leading expert on happiness, and author of TED Talks with millions of followers, has written several bestsellers on what makes people happy. "We're not happy because we're successful; we're successful because we're happy." He goes on to explain: "If you can raise the order of somebody's level of positivity in the present, then their brain experiences what we now call a happiness advantage, which is, your brain in positive performs significantly better than it does in negative, neutral or stressed. [...] In fact, what we've found is that every single business outcome improves. Your brain in positive is 31% more productive than your brain in negative, neutral or stressed. You're 37% better at sales. Doctors are 19% faster and more accurate in coming up with a crack diagnosis when positive instead of negative, neutral or stressed. Which means we can reverse the formula. If we can find a way of becoming positive in the present, then our brains work even more successfully, as we're able to work harder, faster and more intelligently."

YOOX, like many other companies opening at that time, found itself in a constantly changing market characterized by a need for flexibility that was unprecedented in economic history. In 2000 we were happily lost in organizational chaos, which at that time produced more benefits than problems. To bring order to this stimulating growth, I used a model that I like to call "cosmological," where instead of organizational boxes there were circles: my collaborators knew that there were systems around which to revolve according to the problems that appeared each day. Then we apportioned responsibilities with greater accuracy and sought to construct a "neural" model to ensure that everyone knew as much as possible about the company. But in the end even this model had its limits, and I had to look upon YOOX as an organism that needs to change its skin from time to time. What does this mean? It means there's a limit to the sharing of responsibility when a company grows large, and that each person must take their own responsibility. Companies change, and when mistakes are made it's important to find a method, which we recognize as temporary and uncertain but which all the same is a methodology, that enables us to act by observing what we are doing, giving a measure to our actions.

But going back to entertainment, on June 21 each year we celebrate the birthday of YOOX by organizing a party with the slogan "Happy Birthday to You, Happy Birthday to Yoox!" Traditional companies generally have a Christmas dinner with a speech from the CEO, but startups abandon the formalities and have loads of fun.

The June 21 party in 2008 was memorable. It was to be organized by Max, who suggested a musical event and agreed to persuade eight artists to produce a brand-new song for YOOX. The resulting compilation, with the title *We(Ar) Dancing*, would end up on our site so that customers could download it. Remember that Spotify didn't yet exist, and the online music boom was still far away. The party was in a country villa near Bologna and was to involve a contest between impromptu DJs, many of whom were YOOX employees. There were 4,500 people dancing around the swimming pool. Max, from Rimini and a regular clubber, had one line in mind, while I wanted to aim high. We put two or three names together but didn't have that name that made you say, "Wow!"

Then, by an incredible stroke of luck, Max happened to find the contact for Duran Duran's agent who was organizing a tour in Europe. Forty-eight hours later he sends him two links, one of which is an unpublished version of "Skin Trade." Max calls me, mad with joy: "I have Duran Duran's 'Skin Trade' done with the Arctic Monkeys." Within a couple of hours the compilation had reached hundreds of thousands of downloads and the site went crazy.

8

In September 2001, with the attack on New York's Twin Towers, the world held its breath. That day, when the World Trade Center collapsed, our feeling of security also crumbled, and the global economy was in shock. The Towers held much of Wall Street's IT systems (I too had worked here during my training at Lehman Brothers) and when the Stock Exchange reopened on September 17 nothing was the same as before: Wall Street had lost around $1,400 billion. It is reckoned that the physical damage from the attack totaled some $55 billion and that more than 400,000 people lost their jobs over the next three months. People were afraid to fly or to leave their homes: Americans were stunned, depressed, unable to accept that such vicious hatred had fallen upon them. The myth of invulnerability was shattered. As the writer Paul Auster put it: "We all knew this could happen. We have been talking about the possibility for years, but now that the tragedy has struck, it's far worse than anyone ever imagined. [...] We have no precedent for what has happened today, and the consequences of this assault will no doubt be terrible. More violence, more death, more pain for everyone. And so the twenty-first century finally begins."

On September 11, we were in the office when we heard Hilary cry out. She had just seen the first plane crash into one of the towers and was terrified. She was from New York and part of her family lived in Manhattan, not far from the World Trade Center. We rushed to watch the TV coverage. We thought at first that it was an accident, a navigation error. Hilary searched desperately for news, but there was no connection. Soon after, we saw the second plane crash into the other tower and all doubt was dispelled: It was a terrorist attack.

I had studied and worked in New York, yet what was happening seemed so unbelievable. I couldn't imagine what it would be like to be there, in the World Trade Center, imprisoned on a top floor with no means of escape. That afternoon, we all decided to close the website, to make our contribution to the memory of those who were no longer with us. We went to the warehouse and held hands in a circle, to show our affection and our closeness to Hilary. In such a dramatic moment, yoox.com was one of the few sites to suspend business, but the sense of community and respect mattered more to us than anything else. This is what I meant when I spoke about values: putting people before business, believing in relationships, in solidarity, in friendship. If I think about what happened after—during the pandemic, for example, when I decided to close activities in our distribution centers even though it wasn't legally obligatory—I feel there's a golden thread that links us from the time we started until the moment I left the company.

The Twin Towers was a shock. I felt paralyzed, as if everything was at a standstill, waiting to know, to understand how to move forward.

They were difficult times. The predominant feelings were fear, uncertainty, inability to think beyond the next day. No one could predict what the future held, though many things have changed since then, especially for digital technology and for the internet which resumed its inexorable march (despite its ups and downs).

In the meantime, we had moved headquarters from Casalecchio to Zola Predosa, still on the outskirts of Bologna, before making our final move in 2004 to an area that seemed rather like an American campus (the so-called "business park"), a building designed in the late 1970s by the architect Adolfo Natalini. There we put my "Lego strategy" into effect: first we took the ground floor, then the one below, then the one above, and finally a small adjacent building. And when we needed a new warehouse in 2007, we went to Bologna Interporto where we rented a space which we also expanded through a number of adjoining warehouses that each stocked specific kinds of commodity. Data analysis showed us that when customers bought, say, a pair of shoes, they usually bought nothing else, so the package could leave directly from that warehouse without passing through the central warehouse. This network of warehouses later grew further. We then robotized, transforming it into a model of efficiency and experimentation which I will describe later.

In 2001 I also realized that it was difficult to run all operations from Bologna—I couldn't ask brand, marketing, and communications staff to join us there. So I decided it was time to open an office in Milan. I had a tight budget but managed to find a small but magnificent space in the Torre Velasca. The people of Milan have a real affection for that mushroom-shaped skyscraper, built in the very heart of the city in 1956 by the BBPR partnership (Gianluigi Banfi, Lodovico Barbiano di Belgiojoso, Enrico Peressutti, and Ernesto Nathan Rogers), four famous pioneering architects who built one of Italy's first examples of brutalism. The three-room office has a wonderful view of Milan Cathedral: I feel I have reached the summit.

We organize meetings there, but someone might sometimes sleep there in the office and appear next morning at the door, half awake. It once happened to a colleague who came up for an investors' meeting with Net Partners. He tried to get in, knocked several times, and was greeted by Massimiliano Foà, our robot actor from Naples, barefoot, in pajamas, with disheveled hair, who then went straight back to sleep.

Those people were surprised, but for many of us it seemed almost normal. We've all heard stories about tech companies with nerds lying about on the floor. Well, it was just like that, for better or worse. When we were in the middle of a job, it often seemed impossible to break off. For many years we were a community, a tightly knit group in which private and office life merged together. Maybe it was because we didn't see it as a real job, but as a personal challenge. In crucial moments, in times of need, no one held back: at Christmas, for example, all of us went to the warehouse to pack and send the orders off so they'd reach our customers in good time.

THE AMERICAN DREAM BECOMES REALITY

One of our many projects was to open an office in New York, but we needed to be cautious, to wait for the right moment. My growth strategy was closely linked to international expansion. I knew that Italy was a small market, that Europe was certainly larger, but America was largest of all. I wanted to land there, but I also had my eye on Tokyo, for I felt sure that Japanese youngsters were genuine fashion victims, and that Tokyo could become another important center.

I needed money to finance this expansion and what I had received from the first two investment funds was almost finished: I needed a capital increase.

In this tempestuous climate, and in the middle of what had become a hotbed of ideas and activity, something extraordinary happened. Halfway through 2002 I managed to contact the London branch of Benchmark Capital, a Silicon Valley venture capital company, something akin to the Rolls-Royce of the sector. Benchmark Capital, founded by Bruce Dunlevie, Andy Rachleff, Bob Kagle, Kevin Harvey, and Val Vaden, was based in Menlo Park, California, and had been a leading figure in some of the most important tech investments, including eBay in 1997, when it invested 6.7 million dollars for 22.1 percent of the company. Over the next few years Benchmark was behind capital increases in some of the most famous dot.com companies: from Uber, in which they invested $12 million for an 11 percent share, to Dropbox, Twitter, Snapchat, and Instagram. They were involved in what at first seemed a runaway success, but ended in a resounding flop with WeWork, the provider of coworking spaces which—as seen in the TV series *WeCrashed* with Jared Leto and Anne Hathaway—fell flat on its face before the initial public offering, having received many millions of dollars from various investment funds, including Benchmark (which very wisely managed to get out before it went bankrupt).

They offered me an investment of $7.2 million. This, for YOOX, was an enormous opportunity. It meant positioning the company on an entirely different level, becoming a global company rather than always being seen as Italo-centric, even if it sold throughout Europe. Being with them would mean playing in the top league.

I had to choose between two strategic options: I could either continue with the business I had already set up, selling the left-over stock of multi-label stores and designer names without seeking further investment, or I could add a series of articles such as food, for example, like Amazon, which started out with books but now sold everything. For me the most sensible option was to remain anchored to the fashion business without diversifying into other sectors (which might have harmed relationships with fashion designers who were always selective, as they were with physical distribution) while trying at the same time to grow internationally. Espousing Benchmark meant entering the United States by the main door. I aimed to explore new geographical areas and new markets, and America was first on the list. Having Benchmark on board would be a major step forward, also with a view to Stock Exchange listing, which had always been my ultimate goal.

I flew to London to meet Mark Evans, general partner of their British branch, Balderton Capital. Evans spent fifteen years with Goldman Sachs, along with his twin brother (whom I would meet later while dealing with Alibaba in China, as we'll see later), and is regarded as a company "constructor" since he has experience both in the financial services sector and with Silicon Valley, where he lived for two years. Mark was enthusiastic about the business model, understood the route I wanted to take, recognized areas for further expansion, but said: "For us the valuation is too high." When I asked him what I could do, he explained that he needed to buy shares from other shareholders at a lower price in order to reduce the average cost per share. He asked whether there was anyone who wanted to sell. "Honestly, I don't think so," I replied, "but I can put you in contact with Diego di San Giuliano."

Diego's family weren't very enthusiastic, in fact they really didn't want to sell, but Marchese di San Giuliano, Diego's father decided to hand over a small portion of his shareholding to Benchmark to help the project along. He too could see that their partnership would enhance the whole investment. For us it was a true seal of quality. At that time we were—and maybe we still are—their sole investment in Italy.

I obviously also decided to reduce my own shareholding with the capital increase, so that at the end of 2002 we cashed in $7.2 million and Mark Evans joined the board of directors.

I couldn't wait to broaden my horizon, to expand, and 2003 was a truly spectacular year, marking a personal and professional turning point.

ARTICLE OF FAITH

On December 30, 2002, an article appeared in *BusinessWeek*, written by Kerry Capell, their senior correspondent in London, which gave the seal of approval to YOOX. Capell writes:

> When Federico Marchetti founded yoox.com in Bologna two years ago, he reckoned the website would be a big hit with fashion-conscious consumers. With discounts of up to 50% off retail prices on end-of-season merchandise from 300 leading designers, it's easy to see why. But it wasn't until a group of cloistered nuns in Tuscany placed an order for seven pairs of Miu-Miu mules last year that Marchetti realized just how big the market was. "It showed me that Yoox' appeal is apparently irresistible," he jokes.

> Yoox is a rare success story in an industry littered with failures. While most Net retailers are struggling to make money, Yoox is set to break even by the end of 2002, just two years after inception. Sales are on course to hit $12 million by year-end, double last year's.
>
> The site's name is a play on the company's slogan—"Fashion is timeless." [...] Yoox is quickly adding customers in the U.S., where its new site made its debut two months ago. And with more than $15 million in capital from a host of European investors, Marchetti says he has more than enough cash to keep the business on track for the foreseeable future. "Yoox' business model is sustainable," says Jaap Favier, research director at Forrester Research in Amsterdam.
>
> [...] As any serious shopper will attest, buying designer items on the cheap can feel sinfully good. Those Miu-Miu-loving nuns in Tuscany would probably say amen to that.

The mules chosen by the nuns had a low heel and were delightful. When we telephoned the convent offering to let them have them free of charge, they answered that they would pray for us. Maybe this explains our success!

All the same, the words of *BusinessWeek* were music to my ears, and not just mine. A few months earlier, at Modus Publicity, a London communications agency that worked for us, I had met Kerry Olsen, a charming witty English woman with a British sense of humor. She ran the executive account for Benetton and the magazine *Colors* but had been catapulted into a meeting with me to stand in for a colleague who was following the YOOX account and was busy elsewhere. Kerry had graduated in law and had then spent two years in Japan, where she taught children English through a Japanese government scholarship at Tokushima on the island of Shikoku. Back in London, after our brief meeting at Modus, she worked as a buyer and trend forecaster for large Japanese stores and boutiques.

Kerry often tells friends that it wasn't love at first sight, but I intrigued her because I had interesting new ideas. At first, I think, she simply wanted to know me better, so when the article appeared in *BusinessWeek* with a photograph of me sitting on some YOOX boxes, she took the initiative and sent me a congratulatory email.

She suggested we met a few weeks later when she would be coming to Italy. She was often in Tokyo, I was always rushing here and there, but each time we arranged a time and place to meet, one of us was called away and couldn't make it. It took eighteen months before we finally managed to see each other in the same city at the same time. This long wait was truly tantalizing because the messages, phone calls, and emails were bringing us closer, creating almost an intimacy, though we had barely met. A mutual friend brought us together and that was the first spark. For nearly three years we traveled north and south—I flew up to London, she came to Bologna, or we met somewhere else. Slowly I began to realize it wasn't an affair like the others. For the first time, after many brief relationships with women that lasted just a week, I felt she was the person with whom I wanted to have a child. For many years I had devoted my whole time to YOOX and wanted no other commitments; I hadn't the mental space then to do it, but now I felt that things were changing. One day Kerry plucked up courage and told me she was moving to Milan the following week—she had taken a job there with Diesel, the company with which she was working in London. The sudden announcement gave me quite a fright; living together was an important step and if she hadn't done it first, I would probably have waited a few extra months.

Twenty-four hours after Kerry's arrival, I had to leave for America, and she found herself alone in Milan. For some time after, quite rightly, she criticized me for it. She spoke not a word of Italian. To call a taxi she had to go into one of the hotels and ask the doorman to do it for her, pretending to be a guest. It was a baptism by fire, which she passed with flying colors.

Kerry started to enjoy Italian life and in 2011, after the birth of Maggie, we left my bachelor pad—where we had turned the wardrobe into our daughter's room for the first twelve months of her life—for a larger apartment. That period also marked the beginning of our passion, not to say love, for Lake Como, a special place where we decided then to go and live. In 2012 we found a small house and garden to rent at Tremezzina. We used it for weekends and holidays, but in 2014, when Maggie started nursery school, we moved there permanently. Kerry volunteered to teach children English at the local school. But she was still writing, first for *WWD* and *Vogue America,* and now for *The New York Times,* and for *Condé Nast Traveller America.*

AN ITALIAN FLAG ON THE ROOF

In October 2003 we put the finishing touches to our expansion strategies in the United States and opened our first New York office. I'd been told that it made more sense, for tax reasons, to create an American company that would enable us to carry out marketing and be more efficient at a national level. I didn't want to travel there carrying a cardboard suitcase bound with adhesive tape, but it was rather like that in the end. Our accountant, Luigi Perin, was born in Rome and had gone to the United States to avoid military service. Today he is one of the most influential partners in a tax firm but at that time was newly qualified. Our lawyer Giuliano Iannaccone, the son of two confectioners who had emigrated to the States from Treviso, didn't even have an office, but he had a promising future and is now a partner in Tarter Krinsky & Drogin, one of New York's leading law firms. We got on well together, there was a good feeling, and we felt sure they were reliable and honest because they were friends of friends who had recommended them to us.

Our arrival happened in two stages. First, Hilary rented a top floor apartment in Soho with two bedrooms, an enormous sitting room, and a kitchen where she fixed memorable dinners. It was a home and an office; the idea was that she would start off with PR and communication to get us known. We persuaded the other occupants of the building to let us paint the front door with a geometric pattern invented by Alberto Biagetti using the YOOX colors, so that as you walked along Broadway at the junction with Grand Street you couldn't avoid noticing that door, which stood out from all the rest. We had a Starbucks next door where we sometimes held meetings to take advantage of their wi-fi and watched passersby stop to look at the front door—it remained like that for ten years, even after we had left.

Stage two, in 2006, was to open our first real American office. We decided to go to Hoboken, in New Jersey, because Manhattan was too expensive. We needed space and a large warehouse. Max flew there with the task of paving the way. In the meantime, we had employed a young German called Moritz straight from a graduate course at the Bocconi University in Milan where I had given a lecture. I sent him to Hoboken to finish setting up the office, to create a small local team (in keeping with the typical YOOX practice based on the principle of starting small and then growing), to contact suppliers, and to start working on the expansion of YOOX in the United States. We decided at that point to hoist an Italian flag on the roof of the building.

The United States was, and still is, the mecca of online luxury. In 2018 the United States still represented a third of YOOX Net-a-Porter sales. Even if Europe covered a wider overall share of the market, no single country was ever able to equal the United States.

Achieving success there was more difficult. Various Italian companies had failed, and the challenge for YOOX was enormous. We had no similar competitors, apart from the company Bluefly, based in New York, which was local and focused on the American market, whereas Yoox's strong point was its agreements with Italian-made fashion labels that American customers really loved.

Hoboken is where Frank Sinatra was born, large numbers of Italians live there, and waving the Italian tricolor immediately becomes an act of pride. The summer of 2006 was the year of the World Cup. We wanted to announce that we had officially arrived in America, that we're Italians. So we decided to give out free T-shirts to all YOOX customers. They were T-shirts we already had in the warehouse, produced for a previous event, which had a sphere that looked like a football and the slogan "Italians do it better." Italy won the World Cup, and our customers were truly convinced that we could see into the future!

TOKYO, HERE WE COME

By 2004 it was time to look toward Tokyo, where we set ourselves up in Daikanyama, near to Shibuya, a perfect district for fashion lovers. A few years later we moved to the shopping intersection at Omotesandō. Japan had long been synonymous with high, refined, minimalist fashion. I wanted to enter that difficult universe, but I knew I needed to do so cautiously by trying to understand their customs, to respect them, never to offend them.

I was passionate about Japan—and still am. Among the thousands of journeys I have made, those to the Land of the Rising Sun have been particularly special. I've been there some fifty times and think I have almost as many friends in Tokyo as in Milan. I had taken a course in Japanese culture at the Bocconi and learned to speak the language fairly well.

But I decided, before the launch of YOOX, to do some full immersion and spend the summer vacations traveling in places far from the tourist routes. I wanted to really understand my future customers, Japanese consumers, to enter their minds, to discover how they think. At the same time I knew that for the business part I needed a "guide," so I asked the advice of a Japanese friend I knew through Alessandro Guerriero. Kazunori Iwakura is a descendant of Tomomi Iwakura, one of the leading figures in Japan's transition from feudalism to modernity. His face ended up on ¥500 banknotes. Kazunori was refined, chic, creative, had lived in Italy for many years, and was well acquainted with his own country and with Tokyo's finest talents. He introduced me to the right people, revealed to me the unwritten rules, and so I started to find my way in this new territory.

YOOX's only competitor in Japan was Zozotown. Its founder, Yusaku Maezawa, is a billionaire who wants to be the first man to take a commercial flight around the Moon. Zozotown concentrated only on the national market. Their products were all in the medium-low price band, which eased returns: The higher the price of a product, the higher the number of returns, because the potential customer is more sophisticated and therefore more demanding.

Kazunori took me under his wing, let me meet the director of *Vogue Japan*, the local head of Pucci, the top manager of Coca-Cola. He introduced me to various Japanese fashion designers, including Mihara Yasuhiro and his wife Hiromi Uehara, a talented jazz pianist, and Koji Ono, who was the art director for several Louis Vuitton projects. In short, he initiated me into the Japanese business culture. I realized straightway that it was an important market for us, and I wanted to be there.

And that's how it went. YOOX was one of the few international retailers that could really expand there. It was well received by the Japanese, probably because we tried to be as Japanese as possible. In our packaging, for example, about which the Japanese are obsessed. We never sent packages directly from Bologna. We would send them to a local warehouse which would repackage them *ex novo* so there'd be no damage on the international route. The Japanese are fanatical about punctuality, so it was the only market in which we let customers decide the exact time the goods would be delivered.

CELLPHONE MON AMOUR

After my vacation in Japan, I had a sudden realization. I saw loads of people going about with their telephones, from which they are inseparable, and I recognized the potential. Cellphones there used the *keitai* system. They were everywhere, and everyone paid for everything by phone. I was mad about cellphones—they were my passion from when I was a student at the Bocconi. They were bulky at that time but totally revolutionary, and I could see that this object would change our way of communicating—and of purchasing too. The Tokyo office became our world center for cellphone experimentation: From there, I and a small group of technological enthusiasts studied all their possible uses. Bear in mind that the iPhone came out in 2007, but I had staked everything on the fact that we would be shopping through our telephones a couple of years before then. One of the four fantastic members of the YOOX team on our Japanese mission admitted he had been very skeptical, that he hadn't imagined cellphones could spread so massively, but he added: "You were spellbound by them, you followed your own path." The most popular cellphone at that time was the Blackberry, so it wasn't easy to imagine using it for purchases. Some of my team couldn't see what lay in the future, they couldn't picture the high-speed evolution of this object, but I was convinced that an object you always carry with you, that accompanies you everywhere, could only change and get better.

It took only a few years for a visionary like Steve Jobs to revolutionize our life. History has proved me right, and by 2020 most of the shopping on YNAP sites was done through smartphones. In the next few years, nearly all purchases on e-commerce sites could be carried out by mobile phone alone, even though it's possible at that point that mobile phones will no longer exist, that subcutaneous chips or smartwatches or metaverse glasses will replace them altogether. The mission of a tech company is always to keep one step ahead, to have the courage to implement promising new technology, even if it's often at an embryonic stage. The case history of YOOX (I can describe it in this way since an actual case study is being published at the Bocconi) speaks precisely of this: a future which is already present and a present that always looks ahead. Without ever stopping. Those who take the path of innovation know that there's no destination, but only a slow and continuous adaptation to the inventions, and to this planet's occasional revolutions.

The YOOX international teams generally consisted of people from those countries who knew and were a part of the local landscape. Moritz was also replaced by an American manager, Clement, when we moved the office from Hoboken to Tribeca, Manhattan. I wanted to adapt YOOX services and marketing so that they would be seen as American by the Americans, as Japanese by the Japanese, and so on in all the other markets. Even Italians, who have a traditional attraction to foreign things, didn't think YOOX was an Italian company—including our postman who announced each morning in his thick local dialect: "There's post for IOCS!"

In Japan, as in America and then in other countries, we have always collaborated with local organizations and institutions to give the feeling of being closer to the customer. In 2008, during Fresh Faces in Fashion—an event for emerging fashion designers during New York Fashion Week—we gave customers the chance to purchase several looks selected directly from the catwalk in order to extend our US market. The public could watch the show in live streaming, could enlarge the looks on sale, and could buy them months before the garments arrived in the stores. It was certainly innovative.

INNOVATION IN INNOVATION

We were at the end of 2004, and here began the adventure that would perhaps most influence the future of YOOX. Brands were beginning to realize that a website could be useful not just for communication but also for sales. YOOX had impressive skills, infrastructure, logistics and warehousing, as well as enviable technology. All were features that made it unique in a growing market: one which YOOX had the power to shape.

So I invited various brands to let us do the e-commerce for their sites. I was aware that it was more a question of image than of bringing a real increase in immediate sales, but I was sure it would drastically increase the level of interest in our company.

No fashion brand wanted to end up on Amazon: too down-market, too commercial, too many products from other sectors. They had turned to YOOX for surplus stock, but now the game was another: to have a real online presence, and each with their own flagship online store. I felt sure that the creation and management of websites would then, over the years, become strategic and even profitable.

YOOX was by now present in Europe, the United States, and Japan, and soon also in Asia (except for China). It had become truly global. Fashion house sites contained just the usual company information: videos, branding communications, but no e-commerce. The big labels had an antiquated conception of web architecture. They ran along two lines: one elitist, aesthetically perfect, devoted to the brands, and the other more functional and less organized from the visual point of view, reserved for shopping. Madness! I was against this approach from the very beginning. The fashion houses had spectacular stores spread across the international capitals; they needed also to replicate the same atmosphere on the web and to do even more. Content and e-commerce make sense only if they are intertwined.

Another obstacle was the proliferation of subsidiary lines: each of them had at least a couple of them—Dolce & Gabbana had D&G, Armani had Emporio, and so on. It was absurd, wasteful in terms of time and money to create a site for each of these, but that was exactly what they wanted. The right idea, which I suggested to everyone until I was tired of repeating it, was to imagine a single digital building with various floors separated in such a way that each could be "furnished" it as desired. The only one who didn't listen to me was Valentino, who wanted to make a separate site for Red Valentino, before then regretting it and backtracking.

YOOX had the best expertise and, four years after its creation, its know-how was now recognized in fashion circles. I created a team consisting of Max, Alberto, and Gabriele and explained my idea: to prepare complete packages to lease to brands so that they could make their own flagship stores. We set off for Diesel's original headquarters at Molvena, near Vicenza—they are now based in a state-of-the-art building not far away. Renzo's office is the castle tower—you have to cross a drawbridge where there's a display of pictures by famous photographers who portray him in various contexts. It's a scorching September day. We arrive at his office and Renzo is barefoot, wearing jeans and a T-shirt. He sits at the head of the table with all his managers around. Danilo, our sponsor who has been selling us Diesel stock for several years, breaks the ice by showing him the first slide. It says: "One million potential clients for Diesel." We had helped him to do a presentation which began with: "Ten million Diesel customers even today would have liked to purchase our product, but they haven't." It's obviously a provocation: the argument is that if Diesel opened their own e-commerce site, then many of their customers who were buying on yoox.com would be going directly to them. Danilo explains it to Renzo: "Yoox.com is now selling ten million euros of clothing; so if we really want to do our own online store, we have to do it with these guys because they're smart, powerful, competent." And that's how it ended a couple of years later: the Diesel.com site is powered by YOOX and Rosso became one of our biggest strategic partners.

There was a basic stratagem: The brands were all that the final customer saw. We were the invisible partners, the factotum behind the scenes, present during every stage of the process. The project was simple and at the same time complex: This operation could create a virtuous circle for the whole company, because by working with monobrands we could agree to long-term contracts, optimize strategies and pricing, and at the end of the season remove everything that hadn't been sold and put it on YOOX.

We could also share aggregated data gathered by yoox.com relating to customer preferences: not only what people are buying but also what they're not buying. I asked the brand managers: "Do you want to know what color of shoes sells best in Boston in comparison to those sold in Atlanta? I can tell you." I explained not only that they could gain a better understanding of their customers, but that the YOOX algorithms would help them to forecast reverse market trends.

I thought I had struck gold! It was a perfect plan: in fact I later discovered that it was perfect from the strategic but not from the financial point of view. I'll explain why below.

Before creating this new business unit, I approached my investors. The board of directors included Elserino Piol, Net

Partners—which would later change its name to 360 Capital Partners—and Benchmark Capital, through Balderton Capital. Before approving the project, Mark Evans asked me to do a mini roadshow in California to present the initiative to his colleagues. I flew to San Francisco, and in front of Bill Gurley, Bruce Dunlevie, and many other venture capital giants, I explained the idea. They asked me a load of questions and I explained my relationships with the fashion partners and with the technology I was developing. They were convinced, they had faith in the future prospect, so I returned to Italy to put the finishing touches to the plan and create an ad hoc structure.

YOUR BIGGEST STORE WILL BE ONLINE

The fashion houses had to deal with marketing, prices, and aesthetics. We, behind the scenes, had to deal with everything else. The agreement was that we would respect their image but would use our know-how to create tailor-made websites. We decided to ask for a low initial fixed payment to encourage them to take part, but we anticipated a high percentage because we were convinced that these online stores would do very well over the coming years. We agreed to long-term contracts so that there would be time to generate sales, we took items on consignment so as to improve the company's working capital, seeing that we had to buy all end-of-season goods six months in advance and with a heavy use of cash to finance growth.

In short, the project seemed ideal because, from the economic point of view, it went hand in hand with YOOX's end-of-season project: One absorbed cash, while the other generated it.

My thinking has always been long term, and this too was an investment in the future. It was worth being almost in the red during the early stage in order to grow later. We substantially improved our technology so as to give solid performance. We were constructing the most up-to-date center in existence, had strong competitive power, and were offering a service that no one else at that time could offer. My idea was that online stores had to be even more attractive than those offline, and they had to be larger, with all product lines. Once consumers had entered, they had to be captivated by the variety and completeness of what was on offer.

From 2006, one by one, they all arrived. The first was Marni, which had been owned by the Castiglioni family before being taken over by Renzo Rosso and was one of the designer labels of the moment, admired among others by Anna Wintour. It was a small, efficient company, a fast decision-maker. Consuelo was creative, eclectic, and designed some marvelous collections, while her husband Gianni was the CEO and dealt with the management side. They soon decided to come out with "marni.com powered by YOOX," and this was a perfect calling card. Emporio Armani and Diesel immediately followed. These three brands had been courageous and were the forerunners. All the others gradually came later.

There were some memorable meetings. Brunello Cucinelli invited me to Solomeo, the magnificent Umbrian village he had completely restored, where his company had its headquarters. He showed me his empty white desk with not a single sheet of paper or computer on it. "You see, Federico," he said, "I start from zero, I'm a tabula rasa, you have to tell me everything." He trusted me and we launched brunellocucinelli.com. Several years later, in 2012, he was interviewed by John Seabrook, who wrote a piece about me for *The New Yorker* describing me as "The Geek of Chic."

Brunello admitted: “I don’t think democratic luxury exists. I don’t think there’s such a thing as something for everyone. I don’t say it to play the snob. It’s fairly common to sell sneakers online, but not luxury. This is what worries me: How can we put these products on a website without the tactile experience of luxury?” But he said he was satisfied with the YOOX platform, and although he didn’t like the internet, he understood its importance.

Even the greatest skeptics were converted, each in their own way, and each brand came forward with a thousand demands, each of them different. Laudomia Pucci insisted on having her clothes presented by ballerinas instead of models: she wanted lightness and creativity. We obliged.

DESIGNER TECHNOLOGY

The result was that this perfect strategy, from the point of view of the numbers, was mayhem, because the fashion houses each followed their own individual style. There was nothing standard, nothing that we could replicate. Each time we had to customize the site, shape it to their specific needs, based on their preferences and requirements. We’re 100 percent Italian, flexible, anxious to satisfy. I’m sure that if the project had ended in the hands of Americans, who tend to standardize everything, the result would have been different, and they probably wouldn’t have managed to persuade any fashion house. We behaved like artists; we painted each site, starting off each time with a clean, empty canvas.

Our Achilles’ heel was maintenance: it absorbed a percentage of technological resources far greater than the slice of total sales represented by this business unit. This is why, as I’ve already said, the project was both perfect and imperfect. From the purely financial point of view it made no sense in the short term, yet in the long term it was unbeatable.

The business unit continued to grow. Initially it was worth 5 percent, then 10, then 20, until it reached 30 percent of all YOOX Group business. It never reached 51 percent of sales, but it opened the way for all that happened after.

Monobrands, as we called them, brought about a change of opinion among investors. They began to see YOOX as a player that had solid relationships with all the fashion houses, and no longer simply as a factory outlet which could last from one day to the next with no further supplies because some designer perhaps had decided to go elsewhere and the pull the plug.

Sometimes it's necessary to adopt war tactics that lead to certain defeats, but which enable you in the end to bring down your number-one competitor. That competitor, in our case, was Net-a-Porter, which had failed in its monobrand strategy. If you really want to be an entrepreneur you must understand that daily trends, weekly sales, monthly sales, or even annual results aren't everything—they are not the only guide, not the beacon that illuminates and decides. Sometimes it's better to steer into the dark for a while and then to see the light, rather than following the calmer and better-lit course. You need to have a strategy and a vision, to imagine a future more distant than tomorrow, and to follow it.

If I hadn't taken the risk, if I'd chosen once again to play safe, I wouldn't be here telling you the story of YOOX. The company would have been size XS, it wouldn't have expanded, and I would have given up a winning idea. It's sometimes necessary to make significant investments to launch initiatives that can result in a short-term loss, but which promise a robust increase further ahead, and an eventual profit.

At first there were twenty monobrands, then thirty, then they reached forty. Very few brands, Prada included, felt disinclined toward e-commerce. In 2009, after a complete aversion, Patrizio Bertelli, co-owner of Prada, was still saying: "The products we offer on the internet cannot be the same as those of our stores," arguing that it was a mistake to sell their top products online. It wasn't until 2015 that I persuaded them to put Prada on YOOX Net-a-Porter. Since then, their declarations about e-commerce and digital technology have completely changed and, like all fashion houses, a significant percentage of sales today is online, thanks also to the arrival of their son Lorenzo who is very bright and forward-thinking.

Within a few years, from the point of view of business development, we had swept the board and were managing the websites of practically every major fashion house. We looked into their core business; we dissected their entire collection, pricing, new arrivals, strategies for opening in different markets. A kind of two-way relationship was created in which each knew everything about the other. There was always a complete and absolute trust in YOOX and its neutrality. We have never preferred one brand to the detriment of others nor transferred confidential information. Our integrity has always been carved in stone. And this intricate and sturdy network has been one of our assets: It was something which the stock market liked, and subsequently also Richemont, Net-a-Porter's principal shareholder.

I'm proud to say that we have taught the vast majority of fashion houses how to do e-commerce; we have led them by the hand. If they are high performers today, it's partly thanks to us.

YOOX has been an important agent for the kudos of things Made in Italy. We have given a competitive advantage to the online brands in our country—in comparison, for example, with France which had no equivalent to us. In the end, it was the French members of PPR (now Kering), a large group that included such names as Balenciaga, Bottega Veneta, Saint Laurent, and Alexander McQueen, that capitulated in 2012 and asked us to build sites for all their brands, except for Gucci which already had its own platform.

The joint venture with them was a masterstroke; it gave us the title of the world's best player in luxury e-commerce. In seven years we had reached the top, the gates of Paradise had now opened, and we were there among the glamour elite.

The agreement with PPR put Net-a-Porter in serious difficulty. Our rival had tried to turn Jimmy Choo, shoemaker to the stars, into a monobrand, but the result was disastrous. YOOX had all the brands, and they were left empty-handed. They decided then to change strategy and accept a merger that I had proposed on several occasions. They believed that online flagship stores would be the future. The agreement with PPR was what led to the merger with Net-a-Porter and one of the reasons why Richemont decided to buy us a few years later. They saw us rightly as the player who could accelerate the rollout of their brands, as an internal agency capable of speeding up their e-commerce.

If we hadn't carried out the online flagship stores, we probably wouldn't have been listed, we wouldn't have merged, and my company would never have been valued in the end at €5.3 billion.

WHY MONEY IS NEVER ENOUGH

But these years weren't all plain sailing. On the contrary. Money is a recurring problem for anyone setting up a business. It's an endless nightmare. It's never enough because, to develop a company, you always need further funds. It has happened to me several times that I've had to go searching for investment.

I've had many anxious moments when money was about to run out. After a few years of Benchmark funding we had grown exponentially and were in cashflow difficulties. The problem wasn't just finding the money, but also maintaining an appropriate valuation so as not to dilute myself too much with all these injections of capital. It was then that I had the amazing fortune to find two people who at that time were not venture capitalists but more like guardian angels (which is why they're called "angel investors"). Even now it seems miraculous that they decided to make the capital increase at the same valuation at which Benchmark had come in, but which seemed too high for the market situation at that moment, even if they would later be amply rewarded for that choice. One of them was Francesco Marini Clarelli, the other Stefano Morpurgo. I had known Francesco in 1999 when he tried to launch LuxLook, one of the first e-commerce companies operating in fashion, with a significant investment from Mediobanca, but which went up in smoke and closed soon after.

Francesco had this to say a few years later: "I decided, given my own firm convictions, that someone else would succeed, in particular a young entrepreneur, Federico Marchetti, who had just founded YOOX. Investment in YOOX was my first real experience of venture capitalism, stirring my interest in this style of investment which enabled me on the one hand to follow my own innovative investment ideas, and on the other to support entrepreneurs and help them create financial and social value."

Stefano was a consultant in the areas of project management, strategy, finance, and IT. They both worked as private investors and gave me a breathing space for some while.

But as I said earlier, the search for money in a fast-growing company is never ending. In 2008, I therefore needed some more. It was then that a substantial shareholder on the board of directors began saying: "If we don't find new investors to make a capital increase, we'll inject the necessary money ourselves, together with all other venture capitalists, but on one condition: to zero the valuation, and in exchange for this dilution we'll offer you more stock options." They also had a preliminary agreement with a large Swiss fund they had thought of bringing in.

In short, I would have been left empty-handed!

At that point, however, Piol—the only true gentleman I've met among venture capitalists—stepped in. "No. We have to give Federico the opportunity of finding money, a capital increase to the valuation that he considers to be appropriate. And if he finds it, we too will agree on that valuation."

I had very little time—no more than a couple of months—to find some good soul who would accept my valuation. Only in this way could I avoid diluting myself too far and prevent the Swiss from stepping in. Otherwise, I would find myself with a load of stock options like any ordinary manager, but with a zero percent ownership of my own company.

I thought then that the time had come to involve the brands, to further consolidate my relationships not just from the commercial but also from the financial point of view. I contacted the two most innovative—emporioarmani.com and diesel.com—

whose sites we had already developed. It seemed sensible to offer them an investment. Once again, I had a stroke of luck: Each of them knew about the other because I had been transparent and had conducted negotiations in parallel. Unfortunately, at a certain point, the general manager of Armani stopped answering my phone calls. As I waited for an answer, I attended a Giorgio Armani show and saw their lawyer, who came and told me they no longer wanted to take part in the capital increase because the general manager felt I was no longer among their priorities. And as usual I didn't want to call and disturb Giorgio over such matters, so I gave up on that prospect of investment.

I felt the ground giving way beneath me: I panicked because I feared that since Armani had pulled out, Renzo would do the same thing. I telephoned him, told him the truth, and to my infinite surprise he said: "Well, okay then, I'll also take his part." Courageous, loyal, Renzo kept his word. Collaboration with Armani continued just the same however, and grew stronger thanks to Leo Dell'Orco, Giorgio's right-hand man and inseparable friend, as well as Michele Tacchella, the group's top manager.

After Rosso's decision, I went back to the board, thanked Piol for his trust, and pulled my rabbit out of the hat. Thanks to Renzo's investment I managed to go ahead with a capital increase to that valuation, which everyone had to agree upon.

The proposed valuation was around €2 per share. A year later, when we were listed, it went up to €4.3. It had therefore been a great investment for Renzo. He took a 5.5 percent share because five was his lucky number. He resold his shares at €38, almost twenty times more, when Richemont made the public takeover offer on YOOX Net-a-Porter.

I'm a tightrope walker, or rather—given my passion—a surfer. I could have been tossed over by the waves, I could have gone under two or three times, yet I found the impetus to get back to the surface, thanks to people who believed in me and who helped me move forward.

I've learned many things over these years. The first is that you can't make a startup grow without significant means of investment, in other words, you can't do anything on a shoestring. Startup investments in Britain, in Germany, not to mention the United States, were far more substantial but ours had been sufficiently important to allow us an adequate growth. We would never have reached the top if we hadn't worked hard, never taking a break, never losing sight of the target, but if we hadn't had adequate resources, it would have been just as impossible.

9

In 2005, in an article in *Wired* magazine, the journalist and tech guru Kevin Kelly wrote:

> *Today, at any Net terminal, you can get: an amazing variety of music and video, an evolving encyclopedia, weather forecasts, help wanted ads, satellite images of any place on Earth, up-to-the-minute news from around the globe, tax forms, TV guides, road maps with driving directions, real-time stock quotes, telephone numbers, real estate listings with virtual walk-throughs, pictures of just about anything, sports scores, places to buy almost anything, records of political contributions, library catalogs, appliance manuals, live traffic reports, archives to major newspapers—all wrapped up in an interactive index that really works.*
>
> *This view is spookily godlike* [...] *I doubt angels have a better view of humanity.*
>
> *Why aren't we more amazed by this fullness? Kings of old would have gone to war to win such abilities. Only small children would have dreamed such a magic window could be real. I have reviewed the expectations of waking adults and wise experts, and I can affirm that this comprehensive*

> *wealth of material, available on demand and free of charge, was not in anyone's scenario. Ten years ago, anyone silly enough to trumpet the above list as a vision of the near future would have been confronted by the evidence: there wasn't enough money in all the investment firms in the entire world to fund such a cornucopia. The success of the web at this scale was impossible.*
>
> *But if we have learned anything in the past decade, it is the plausibility of the impossible.*

Technology was in ferment. The web had emerged from its niche to become a global reality. The new economy—a term coined by Kelly himself in 1997—had come of age. The process of technological innovation was generating a hitherto unknown "web economy," capable of expanding the size of markets, of speeding up their operation in terms of production, distribution, and consumption.

Robots were entering factories, and those like me who had created a tech company fully shared this enthusiasm and this sensation that many of our dreams were turning into reality. In the blink of an eye we had been transported into another dimension; many of the things we were once accustomed to were disappearing, leaving space for new practices. In my case it was already apparent that it was no longer simply a matter of selling clothes online but of drastically changing the lifestyle of millions of people—of entering into their behavior patterns, disrupting them, and demonstrating that we could easily dress creatively while still at home and without going to a store, changing clothes, trying them on virtually. It was a leap into the future, and many people were ready, and even looking forward to doing it.

A GENIUS BY THE NAME OF JOBS

The first decade of the new century witnessed a flurry of online activity—Facebook was created in 2004, Twitter in 2006, and in 2007 Apple would launch its first iPhone, the progenitor of all the smartphones that have revolutionized our way of interacting with those around us, and with ourselves. The scene was now crowded with new players.

In early 2006 I wrote an email to Steve Jobs and proposed a meeting to bring together fashion, technology, and omnichannel, namely the integration between physical and online stores, what is now called "new retail." Before going to Cupertino, I contacted Steve Jobs's office (his email was iCeo@apple.com—beginning with an "i" like all the products he would design later). His assistant asked me to send him a list of the points to be discussed.

We had—relatively speaking—several things in common: He had found an impeccable way of combining aesthetics and functionality, and in doing this he was certainly inspired by Olivetti and by Italy. Olivetti's story is interwoven with his, and to some extent with my own story. But few people know that the world's first transistor computer was produced by Olivetti thanks to the brilliance of Mario Tchou, the son of a Chinese diplomat. Tchou was born in Rome where he began his studies in engineering before flying to America to gain a master's degree at the Polytechnic Institute of Brooklyn and to begin teaching, first at Manhattan College and then at Columbia University. Adriano Olivetti, on the recommendation of Enrico Fermi, met him in the United States and persuaded him to return to Italy to run the Electronic Research Laboratory at Barbaricina, near Pisa. In 1959, after designing several data processors, he came up with Elea 9003, the first fully transistorized computer, produced a few months before IBM produced theirs. The design was by Ettore Sottsass, who created an ergonomic console with easily controllable commands that gave central importance to the operator rather than to the machine, and for this he was awarded the Compasso D'Oro industrial design award. It marked the beginning of the battle with the United States for supremacy over computers. Even the CIA kept a close eye on Olivetti, and when Tchou died at the age of just thirty-seven in a road crash—he had recently bought a black Buick—many thought the American agency was behind it. According to his wife, Elisa Montessori, there was no proof of American involvement, though the suspicion remains, and it just so happens that the electronics division of Olivetti ended in the hands of General Electric a few years later.

Many coincidences, many things in common: Sottsass, a partner of Alberto Guerriero as well as a leading figure in our "Dressing Ourselves" show at the Milan Triennale in 2003; Piol, from Olivetti to venture capitalist and my first financier; Bellini, the designer of Programma 101 who had met Jobs at Aspen and then in Italy; the Apple technology that brought together American functionality with Italian aesthetics. For this reason I thought Apple could be a perfect tech partner for YOOX in launching the sites of Armani, Marni, Diesel, and others. I knew I couldn't manage the whole ambitious technical project I had in mind if I worked alone and thought Apple might be interested in fashion. I felt the new virtual stores ought to mix technology, music, entertainment, and much more—and that we could do it together. I suggested various points of discussion so that Jobs could choose, but after a couple of emails I heard no more about the meeting.

A few years later, in 2013, when I read that Angela Ahrendts, CEO of Burberry, was moving to Apple, I thought I hadn't been so far off track—this time just a little too early.

A MAN NAMED ELON MUSK

In May 2006, we were invited to a meeting organized by Benchmark Capital at Half Moon Bay, a town south of San Francisco famous for the Mavericks, an area of fifteen-meter-high waves reserved for super-skilled surfers. It was a mega-reunion of all the startups in which they had invested, with such leading online figures as Google, eBay, PayPal, and Expedia. I also met a man named Elon Musk with whom I exchanged a few words.

At the time he was a young South African brimming with enthusiasm and many ideas, some brilliant and others impracticable. Over these years he has become the richest man in the world but also one of the most powerful. After having contributed to Donald Trump's election as president of the United States, thanks also to his social network, X, and to his substantial financial donations during the election campaign, many now regard him as the man who has influenced many of Trump's choices. The world is keeping its eyes on him to understand what he will actually do, and where his ambitions will take him.

I haven't seen him again since then, but in May 2023, when my region of Emilia-Romagna was hit by disastrous flooding—the rainfall in thirty-six hours was of half the quantity that would normally fall in a whole year—causing dozens of deaths and billions of euros of damage, I wrote a post on X which said: "Elon, have you read about the horrific floods in Emilia Romagna in Italy? Schools are closed and people fled their houses. Any chance you can help with @starlink?"

A few days after my post, an article appeared in a leading newspaper that is widely read in Bologna and in the region, and which had launched a fundraising campaign: "The Unipol Group, in collaboration with the American entrepreneur Elon Musk through his company SpaceX, has purchased Starlink terminals that will enable rescuers, essential and strategic services (such as hospitals) and the population to have internet access. How did this initiative come about? Federico Marchetti, the digital entrepreneur from Ravenna, one of the very first to give funds in support of the populations hit by the flooding, launched by the Monrif Group and by our newspapers, had sent a tweet inviting Musk to help Emilia Romagna." I don't know whether it was entirely due to my message, but Elon Musk later declared: "SpaceX, Starlink and Tesla are happy to be of help in any way to Italy and its population afflicted by the flooding." And the satellites worked.

Returning to the meeting of 2006, my team were the only Italians, and we managed to get ourselves noticed. Max won a game of poker against the founder of Expedia who, as a forfeit, hung vertically upside down in front of us all, whereas I arrived for my speech wearing a white sweatshirt with an Eminem-style hood and, after three days in which everyone had mangled my name in every possible way, I said: "I'm Federico *Marketti*, not *Fedrico*, not *Marcetti*," causing general hoots of laughter. It was the first time we had appeared at such an important international gathering, and from here, we joined the network of all those companies like us who were growing fast; this time, networking was opening doors to new business opportunities.

GROWING BIG

The digital revolution was now at the height of its development and to be there required all available weapons—those of technology on the one hand, and of scaling-up on the other. Growing big, conquering new countries, wasn't just an option but a pressing need.

For us, this meant establishing a new YOOX organization as well as setting off in new directions. We started with the question of organization. In 2006, after a year that ended with figures rather lower than expected, I decided to stage a revolution and move the existing managers to other jobs, offering the key positions to a group of more experienced managers who could guide me toward a sustained growth with a view to a Stock Exchange listing. The venture capitalists were pressing for novelty and better performance, so I told myself: "It's time for a major upheaval."

Max, Alberto, and the others had grown up here, many of them had no other experience, they knew no place else. I was therefore convinced that YOOX needed to grow up, needed to retain its modern tech character but become more mature and more structured. I chose several managers who seemed perfect on paper but, as soon as they arrived, they proved to be disasters: The culture gap between them and the original team, which I had wisely kept and moved to other positions, was too great. The original group was passionate, they felt as if YOOX was theirs, many of them knew nothing about fashion but they were young, they understood the customers, they had fun, they were in their primordial soup. The new ones, on the other hand, were bright, they were competent, but they wandered around the corridors like Martians. They didn't understand the essence of YOOX, they didn't feel part of the company's culture and its spirit. There was no osmosis between the two groups, and I eventually recognized my error. Not one of my choices was right; each person turned out to be wrong—or at least wrong for YOOX. By April, during a meeting at a spa center at Sasso Marconi near Bologna, we took a break and while we were in the swimming pool I slipped into a flamingo-shaped inflatable ring, looked at the new sales director, who should have been our springboard toward the first public listing, and I was already hoping deep down that he'd be out of the company by Easter.

And so it was: In 2007, I staged a counter-revolution, reinstated the original team, and we restarted from there. Meanwhile there was a reshuffle in which everyone switched jobs: Max became marketing director, and Alberto became sales director. We spent a few days in the Langhe in Piemonte, where a friend owned a villa near Serralunga d'Alba, and in seventy-two hours we rebuilt the organization that would launch us in 2007 toward the public offer that will take place two years later.

Making a mistake is the easiest thing to do—you're convinced about something, you go ahead with it, and at a certain point your castle of playing cards and all your dreams tumble. You realize that the organization, which seems right on paper, doesn't work in practice. At this point you need to respond quickly; once you've recognized your mistake, you must put it right. And do it fast. There's no point being proud, or feeling sorry for yourself, or putting on sackcloth. It's better to be pragmatic and to move quickly, looking for alternative solutions which, if possible, don't take everything back to the status quo but anticipate some imaginative new symmetries and experiments. Asking people to try out something entirely new is stimulating for them and potentially very useful for the company. Innovation and experimentation are essential at every stage in the growth of a startup company.

A WAREHOUSE AT THE FOREFRONT OF TECHNOLOGY

On the evening of December 21, 2007, when the company was already larger and the warehouse had moved to Bologna Interporto, after a hectic week of Christmas orders, the company managers and I decided to go down to the warehouse and open a bottle of champagne to celebrate the sales boom with all the young workers who were still working away. It was a cold night, and the warehouse was three to four degrees below zero centigrade. Extremely difficult to work in such conditions. This spurred us to speed up the timescale, to automate the warehouse for storing and picking, and to create a separate area for parceling that was warm and comfortable for staff.

This first great step perhaps marked the beginning of the relationship I have always preferred to have with machinery: making them do the harder work and leaving the more delicate part to people, where the human touch is necessary and makes a difference. I have complete faith in technology and its potential, and I'm convinced that knowing how to use and guide it to improve the quality of our life will be increasingly crucial in the coming years. I confirmed my belief in it from the very beginning, from the name I chose for YOOX, where technology finds space inside the chromosomes of humanity.

For us, 2007 and 2008 were the two most intense years of automation, a pioneering decision far ahead of the times.

Interporto was now a distribution center that has grown to over a million square feet. Automation has turned it into a kind of cacophonous orchestra, where machines and humans know exactly what and when to operate.

Much has changed since the first industrial robot was patented in 1954. At that time, it weighed a little over 1.6 tons but when it was introduced at General Motors in 1961 it revolutionized the assembly lines of the whole automobile industry. For YOOX, from the very first time they were used, they became indispensable, efficient, versatile, invaluable work companions. And while there were very few robots in the warehouses at the beginning, they would eventually grow to several hundred—those that transport the pallets, those that turn the mannequins, and the great mechanical arms (nicknamed "Aliens") that deal with storage and picking. The first robots we acquired weighed around one-third of a ton, cost around €300,000, and had to be isolated, kept away from people. Then, as often happens in technology, everything was miniaturized: there were small, light, cooperative robots with which we could easily interact. The coming years will be fundamental in deciding what to teach them and how far to involve them.

The new models of today are light years ahead of the first prototypes, and I'm convinced that each of us in the future will have a robot among our collaborators and even among our friends!

By the time I left my group, sixty thousand items were arriving in the warehouse each day, and the same number leaving. The space contained an average of seven and a half million objects, stockpiled entirely by robots but checked in, controlled, and packaged at the time of dispatch by real people. Everything was synchronized and, thanks to innovation, finding an item in this wonderful, colorful, modern souk was very simple. We made so much progress that we were the first in our sector, in 2010, to replace the barcode with RFID (radio-frequency identification). This enables us to monitor in real time what is happening to an article through the whole supply chain, preventing any mistakes from going to the final customer. It's a philosophy similar to that of the Japanese who promptly and meticulously check every phase, from purchase to delivery, so as to eliminate errors almost entirely. The RFID tags are used to identify articles at every point of their life cycle through the warehouse, from arrival to picking, parceling, and dispatch to the customers.

The modernization process lasted several years up to 2010, when automation of the warehouse was completed. What does it mean from the point of view of workflow? A revolution, the result of which was a new organization that made it possible to move from physical to digital and then back to physical. It was a type of complicated dance with a great number of well-trained extras that entered and left the stage in perfect synchrony. The algorithm constantly interacted with the human. Interporto had been transformed into a warehouse-city of the future, where robots of different sizes and capacities worked with humans to create a unicum in which the clothes that entered followed an automatized procedure up to the moment they left, when they were ordered by a customer. A marvel of technology where fifty-five photographic studios took between nine and fifteen thousand pictures every day. A business where humans were tasked with receiving the products that arrived, doing the quality control, dressing the mannequins, taking the photos and dealing with the packaging of the products when they were sold, sometimes with tissue paper or with a ribbon according to the requirements of the brand. You wouldn't expect such perfection from an Italian company, with an error-factor of approximately 0.001 percent! Precision was fundamental: You couldn't send a Saint Laurent product to an Armani customer. We'd risk losing our credibility. And above all, we treated all our customers the same, whether they were the Queen of the Netherlands or a penniless student from the remotest part of Sicily.

In short, it was a mesmerizing spectacle of precision and harmony, a kind of orchestra formed by so many robot musicians and with a computer as its conductor—like the second pitch I wrote at Columbia Business School!

TECHNOLOGY AND HUMANISM

There are two parts to me that happily coexist. I believe in technology and in a new humanism. Technology has been a part of my personal story, of my professional life: I discovered it at the very start, in the mid-1990s. I put my money on digital technology when no one in Italy believed in it. I developed and pursued it.

I love technology because I'm firmly convinced that innovation comes from here, from one of its characteristics; it's never-ending. When you think you've achieved something, it's not an end result but just an intermediate step along a path whose beginning you know but whose ultimate destination you can only imagine. It's rather like the journey of an explorer. It's fascinating! I read the future through digital technology. It has allowed me many times to predict the future, to get there first, and I think that if we know how to use technology intelligently then it will help us take a further step in fulfillment. It won't just be a system for innovating but also for anticipating and satisfying people's needs, wants, and desires. Technology is a means, not an end, but it can help us create projects—for cities, schools, and hospitals as well as everyday objects—that are dictated by the requirements of citizens and consumers. Statistics help us to study macrotrends, to understand why some things meet public favor and others don't. We just need to learn how to use them properly, not invading privacy but listening to what they tell us.

Then there's the other part of me, the side that looks at creativity, at unpredictability, at the surprising and unlikely human capacity to venture into the unknown, inventing works of ingenuity never imagined before. There's the beauty of imperfection, failure, starting all over again. There are thousands of human sentiments that mean no one is quite like anyone else. After all, it's always been like this; man has created machines that then evolved to such a point as to seem autonomous—and yet, behind everything there is still the human hand. I try to make these two parts coexist within me and in my exploits. YOOX—the name I gave to the company I founded—brings together humanism and technology. I welcomed robots when they were still immature and prehistoric, I watched them grow, I filled them with data. In the beginning they were large, cumbersome, sometimes clumsy and "obtuse," then thanks to the data they became increasingly intelligent and able to solve sophisticated problems. The coexistence between humans and machines must be harmonious, and the new humanism is a close and friendly collaboration between machines, information, technology, and humans. Together we can change the universe. And improve it.

According to Klaus Schwab, founder of the World Economic Forum, we are at the beginning of the fourth industrial revolution, distinguished by the presence of new technologies that bring together the physical, digital, and biological spheres and influence all disciplines and economic and productive sectors to the point of questioning even the meaning of "human being":

> *We stand on the brink of a technological revolution that will fundamentally alter the way we live, work, and relate to one another.*
>
> *In its scale, scope, and complexity, the transformation will be unlike anything humankind has experienced before. We do not yet know just how it will unfold, but one thing is clear: the response to it must be integrated and comprehensive, involving all stakeholders of the global polity, from the public and private sectors to academia and civil society.* [...]
>
> *Already, artificial intelligence is all around us, from self-driving cars and drones to virtual assistants and software that translate or invest. Impressive progress has been made in AI in recent years, driven by exponential increases in computing power and by the availability of vast amounts of data, from software used to discover new drugs to algorithms used to predict our cultural interests. Digital fabrication technologies, meanwhile, are interacting with the biological world on a daily basis. Engineers, designers, and architects are combining computational design, additive manufacturing, materials engineering, and synthetic biology to pioneer a symbiosis between microorganisms, our bodies, the products we consume, and even the buildings we inhabit.*
>
> *We need to shape a future that works for all of us by putting people first and empowering them. In its most*

pessimistic, dehumanized form, the Fourth Industrial Revolution may indeed have the potential to 'robotize' humanity and thus to deprive us of our heart and soul. But as a complement to the best parts of human nature—creativity, empathy, stewardship—it can also lift humanity into a new collective and moral consciousness based on a shared sense of destiny. It is incumbent on us all to make sure the latter prevails.

INTERNATIONAL INTRIGUE

We were at a turning point once again. In 2009, nine years had passed since the founding of YOOX. The company had grown, it had had various capital injections, but the venture capitalists that had financed it now wanted their money back (ten years is generally thought of as the maximum time for a return from investments in venture capital).

The story I'm about to tell is like the plot of a spy story. The international intrigue, played out between London, Seattle, Milan, and South Africa, is a power game: the main female character is elegant and ambitious, the story is intricate and filled with walk-on parts, disappearances, and spies listening in. It lasts seven long years and, in the midst of it, you'll find me trying at all costs to merge with my rival but failing repeatedly, you'll find an American tycoon, a "predator" who wants to buy us cheaply but to no avail, and you'll find a stock exchange listing obtained, once again, just in the nick of time. But in the end, Federico, the "small fry," having swum in a sea of sharks, will manage to survive and get the better of his adversaries.

SCENE ONE. Early 2009. London. We were at the Electric House, a very cool private club in Notting Hill. There I met Natalie Massenet, Anglo-American, ex-journalist, now running her splendid creation, Net-a-Porter, a luxury fashion e-commerce site based in London, founded in 2000, similar and yet different from YOOX. We had first met in 2003, once again in London, once again in a restaurant. She was my number one rival, and I was curious: I'm not the type who likes viewing things from a distance, or spying on others, or puzzling over what they are doing. I prefer the direct approach, to look the devil in the eyes, to see what's in her mind, how she moves. I remember that Natalie appeared at the first meeting with her CEO, Mark Sebba, (may he rest in peace); I was alone, and I recall that she mocked the name of Armani, which I obviously defended.

This time, six years later, I invited her to dinner, but she said she could only manage an aperitivo. Knowing that she'd be coming with her husband, I asked Fabio Canè to come along so that we'd be two against two. I proposed the merger of our two companies, but Natalie was very blunt. "I don't think it's a good idea to tie two ships together during a storm," she said.

Only later did I find out that Natalie likes metaphors and set phrases. She was telling me, in effect, that Net-a-Porter had just emerged from a difficult financial year. I, on the other hand, had stepped on the gas with YOOX and had managed to overtake them in terms of turnover. The prospect of a merger vanished with her first remarks. We said goodbye and, while I was in the taxi on my way back to the hotel, I thought the best exit strategy for returning the money to the venture capitalists was by listing YOOX on the stock market, even if I knew the investors wouldn't assess the company at the value it deserved. All the same, I needed to try.

Making a startup grow sometimes means going against everyone and everything. No path is without its risks, but you need to make a choice. Being an entrepreneur always means choosing, and the path you choose to follow will determine the fate of your creation. It can lead you toward growth or into insignificance, to supremacy or subjection, to success or disaster.

FLASHBACK. On September 15, 2008, the Dow Jones index had closed at 500 points down, the greatest fall since September 11, 2001. You all know what had happened: Lehman Brothers shares had collapsed and the whole planet had witnessed the most cataclysmic crash in American history. Lehman had bank debts of $613 billion, debenture debts of $155 billion, and $639 billion of assets. All evaporated into nothing. "Too big to fail" was the slogan that everyone believed or wanted to believe. It had happened a little earlier to Bear Stearns, an investment bank that had been on the brink of bankruptcy but had been bought out by JPMorgan Chase with the United States government guaranteeing its trading debts. It was thought then that the same would happen to Lehman Brothers. But it didn't. On September 9, Lehman shares dropped almost 45 percent, and on September 11 they fell by another 40 percent. On September 13, the governor of the New York Federal Reserve Bank, Timothy Geithner, made a last-ditch attempt to save the bank, but he failed, and on September 15, 2008, Lehman announced that it would invoke Chapter 11, the federal law that guarantees protection in the event of bankruptcy. There was pandemonium on the stock market; the television showed pictures of employees—the bank had twenty-six thousand of them in all—

leaving the building in Wall Street with their belongings in cardboard boxes.

Lehman, the company for which I had worked and where I had been trained fourteen years before, had exploded, evaporated from one day to the next, leaving behind it a pile of debris.

The situation was chaotic, the markets were in the grip of instability; the last three months of 2008 would not allow enough time to recover from the losses and start again. It would take a while to return to normality.

At the beginning of the new year I was back with the venture capitalists who had invested in YOOX—they were increasingly impatient and wanted an exit strategy. Yet our competitive situation and the possibilities of success were clear, at least to me—and not just to me. Our growth in the first decade was explosive and in 2005 we had a positive EBIT (earnings before interest and taxes). In comparison to non-Italian startups, YOOX had obtained much less financing but had known how to maximize and successfully invest the money it had earned. Moreover, while losses are acceptable in the first ten years for American and British startups, Italian investors always look for operations that could produce short-term profits. And YOOX was no exception. Apart from the first three years, in which costs exceeded revenue (as generally happens for startups), after 2003 revenue and costs had begun to level out. In the last quarter of 2004, the EBITDA (earnings before interest, taxes, depreciation, and amortization) was positive. Breakeven point had been reached. In the first months of 2009, the venture capitalists were doing all they could to disinvest, to get out of the company, and to cash out all their gains.

At this point the so-called dual track generally arises, which provides two options: Stock Exchange listing or sale. This is a difficult moment because very few companies have the courage to appear on the stock market for fear of getting burnt. The only alternative is to consider offers of purchase.

THE SEATTLE TYCOON. In early 2009 I received a call from Diego Piacentini, Jeff Bezos's right-hand man. He had been vice president of the European division of Apple until 2000, when he joined Amazon as senior vice president of international consumer business and was one of the few Italians to have made an outstanding career in Silicon Valley. He asked for a meeting in Seattle, at the Amazon headquarters. Alberto Grignolo, Max Benedetti and I flew to the United States, looked for a hotel (at our own expense, they don't even offer us accommodation!), and we spent a whole day between one meeting and another with all of Amazon's front line who wanted to check us over from head to toe, not just from the business point of view but personally too. Next day we arrived at the Pacific Medical Center, Beacon Hill—at that time, the Amazon central office—a cramped, gloomy ex-hospital with long shabby corridors.

Before we enter the meeting room, I said to Piacentini: "I have a gift for you, if you don't mind." As you will have gathered, gifts are my secret weapon. I like to create surprise and to study people in such a way as to alleviate the situation with a touch of irony. I knew that Diego was a fanatical supporter of Inter Milan, and through a team masseur who was also my physiotherapist I had managed to get a jersey signed by Zlatan Ibrahimović with a dedication (I confess I'm not 100 percent sure the signature was genuine...). All the same, he was pleasantly surprised and appreciated the thought.

He took us into the presence of the "emperor" at the center of a large meeting hall, surrounded by twenty or so of his managers with an aggressive air, expressing power, business, and money. On the other side of the table, just the three of us. Being a good Romagnolo, I tried to defuse the atmosphere and create a relaxed climate, and I made a stupid joke. Bezos burst into thunderous laughter. His laughter is now well known and described in all the books that talk about him, but I was caught unaware, and his team, the day before, had told us countless things but hadn't mentioned this. So I imagined at first that I was being extraordinarily funny, then realized it was not the case, and his outbursts have a loud and deafening intensity that had nothing to do with my wit. They asked countless questions, he laughed a great deal, like a fairytale ogre, and they finally ended the meeting.

When I got off the plane, back in Milan, I found a message from one of his entourage: "Jeff really liked you, we want to make you an offer." I was puzzled; I didn't want to sell my company to the Americans. Most of all, Amazon was trying to enter the luxury market without understanding its rules. His managers during the meeting had shown a total lack of awareness about fashion. They didn't even know the difference between the first and the second line of a brand. And even later, up until the present day, the problem with Amazon is that the people Jeff has chosen to run his "fashion" division (which in reality, due to its medium-low content, ought to be called "apparel") don't recognize the peculiarities of European luxury. For this reason, someone like Bezos, who is trying to fly into space, still hasn't managed to break into luxury fashion.

The offer they made was really low and I was pleased it was, because I had good reason to say: no, thank you! I had decided to run the risk of keeping the board of directors in the dark about this flirt with Amazon. I knew that if I had said "Bezos wants to buy us," they'd have immediately replied: "Sell!" They wanted their money back as quickly as possible. I kept quiet because I was convinced it wasn't the right path, and felt that Amazon's offer, which really was too low, confirmed it. The IPO (Initial Public Offering) price in December 2009, just a few months later, was almost double—therefore, in the end, I had protected the interests of my shareholders but had run the risk of not getting to the Stock Exchange and of not selling. If I'd failed to reach those two objectives, I'd have been finished.

MILAN STOCK EXCHANGE. At that point, having abandoned the marriage with Net-a-Porter, having rejected the sale to Bezos, I pushed for listing. It had always been my first choice: I had founded the company just nine years before, my creation was still young, and I could see very many possibilities for growth. There still seemed much to do and to innovate in e-commerce: I didn't want to sell YOOX, and the time for a merger wasn't yet ripe. I therefore approached Mediobanca and Goldman Sachs, followed the whole procedure, and in fall of 2009 we arrived at the Stock Exchange.

But here too, there was a moment of suspense. A few days before the listing, there was a sudden turn of events in Dubai. After years of economic boom, the global financial crisis had hit the Arab emirate, causing the loss of thousands of jobs and dashing real estate projects worth billions of dollars.

Dubai would try to create a minimum of optimism in January 2010 with the opening of the Burj Khalifa, the record-breaking skyscraper and symbol of resurgence for the small Gulf state, but many still remember the two thousand automobiles abandoned at the airport, the trash cans filled with credit cards, and the empty houses left hurriedly by those fleeing abroad. I watched the TV and thought: If I don't manage to reach the stock market at this moment, who knows when I'll have the chance to do it.

I was seriously worried because time-windows are often very short and—as you'll have realized—it's essential to get in before they close. We decided to go ahead and started off with a special road show that was not of the usual kind. No press conference where the data is explained to analysts, no long boring speeches. We hired a movie theater in Milan where we screened a particular film for one hundred people who worked in the banks. *Avatar,* the 3D science-fiction masterpiece and box-office hit directed by James Cameron, had just been released. It tells the story of Pandora, a planet covered by a gigantic rain forest in which avatars, hybrid creatures created from human genes, move among the natives.

Our movie was a short film of eight minutes, also in 3D, that showed the YOOX ecosystem, imagining it as a universe with planets around it—the stores of our brands, from marni.com to emporioarmani.com—and to watch it we gave each viewer a pair of glasses. The general surprise left a good impression on the invited analysts and so, at the end of our roadshow, on Monday December 3, 2009, we turned up at the Milan Stock Exchange.

The YOOX shares were valued by the investment banks at €4.3 for a company valuation of around €220 million. In the cold December of that year we were the only Italian-made IPO on the main market. The ordinary shares listed were €27.9 million and the value of the total offer was around €120 million, attracting Italian and foreign investors. The figure at which we arrived wasn't much but I was happy—I like going against the general trend and doing something that no one else at that moment would do. A few years later we would become the first, and for many years the only technological unicorn—a company with a valuation above $1 billion—in Italy. Therefore, looking back, I can say it went very well! And that evening, to celebrate, instead of the rivers of champagne seen in every American movie on the Stock Exchange and finance, I chose a bowl of warm minestrone soup at home with my wife. Call me a neo-Calvinist, if you wish!

DIFFICULT, MYSTERIOUS CHINA

Anyone who thinks I'd take a break for a while after the Stock Exchange listing would be wrong. Two days later, I decided it was time to go to China—a growing market with great potential. The question was: how to get in? How to win over customers? What were they looking for? What brands did they like?

A few years earlier, in 2004, I went to explore Shanghai, once again with my faithful team. We wanted to meet as many people as we could and to look at the possibility of opening there.

We had met the daughter of a prosperous owner of a large store to whom we wanted to pass on our surplus stock in order to make our journey financially worthwhile. She invited us to dinner even though she had five or six other dinners at the same time and spent the whole evening moving around like a spinning top. Alberto Grignolo, a firm advocate of animal rights, felt ill when they served a live lobster at table, to be eaten while it was still moving. It all came to nothing, and the Chinese didn't buy a single garment from us.

In the case of China and Japan—two cultures far from my own—rather than just doing market research, I went off, visited each place, tried to immerse myself in their customs, in their way of life, to understand the potential. I wanted to make physical contact.

This time we decided to take our first step with emporioarmani.com powered by YOOX. I was convinced that arriving with a name that was already established and famous at every latitude might make the operation easier. Preparation took us twelve months of extremely hard work. When I explored the United States and Japan, I had compiled lists of things to do with some 30–40 headings. For our arrival in China, the list stretched to 101 headings. There were countless things to resolve, to consider, and we could not leave anything to chance. Through John Hooks, Armani's sales director at that time, we found an intermediary; foreigners at that time couldn't operate directly in China. We selected the license holder for the Emporio Armani stores, a serious and honest businessman, who in return for a percentage of turnover agreed to create this company from the legal point of view. In 2010, Emporio Armani was the first international retailer to launch an e-commerce site in China. It had all the indications of being a success, but instead it was a partial flop.

I've asked myself many times: "Would you do it again?" And the answer is no. I got it wrong, partly in underestimating the problems, and partly in not properly understanding the country I was going to. It was a place not yet ready for fashion. I discovered only later that many Chinese people hadn't even heard the name Armani, and the other brand names were completely unknown to a large majority of citizens. I went to Beijing for the 2008 Olympics and when I wandered the city and entered the stores, I found them empty with no goods on display. Fashion, over which they are now all going crazy, didn't exist at that time, or was the prerogative of a tiny niche, and luxury e-commerce was an unknown specter. The other problem was the potential partners I had contacted before our arrival, who were totally unprepared on the subject. I was looking for a joint venture with JD: I wanted to avoid arriving in China straightaway as YOOX and knew that our entry would be helped by relying on a Chinese company that understood the bureaucracy and procedures to be followed. But the agreement didn't materialize. JD wasn't able at the time to deal with a business like ours, linked to glamour and luxury. Its founder came from an experience in fruit and vegetables, and none of our brands would ever end up on such a portal. All the same, I chose a communications agency for the launch, encouraged the local team by displaying my baritone voice in a karaoke performance singing David Bowie's "China Girl," and we did a magnificent launch film, *Lost Paradise,* shot by Wing Shya, set photographer to Wong Kar-wai in the film *In the Mood for Love,* with the famous actress Gwei Lun-mei, but despite all our fireworks there was nothing we could do. It didn't take off.

Maybe I made the mistake of not calling Jack Ma of Alibaba—the wizard of e-commerce, founder of the world's largest online sales platform—with whom we did a joint venture many years later; maybe I thought I could go it alone, or maybe the protectionist politics of the Chinese government were preventing initiatives like ours from taking off. As a result, things went badly: China didn't manage to rise above 1–2 percent of our global sales. Asos, Neiman Marcus, and others followed YOOX, but they closed their companies in China a few years later. The Chinese government decided to create and support local companies and to limit and control the entry of large tech companies from abroad, particularly from America, with the results that have been seen over the years.

I've always been so conscious of timing in business and realize that arriving too early can be disastrous: many good ideas are in danger of being misunderstood if they're carried out too soon. They don't satisfy the need of the moment. It's important to know and understand the market where you want to expand: if it's not ready it will reject you, or at least ignore you. I would return to China a few years later, but quite a lot of water had to flow under the bridge before then.

THE ANGLO-ITALIAN MARRIAGE

Let's now get back to our spy story.

A couple of years went by after that meeting at Electric House when, on May 6, 2011, I received an email from Mark Sebba, CEO of Net-a-Porter, saying that he and Natalie thought the right thing for them would be to consider a merger with YOOX! We managed to fix an appointment in Milan at the end of May 2011, which went very well, to the point that Mark wrote immediately after, telling me that they were "inspired" by our meeting.

This formal approach began much *to*ing and *fro*ing that ended, years later, with a marriage between the two companies.

In truth, I was crystal clear from the very beginning: YOOX was listed, and my professional life was still entirely centered on the shares I held in my company, whereas Natalie had sold the whole of Net-a-Porter to Richemont a year earlier and had collected a lot of money (then reinvesting a small part of it), so that if she wanted to become CEO it would work only if I too could sell all my shares; otherwise it was obvious that, since I was the one who was risking the most, I would take full responsibility for the final outcome in my capacity as CEO.

Many meetings followed in summer and in fall of that year, also at Richemont's offices in Geneva, up to Christmas 2011, when Mark wrote me again and, with the season's greetings, said that their lawyers were studying a company structure and needed a little time to digest it. He ended by saying he would get back to me in early 2012.

I'll save you every detail, but in March 2012 I decided to write an email telling everyone we'd been going round in circles and this marriage wasn't going to happen. Meanwhile, in late spring I concluded my fantastic deal with PPR/Kering to launch the sites for their brands on our platform. The deal left everyone (Massenet, Sebba, and Richemont) flabbergasted and reopened discussions over the merger with Net-a-Porter, because it was now clear that our competitive advantage on monobrands, thanks to this agreement, was unparalleled.

In November 2012 I received an email from Mark Sebba in which he and Natalie proposed an organizational structure in which she basically became the co-CEO (with the role of Chief Strategy Officer): I said no and explained that this division of responsibilities would have a deleterious effect on the organization because no employee would ever know who to report to and which of the two to listen to. We were back to the beginning, and yet I had been extremely clear: one person alone could be CEO, and I was prepared to stand aside if someone bought my shares as they had done with her.

THE RELECTANT BRIDE. Natalie and I met again in February 2013, this time at my apartment in New York during fashion week. Natalie suggested a name to give to the company: Co&Com (Content & Commerce), which didn't convince me. The most important point was the figures: While YOOX was profitable since the end of 2004, Net-a-Porter was less so. Valuing the two companies on their ability to generate profits and with assistance from the valuation of Goldman Sachs, I proposed an exchange ratio in which YOOX was given a higher value. We were ready with all the documents in late spring of 2013, after two years of complicated gestation, when I received a phone call from Richard Lepeu, then CEO of Richemont and the person who had negotiated over the last two years with great distinction and insight, in which he informed me that the deal was cancelled.

For a while I put my merger project aside, without abandoning it all together. A few months passed, and in June 2014 we were about to complete several contracts with Richemont for the running of chloe.com, dunhill.com, and lancel.com (then sold by Richemont to Piquadro), each powered by YOOX, when that agreement was also suddenly cancelled. I was extremely concerned because I had let it be known in the market that we were about to conclude a deal relating to monobrands, our jewel in the crown, with one of the world's largest luxury groups.

I summoned my courage and, for the first time in my life, I called Johann Rupert, chairman of Richemont, South African plenipotentiary of an empire that included such labels as Cartier, Montblanc, Bucellati, and Chloé, as well as the most important brands of luxury watches. I had met Mr. Rupert only once, exchanging a couple of remarks in New York at a gathering organized by Amex, and wished to complain politely but clearly about this umpteenth about-turn. At that point I took the opportunity to ask for a meeting. He suggested a meeting in July in the Hamptons on the golf course. I couldn't play golf, I didn't have the right shoes, but I obviously accepted the invitation. I spent a day and a whole night at his family chalet with his delightful wife, Gaynor, and son, Anton, a bright kid and a nice guy too.

I realized that I was playing for everything, so I told him also about my dream regarding the merger, namely a new technological platform that would allow Net-a-Porter to be competitive in the mid-long term, and I told him that insofar as my remuneration, he could happily decide everything himself, as I had indeed let my shareholders do from the start of my adventure. I still remember him saying to me: "You're more American than the Americans!" Having spent a little time together, I think the South African visionary magnate was convinced that I was a pragmatic self-made dreamer.

After that meeting, discussions with Net-a-Porter resumed, with Richemont as shareholder, and once again there was indecision about the structure of the company in Italy, until Richard Lepeu took the situation in hand again, in January 2015, with the blessing of Mr. Rupert, but with an exchange ratio reduced to a simple and diplomatic fifty-fifty, valuing the two companies therefore at the same figure. Mr. Rupert obtained a better negotiation compared to two years before, and as usual his instinct as dealmaker worked. A few weeks before the agreement, while I was swimming in the pool, the telephone rang. I read the display: it was Johann Rupert. I was in the changing room, there was a crazy commotion, and it was ten in the morning. I was overcome with guilt: I ought to be in the office, how do I explain that I'm dripping wet and about to take a shower? I answered quickly, saying: "My battery's run down, I'll call back in an hour," and ended the call. Sometime later Mr. Rupert admitted that he thought I'd been very clever in playing for time. He thought I'd done it on purpose to think up my answers. When chance is transformed into strategy, never let it pass or ignore it!

In order to conclude the deal, the big boss of Richemont, being a true gentleman, offered Natalie the prestigious position of Executive Chairman, and Richard Lepeu and I clarified our roles and responsibilities for a clear and unambiguous company governance. Soon after—following more touch and go and before the official announcement—Natalie accepted the title and all that went with it.

ALL THAT GLITTERS IS NOT GOLD. The state of Net-a-Porter, however, was causing some concern: cracks were appearing in its technology (they had just had seventy-two hours of downtime during Black Friday/Cyber Monday—in other words, an etailer's busiest time of the year for orders), the warehouses were full because they had postponed investment in logistics to save money, customers in certain Asian markets were buying on discount, and the brands were alarmed by this short-term practice. The management, however, had been reassured with promises in terms of pay increases as well as promotions.

I therefore found myself handling a beautiful trademark that was glamorous and glittering on the outside but with several internal problems. YOOX had managed to engineer monobrands, but Net-a-Porter hadn't: they had been positively late in launching their menswear site, Mr. Porter, whereas we had been selling menswear from the very beginning. We had worked hard on smartphones and had many specifically Italian brands, such as

Moncler and Cucinelli, which they didn't have. In short, YOOX was well ahead in many things.

But in the end, we had much in common on which to work. We had started up with end-of-season, they with full-price. They had then added end-of-season (with The Outnet), while we had added full-price with The Corner, an online department store, and Shoescribe, a site for shoes only. We had the monobrands, because we were good at backend and logistics, and they had launched editorial content, because they were good at frontend and marketing.

On paper it really was a perfect merger with one complementing the other.

I became the CEO with all-round management of the company, and Natalie became the executive chair with powers in certain limited areas.

After the announcement I went to meet the company management. Natalie had just done a mega-show to glorify the merger, enchanting the crowds—she was certainly a skilled performer—and now it was my turn. I knew the climate was hostile: Many employees and executives were against the merger. An Italian who technically buys out the English—even though it's a merger—is unacceptable! I flew to London, stayed at a hotel close to Westfield where their offices were, and that evening I had the unfortunate idea of eating a tranche of salmon that looked immediately suspect. I was sick throughout the night and felt like death warmed up when I woke the next morning. I had no desire to go to the meeting, was not in top form, and was not even a cheerleader like Natalie. I'm calmer in character, and after the food-poisoning my energy was down in my boots.

Once the meeting was over, I realized I'd made a load of promises: salary increases, promotions, and the like. But I needed someone who could represent me in London because I knew I couldn't spend more than a third of my time there.

There were already three or four candidates. Natalie was keen to promote Stephanie Phair, her protégée, while I wanted to have an objective assessment made by an independent agency so as not to create favoritism. Stephanie did not come out strongest. The right person turned out to be Alison Loehnis, a true "woman for all seasons," described by *The Fashion Law* as "a PR and marketing-focused executive," who I would later appoint as president of Net-a-Porter and Mr. Porter and, after my departure, would become interim managing director of YNAP. Despite all my efforts to involve her as much as possible in the preliminary months, Natalie was evasive. She canceled a meeting with me in London when I was already on the plane and, soon after, informed me she would be taking about two months' summer vacation. "Not bad," I thought, "in the middle of your company merger!"

At the height of the negotiations, while we were defining our respective roles, I was driving toward Lake Como when she called me. I switched on the speakerphone and said: "Natalie, I'm driving, but we can talk just the same." She replied: "But Federico, it's something important!" She was thinking I'd be prepared, that I'd be fully concentrated, that I'd have forty sheets of paper in front of me, and instead she discovered that I was improvising. She interpreted it as a show of strength and confidence and realized I was at ease.

Sometimes improvisation works better than planning! And a good dose of luck always helps. Maybe the people at Net-a-Porter weren't of the same opinion. Very shortly after my arrival, they revealed that in the past they had created a micro-team that knew everything about YOOX and even knew my movements in advance: they knew if I was going to Paris, and were informed if we were organizing an event. They did business intelligence, an art at which the Anglo-Saxons are one hundred percent better than we are, and which for us is unthinkable; we would never even dream of creating a structure of this kind.

This was how things went, and this was how my adventure on the other side of the English Channel began. The climate inside was not idyllic, the British press joined the war against the "invader": one of the most relentless was *The Business of Fashion,* a site created and directed by Imran Amed, a former consultant with a high regard for Natalie and her associate Carmen Busquets, who wrote various unflattering articles about YOOX and about me, so that at a certain point the famous investigative journalist Oliver Shah, responsible for the fall of Topshop founder Sir Philip Green, wrote a piece in *The Sunday Times* of June 28, 2020, with the title "Business of Fashion Ruffled by 'Bias' Allegations." "Ex-McKinsey consultant Imran Amed has won friends and influenced an industry, but his website is drawing flak for alleged conflicts of interest." Bingo!

The atmosphere was hostile: I was concerned about a possible hemorrhage, a mass exodus that I'd have had difficulty managing. I decided then to handle the situation with kid gloves, but in doing so I was harming myself, going against my own more decisive nature. I used fair play and pliancy, I gave everyone a second chance, knowing that the objective of many was simply to boycott me. It was a tragic error—if I could go back, I'd never do it again.

I'VE MADE MANY MISTAKES...

Ah, I've made many errors, all connected with trust. I've trusted people too much. I've been naïve, to put it mildly. I trusted my PR advisor who hadn't pointed out to me the risk of giving an interview to a major international financial newspaper at a moment like that, and I trusted the journalist who asked me a series of questions to highlight the war between me and Natalie. The result was a totally misleading article that suggested I was the boss, whereas throughout the interview I had repeatedly recalled that my objective was a governance that was clear and, above all, functional to the success of the new group and not to my own self. The journalist then asked what I expected from my management and from the people who worked for me, and I replied that I wasn't interested in being worshipped like a nineteenth-century ruler, that I liked to disrupt hierarchies and work democratically with everyone, that I wasn't looking for the adulation of brown-nosers but for results, respect, ethics, integrity. The journalist ended by emphasizing the two styles of management: on the one hand, Natalie, cheerleader with a company that was losing money, and on the other hand, Federico, who had orchestrated the merger with a listed and disciplined company, and speaking about my relations with the team he wrote the fateful words: "I don't need love, I need results," ignoring many other things that I had told her.

Many newspapers reported these words. Even the Italian weekly magazine *Famiglia Cristiana* attacked me with a vitriolic article, and a meme circulated widely on the internet with the phrase: "YOOX Net-a-Porter has only one boss, and that is me."

At the beginning of September, maybe also due to the contents of this article, Massenet notified Richemont of her resignation. I asked her why, and she replied in vague and enigmatic terms. Since that moment I've had no contact with her. Indeed, she has even blocked me on Instagram!

If I ever had to conduct another transaction like this, or if more probably someone asked my advice in a similar situation, I would tell them not to react in the way I had done. I would tell them to make a clean break with those who did not embrace the project. My advice is: "Free yourselves as far as possible from the old guard if it's hostile." I could have done it; the employment market in England allows it. Instead, I chose the more acquiescent route.

I've made other serious errors, always based on a misconception of people. I delegated one of the most complex and sophisticated re-platforming operations (in other words, the transfer to a new technological platform) to a new chief technological officer specially recruited for this project (while Gabriele moved to run the research and development department), a manager who assured me for over a year about results which, alas, he couldn't achieve. He had an impeccable track record and had worked for Walmart, the number one chain in the American retail trade; he really seemed the right person, even for the shareholders who interviewed him. All the same, I placed two joint general directors, Alberto Grignolo and Irene Boni, over him to keep an eye, knowing that he posed the greatest risk for integration, but neither of the two raised their hand in time to tell me we were miscalculating certain fundamental aspects of the operation. Despite the mayhem of the first migration, that of theoutnet.com, he kept smiling even when he knew he was in the wrong. He never admitted errors, covered them up, and said that in a couple of weeks everything would be fine again, when in fact it took us many months. I underestimated the complexity and, as always, accepted full responsibility: It took us twice as long, we spent twice as much money, and we even lost in market share.

I made a mistake in involving myself in a project as ambitious as it was necessary; pure technology is my Achilles' heel (who knows how it would have gone if Steve Jobs had listened to me when I wrote to him). I'm able to supervise all company processes, but I'm not a programmer like Mark Zuckerberg and, for the whole technological implementation aspect, I needed to rely on others. Creating a single customized platform for the different brands made a colossal logical sense in terms of investment and maintenance in the coming years; it was the right path from the strategic point of view. But passing from one platform to another is a woeful experience, as it is for many digital companies. Thinking about the long term, about what happens in the next five years, made me lose sight of the short term, which is equally important when you're in a highly competitive market.

When the process was complete, I could say I had exchanged a battered old automobile for one that was fast and elegant, like moving from a Fiat Panda to a Ferrari. But in the years of transition, the suffering caused by all those things that failed to work was truly enormous.

THE HAPPY COUPLE

The marriage between YOOX and Net-a-Porter was celebrated on March 31, 2015, after a very long engagement with quarrels and reconciliations. I had managed at last to fulfill another of my dreams.

I wanted the two companies to merge, I strongly believed in it, and did everything to make it happen. In 2015, by creating YNAP (YOOX + Net-a-Porter), we were the first to merge two great e-commerce companies. It was an innovative, disruptive merger, the first in the luxury online sector, and the industrial rationale behind this transaction was remarkable.

It seemed almost like a trick of fate: both companies had been founded in June 2000, they had taken different routes, but both had a clear objective—that of becoming number one. Both had achieved it differently. They sought to transform differences into a strength, as in the opening years of YOOX.

It was a union between two winners, two equals, based on a complementary relationship. Net-a-Porter, based in London, was the most prestigious luxury e-commerce site in existence, a perfect mix of editorial and commercial content and extremely powerful in English-speaking countries. YOOX was my creation, and as an Italian entrepreneur I had the idea of becoming the global partner, the internet retailer for the leading names in fashion. YOOX was ahead in technology and well established in southern Europe and Japan. Net-a-Porter published a beautiful magazine and had launched mrporter.com and theoutnet.com, whereas YOOX represented the state-of-the-art in digital marketing and sustainability; the mutual potential was enormous. We had many things in common: our central focus on the customer, innovation, our aim of growing and attracting the best talents in the sector. The difference made us stronger. We put together an international team with no cultural barriers. Together, we wanted to reinvent the future of online fashion. And we succeeded.

It certainly wasn't easy. They were glamorous but they didn't have an industrial focus which is generally what we Italians have always been good at, from the 1950s onward. Nevertheless, we complemented each other and were very strong together.

My idea of mixing diversities, of joining two distant cultures, was achieved. It was now clear to everyone that this project was not aggressive—as some had suspected—but defensive: only by working together could we compete in the coming years whereas, alone, we would have suffered too much. I wanted to defend my YOOX, but also Net-a-Porter.

In conclusion, do you remember I spoke about Federico the small fry that swam in a sea of sharks? Now you understand why. In the beginning, digital technology was a desert with very few players and no competition, but in the space of fifteen years it had become an aquarium of piranha fish, all of them ready to eat you in one gulp and spit out the bones. The birth of certain giants has changed the balance of the world economy, and it has become a titanic enterprise to survive, not to be gobbled up. I have continued consistently along my path, bringing together Italian creativity and American business. I have surfed between fashion companies that have never worked together and which—as we know—are super-competitive and mutual rivals. I have sailed in stormy waters and reached agreements with people of immense power without ever feeling inferior; I went to visit Mr. Rupert as myself, whereas some people had painted me as the bad guy; I held firm for years until I successfully merged with Net-a-Porter. I was determined, never conceded an inch, and never let myself be frightened by anyone. I wanted to grow and become big.

Maybe I too was a shark—but disguised as small fry.

10

On October 5, 2015, the Italian Stock Exchange in Piazza Affari, Milan, was decked out with a large black bow that transformed it into a gigantic gift pack. At exactly nine o'clock, after my speech on a platform on which I was joined by colleagues and many leading Italian entrepreneurs, I rang the opening bell that signals the start of trading. I was happy and excited because my new company was making its debut after the merger between YOOX and Net-a-Porter. The Italian digital economy had taken off, and we were its leading players. With total sales of €1.3 billion a year, YOOX had become an e-commerce colossus.

It hardly seemed true! In fifteen years, we had moved on from a "garage" in Casalecchio, when the word *startup* barely existed in Italy, to an amazing merger. We had started off with Elserino Piol's L.3 billion (€1.5 million), a figure that seemed large but wasn't, to become one of the key players in the digital world; from a group of kids from Romagna we were now a workforce of eight hundred in YOOX alone—most of us in Italy—which, when I left in 2021, had reached several thousand at group level, a large proportion engineers.

YNAP is the acronym we chose: Natalie Massenet had wanted to call it Net-a-Porter YOOX Group, but I couldn't agree because it sounded better turned round into YOOX Net-a-Porter. It started off with a capitalization close to €3.8 billion and a price per share that immediately shot up to €29.95 (+6.7 percent). The following day, October 6, it rose again to €30.50. According to the analysts it was an unqualified success, and YOOX stock price gained 2.5 percent that day.

In the new company, since it was a "merger of equals," 50 percent of the shares would be held by YOOX shareholders; the remaining 50 percent would go to Richemont but with a voting right of only 25 percent, with the remaining 25 percent without voting rights so that it didn't have control of the company. YNAP would cover 180 countries with a distribution that was expected to be 28 percent of revenue in North America, 15 percent in Great Britain, 7 percent in Italy, 30 percent in the rest of Europe, 15 percent in Pacific Asia, and 5 percent in the rest of the world. We could count on more than two million customers worldwide.

FASHION VALLEY IS BORN

The idea of creating a mega conglomerate of virtual luxury had happened! It seemed like a Silicon Valley story, and yet we were Italian through and through, while technically we had bought a Swiss-owned English company and become world recordholders in luxury e-commerce. When I founded YOOX I knew that, since Italy is the top manufacturer and the world's third consumer of high fashion, its heart could only be here. When I brought fashion onto the Web, I carried with me all the great names of fashion, explaining the importance of the internet to them, even before it became indispensable: I like to think that I ferried them into the new century. My idea then—and time has proved me right—was that bringing together different skills would allow us to strengthen the connection with luxury, offering them a store on an independent, comprehensive, and specialized platform that operated at a global level. The whole of Italian fashion was now online, largely thanks to us. Our next task was to raise our sights and conquer the rest of the world. And that morning at the Stock Exchange I was in seventh heaven. In my speech, I remember the laughter among everyone present when I said it was the second time that I was ringing the bell but there wouldn't be a third.

At the same time, those images came back to mind of my appearance as a film extra when I was at the Bocconi: I was a dealer then, wandering around the Milan Stock Exchange, and twenty years later I was there as a real protagonist!

I had worked hard, had never given up. I wanted Net-a-Porter and in the end was able to get it. I knew that in a market now so highly competitive there was no space for small fry—only the big fish survive and can swim in peace. I had become one of them.

Since the merger we were now fully-fledged members of the world net economy and over the years I would meet various key figures in this galaxy. Mark Zuckerberg came to Milan in May 2022, during the COVID pandemic, and wanted to organize a meeting with a few Italian entrepreneurs. Americans obviously had their own policy, and Meta asked us to take a molecular swab test before the meeting, which had been arranged for a Monday. The day before, on the Sunday afternoon at five o'clock, an Italian doctor rang my doorbell, accompanied by an American guy six feet two inches tall, of muscular build, looking like a secret agent in a spy movie. They produced a machine for carrying out the test, and in ten minutes they certified that I was negative. It had all the appearance of a special military operation. Meta wasn't going to trust us Italians to do the test ourselves; it wanted absolute control over every stage.

The next afternoon, I was the only person at the meeting who wasn't the owner of a brand. There was Brunello Cucinelli, Diego Della Valle from Tod's, Lorenzo Bertelli from Prada, Remo Ruffini from Moncler, and Renzo Rosso from Only The Brave. I thought of the past and almost felt it my duty to play the host, to be the go-between once again between tech and glamour. We talked about the metaverse and the prospects it might offer for those who do fashion. Zuckerberg is determined, cold, knows exactly where he wants to arrive, and his journey to Italy was a foray into the country where style is created and developed. At a certain point, while we were talking about the new glasses created by Luxottica for navigating in 3D, I jokingly told him he ought to replace them with contact lenses, but he replied that he's as blind as a bat, that he's many diopters short and wouldn't see anything with Meta glasses. Everything was very algorithmic, interesting, but chilly. He wrote a few days later to thank me for the meeting, and the funny thing I noticed is that he too, like all tech guys, uses his initials as a signature. I'm the same—I've always been FM—and then everyone in the company calls us like that.

Several years earlier, I met Tim Cook, CEO of Apple, who took over on the death of Steve Jobs and has brilliantly steered the company to meteoric levels. I was at Cupertino to meet Luca Maestri, Chief Financial Officer of Apple, whom I'd known at the Bocconi—he had invited me to visit Apple Park, the "spaceship," an enormous ring-shaped structure of 2.8 million square feet, covered by solar panels, with park and lake inside. It had been the idea of Steve Jobs and Jony Ive, Apple's chief designer at that time, who decided to entrust the project to the great architect Norman Foster. It's a spectacular place, both technologically and visually.

I felt proud that an Italian like Luca had risen so high; that same year he had made more money than Cook! I spent the day there but met Tim only in passing.

A few years later, I was on the Florence-to-Rome train, in the executive carriage, when I realized the person sitting next to me was Cook himself. He seemed on vacation, an American in Italy, and no one had recognized him. I, shameless as always, decided to introduce myself: "We met briefly when I came to Apple," I said. "I was with Luca Maestri. . . ." He knew who I was, knew all about me, and about YOOX. We spent an enjoyable half hour on the train, over coffee, and I gave him a few suggestions about where to go, what to eat, and places not to miss in Rome. No business, only holiday!

BREAKING THE MOLD

But let's return to our merger and to D-day. After that, many things would change. I fulfilled my dream but realized that this really was a turning point: We were now a group or, better still, a large corporation. I needed to find a way to integrate two companies, two cultures, two methods of working. I needed to abandon old ways of thinking and construct new ones. Never follow old practices, never stick to convention. What worked well for YOOX needed to be reinvented for a new differently sized company with employees that lived in different countries and whose work practices weren't always compatible.

I could see very much in common: We could combine our technologies and our logistics, we could improve the geographic localization of our stock assortments, bringing them closer to the customer. And above all we could share the best practices of both companies without harming the current quality levels of service.

When we merged with Net-a-Porter, we brought them our own logistical model. This provided for a central warehouse, which was the departure point for all goods, and other peripheral warehouses that served to manage returns and certain products that sold well in that area. They, on the other hand, had previously followed the opposite course: They had opened a warehouse in each main market containing all products, with the result that unsold stock remained there, whereas we, having a central warehouse, distributed the goods everywhere. The technological infrastructure was also different: They had many sites whereas we had just one that relied on many distribution centers. With the merger we now had two central warehouses situated in Italy (one in Bologna and one in Milan) and distribution centers in the United Kingdom, United States, Hong Kong, Dubai, China, and Japan.

The merger opened the way for many negotiations and the conclusion of several international agreements, such as one with Mohamed Alabbar, regarded as the mastermind behind Dubai's economic growth. Alabbar founded Emaar Properties, the owner of the Burj Khalifa, the world's tallest skyscraper, and Dubai Mall, one of the world's largest shopping centers. He's a visionary entrepreneur whose real focus is on the business of the future, and we became immediate friends.

I was introduced one day by Franca Sozzani, with whom I established so many magnificent initiatives. I mention Franca because she was a figure of great importance to me. I had been off the glamour radar from the foundation of YOOX to the time we were listed in 2009. From then I gradually entered this inner circle over which Franca was the undisputed queen. *Vogue Italia*, the magazine on which she was editor-in-chief, dictated the line on image and international glamour trends: she was the point of reference for so many creatives. Franca had curiosity, wit, intelligence, and contagious energy. She was fascinated by the internet, and for her I represented the new. We were among the first to use the English word *talent,* and we worked on discovering and promoting many young stylists such as JW Anderson, Simone Rocha, and Aquazzura. Every year we organized a mega-event at Palazzo Morando in Milan coordinated by the wonderful Emanuela Schmeidler and, having selected the best designers from all the countries—from Italy, Africa, South Korea, and so on—we put them before a jury for the final awards. It was an evening not to be missed: the heads of every fashion house were there, from Domenico Dolce and Stefano Gabbana to Donatella Versace and Giorgio Armani, on the hunt, too, for young collaborators.

No one could resist Franca; that was her strength. Our event gave great space to young people from all countries, more than I've seen done in America with the CFDA (Council of Fashion Designers of America) or in France with ANDAM, the French association whose mission it is to identify and support the talent that will produce tomorrow's fashion collections. I was a member of all three associations, but what we achieved with Franca was unique: we were inclusive and were looking for young people from every country, unlike the others who focused only on the United States (in the case of CFDA) or France (with ANDAM). We often had brainstorming sessions, invented projects to carry out together, and our motto was "no sooner said than done": we enjoyed it, we worked fast, our ideas soon became reality. Working with her was a pleasure and our two teams knew that things were concluded well and quickly.

Franca was one of the great supporters of the merger with Net-a-Porter, backing me with Mr. Rupert. We were friends, we understood each other, and she kept on saying: "Federico, you've got to look to the Middle East, because it's going to become more and more interesting and innovative. Believe me, don't underestimate them. And then, if you come with me, I'll introduce you to Alabbar, he's someone very special; you'll see, something will work out between you."

So one day I went to Dubai to take part in a *Vogue* event in honor of Franca and to understand this new galaxy; I ended up at a memorable party with lots of celebrities and top models when, at a certain point, Franca called and asked me to go to her suite: "I have to tell you something." I arrived in this gigantic penthouse that Alabbar had provided for her, together with a private plane. "I have lung cancer," she told me. "I don't think I'll make it." It was two years before she died, and I think I was one of very few who knew about it; I burst into tears and felt an immense grief. I visited her several times during her treatment at the European Institute of Oncology in Milan, founded by Umberto Veronesi. Franca fought like a lion to the very end. She had a tremendous work ethic; she never stopped, even when she was exhausted by the pleural mesothelioma, a cancer caused by exposure to asbestos that was now consuming her. No one knows how the hell the editor-in-chief of *Vogue Italia* could have been in contact with asbestos! Her funeral took place on December 24, at her beloved Portofino.

After Franca's introduction, Mohamed Alabbar came to visit me in Bologna with his son Rashid. They wanted to talk to me about Salama, Mohamed's beautiful daughter, who was trying to launch a luxury e-commerce site in Dubai. Rashid had with him a suitcase bearing the name Mr Porter. I looked at him and said, with a smile: "But how can you turn up carrying my competitor's suitcase?" At the time I hadn't yet carried out the merger, though it was already in the air. We concluded nothing with Alabbar at the first meeting.

The acquisition of Net-a-Porter not only extended YOOX's trading borders but gave us prestige in several countries such as Dubai and America, where they were more famous than us. Negotiations with Alabbar resumed in 2016. He lined up a powerful team of lawyers while I had Silvia Scagnelli, my investor relations manager, precise, insistent on detail, very cautious; they made impossible demands, and we made requests difficult to satisfy. When I saw that the agreement was in danger of foundering, I called Alabbar, and he and I dealt with the last few—but important—details via WhatsApp. It was the first deal I had completed in this way. We reached a compromise to deal with a complicated market where you certainly need a local partner; I had learned my lesson in China, so in Dubai I did the contrary of what I had done there. I chose the number one and we built a company together in which he had the 40 percent minority share and we had 60 percent—the owner of the brand must always have the majority; he had to put in the capital and had to finance the whole startup phase, and we had to bring the products from our central warehouses in Italy. We recruited a local manager and opened an office in Dubai that dealt with local customer care and marketing; they had a better knowledge of their clientele. They decided what kind of promotion to do, what pricing policy to apply, what products to push more, what to push less, what to select from our enormous warehouse in Bologna, and whatnot. They managed returns according to local legislation and knew how to handle privacy problems. They answered telephone calls, made sure the packages arrived. We sold directly to the customer at first, but then we moved on to a local warehouse.

I am still friendly with Mohamed Alabbar and often visit him in Dubai. He once invited me to his estate in the middle of the desert. I insisted on driving his dune buggy, having great fun until we got stuck. He calmly called for help and a second dune buggy arrived, which, instead of rescuing us, also got stuck in the sand. Then a third arrived and ended in the same way, at which point we left all the dune cars in the sand and at last, with a real automobile, we arrived at his marvelous residence where we ate a perfect Italian-style pizza cooked in an enormous wood oven.

RETURN TO CHINA

By 2018 YNAP was the leading figure in luxury online. There was only one piece missing: China.

As you will have gathered, since my foray with emporioarmani.com powered by YOOX in 2010, China had been one of my fixations. But I had learned my lesson and knew that if you wanted to get into that enormous and fast-growing market you needed to rely on a local partner—doing everything alone was impossible, particularly there. In 2018 I therefore contacted Michael Evans, right-hand man of Daniel Zhang, the CEO of Alibaba. Michael deals with the international side and is the brother of Mark, the venture capitalist at Benchmark, which had given me money in 2003. The Evans brothers are ex-Olympic rowers, intelligent, and have been crucial at two different moments in my career. We started negotiations with Michael before Zhang took over. I fought strenuously to establish our arguments: I lost my cool, made scenes even with Zhang, but I knew they too wanted to reach an agreement because Alibaba, without us, would never manage to carry true luxury onto their platform. I always felt like David against Goliath—negotiating with such a big company wasn't easy.

We'd had meetings with our competitor, JD, even after my first meeting with the founder of the company, but I had finally understood that agreements needed to be made with the number one player, the strongest, and Alibaba was the undisputed e-commerce leader in China. Halfway through the negotiation, which maybe lasted too long and was close to deadlock, Richemont fortunately stepped in with a negotiating power different to mine. We found ourselves at Hangzhou, the former silk capital once visited by Marco Polo, now a metropolis where Alibaba had its headquarters, a place so vast that it was a city within a city. Those present were Jérôme Lambert, CEO of Richemont, Daniel Zhang, CEO of Alibaba, Michael, and me: a truly top-level meeting. The evening before, I had dined with all the number twos who were staying in my hotel, I arranged with Michael Evans that we'd have breakfast together and would then go with his driver to the mega meeting, and I went to bed.

I set the alarm for an early call, seeing that breakfast was at seven-thirty and the meeting was at nine, but at a certain point I opened my eyes, saw on the telephone that it was already nine, and realized that the alarm hadn't gone off. Help! I found all the missed calls, saw the messages from Michael Evans, those from Silvia who had tried twenty times, saying: "Okay, we're leaving, we've already left." I dressed as fast as I could, rushed out, hurried to find a taxi, and arrived at the meeting at least half an hour late. I looked disheveled and said the first thing that came to mind: "I was sick last night...something I'd eaten" (this time it was nonsense, but I hadn't the courage to tell some of the world's most powerful people that I hadn't heard the alarm...).

The Chinese took me straight to a clinic, a kind of super outpatient clinic with several doctors on duty. There was nothing wrong with me, I was fine, but without batting an eye I swallowed two pills they gave me and felt I had also mortally offended them by talking about food that was off, which for them is unthinkable. In actual fact, I'd had food poisoning in 2008, at the Beijing Olympics, after eating Peking Duck. It was good but extremely heavy, and I really did have a night of hell that time.

Luckily the meeting continued with no further hitches. I made my contribution, and the deal was at last done. Johann Rupert then happily completed it in 2019 when we announce a joint venture to bring the European luxury market onto Tmall, the largest e-commerce platform in existence, and into his Luxury Pavilion, specially invented to host luxury products.

By strange coincidence, I came across Jack Ma not once but twice, on the Strait of Bonifacio, in Corsica. On the first occasion I didn't feel able to stop and introduce myself, whereas the second time we were in the middle of negotiations with Alibaba. Every summer I hire a boat, the *Puritan,* for a couple of weeks. It's a yacht built in 1930 by John G. Alden, one of the great American naval architects. It's had numerous owners since it was launched. it was in the service of the United States navy during World War II, then became an exploration ship, then belonged to the Ferruzzi family of Ravenna, and to Arturo Ferruzzi (may he rest in peace) in particular, and lastly to the current owners, who have restored it and put it into service as a charter vessel. It's a gaff-rigged schooner, all manual with no electronics, which has sailed from Nova Scotia to Cape Horn and from the Caribbean to the Mediterranean, where I spend a part of my August vacation. To sail with no engine is magnificent—and truly sustainable. That year, we went first to Sardegna and then, having reached Corsica, we stopped at Bonifacio, a magical harbor where we came ashore for dinner at a very simple pizzeria. While I was there with a beautiful pizza Margherita on my plate, I saw a man in the distance followed by a swarm of people. "That looks like Jack," I thought to myself. And as he gradually approached, I became sure: "But goodness, this is Jack Ma."

As you can now imagine, I was no longer seated, nor silent. I got up from the table and called him. He stopped to see who it was, who had recognized him—like Tim Cook, no one knew who he was—and I told him I was in negotiations with his people. He replied that he'd heard about it. I asked him which boat he was on, and he pointed calmly to the cruise liner anchored outside the harbor, a thousand-foot vessel. Friendly, easy-going, he hadn't flaunted his power or his wealth for one instant.

SELL OR KEEP?

The time has come to tell you about the sale to Richemont. At the end of 2017 I was at another turning point. In Italy there's a well-establish line of thought in family-based capitalism that 51 percent seems to be the only option. YOOX was financed first by Italian venture capital and then by several Italian funds and by an international fund, Benchmark Capital, and finally Renzo Rosso also put money into us. After the merger, I dropped to 4 percent of YNAP; I never felt it a priority to have the majority of a company. What matters is the results, growth, market power, the involvement of the team, being generous. On January 22, 2018, I announced on Instagram:

Today marks an historic event for the YOOX NET-A-PORTER GROUP. Richemont, already our largest shareholder, has decided to make a tender offer to buy all of YNAP's shares, valuing our Group at around $6.4 billion! Richemont expressed its admiration for the quality of our teams across the UK, Italy and worldwide and appreciates YNAP's solid track record of growth. It is ready to put even more resources behind us to further strengthen and accelerate YNAP's long-term leadership in online luxury. Richemont is one of the world's leading luxury groups. Its portfolio of Maisons includes Cartier, IWC Schaffhausen, Jaeger-LeCoultre, Van Cleef & Arpels, Chloé, Montblanc and Officine Panerai in Italy. As a passionate entrepreneur, I remember with pride the hard work and excitement of YOOX's IPO in 2009, when total revenues were around $200 million. It was always my dream to create something much bigger. This became possible in 2015 through the combination of YOOX and NET-A-PORTER. The merger allowed both companies to flourish, creating the world leader in online luxury. This Anglo-Italian collaboration brought total revenues to around $2.4 billion in a couple of years. I'm very grateful to everyone who made it all possible. Nearly 20 years after inventing YOOX, YNAP's magic excites me even more. The prospect of no longer owning my 4% of the share capital does not change my entrepreneurial commitment to YNAP. Dreaming and innovating to the benefit of our customers has always been my motivation; it will remain so in the years to come.

Shortly before, in fact, YNAP's board of directors had received an offer from Richemont. The board accepted and Richemont therefore launched a tender offer at thirty-eight euros a share for YNAP, delisting the stock from the Milan Stock Exchange.

I had been clear with Johann Rupert: I had told him that I didn't want the role of manager, that I would honor my contract and support a phase of transition but would not remain in the group forever.

Being independent is the right position for an entrepreneur who wants to break the mold, who has no intention of falling into line but prefers to smash everything so as to then build something new.

My young, anti-establishment, and let's say rather punk attitude has never vanished. I'm a rebel but I also have the fragilities that I've carried with me since I was a student: One of these fragilities is impostor syndrome. What is it? It's the feeling of not being worthy of the success achieved. I have a recurring dream: I'm at university and, after four years, I still haven't taken a single exam. I wake with a jolt, and start thinking how I've often played with fate, that I've had a long succession of lucky chances which have gone better than I deserved. I feel more like the bungling Johnny English—played by the brilliant Rowan Atkinson—who always somehow manages to get through, than like the super determined Mark Zuckerberg. I prefer to observe life with a touch of irony, at the risk of feeling an intruder, or Gladstone Gander, the lucky character in the *Mickey Mouse* comics.

The situation reverses when I go to America—back, for example, to Columbia University. There they roll out the red carpet for me and I've discovered that I'm in the Columbia Business School magazine as one of their star alumni, one of the real examples of success, alongside the inventor of Beyond Meat. Even my retailing professor at Columbia (Alan Kane) continues to tell me he is puzzled that it was an Italian and not one of his American students who had managed to create such a large global retail company. America restores some feeling of pride, otherwise I would continue fighting against my syndrome. Yet there's one thing I know I'm good at: timing. All the key moments of my business have happened through perfect timing, from when I began until when we were listed and when I sold. I started at the very last moment before the internet bubble burst; we discovered talented people early on; we put our hopes in the cell phone before all the others.

I sold before the umpteenth slump, before e-commerce lost its innovative edge to become the prerogative of the great giants, acquiring a different aspect, becoming less creative and disruptive, focusing mainly on the management of costs and investments.

LOSING MY HEAD OVER TITIAN

I'm quite a thrifty person; I don't squander money on jewelry and luxury boats—which I only hire—but I have two passions that I've been cultivating since I started to earn good money: the first is houses, and the second is art. With part of the money from the sale of YNAP I decided to gift myself something of real importance, which I would never have imagined or sought to possess. I bought a painting by Titian portraying Salome with the head of John the Baptist. Yes, a work by the great Italian master and Renaissance genius.

I had begun my art collection a few years earlier, in my usual unpredictable manner. In 2015 I returned home from hospital after a cartilage operation when Kerry and Maggie decided to go to Lake Como to prepare for Halloween, two days later. They left me at home alone, and I did something crazy. That evening, my friend Francesco Bonami, the famous critic and art curator, had organized an auction at Phillips in New York devoted entirely to Italian art. "There are some lovely pieces, if you want," he said. "For example, there's a beautiful Morandi that belonged to the Pulitzer family" (the same family whose name was given to the prestigious American prize for journalism and literature). I said: "Okay, Francesco, but let me know the estimate because I don't know that I can afford it." He told me the auction starting price is $800,000 and, according to him, the right price is between $1.3 and $1.5 million.

I was alone and might still have been under the effect of the anesthetic when I started taking part in the auction, almost for fun: I'd never bought anything of that caliber, or for those sums, and had absolutely no intention of spending a million. They opened the bidding for the Morandi at $800,000, and I bid, feeling sure it would rise and that someone else would buy it. I waited, but no one offered any more. They knocked it down to me! I panicked, called Kerry, and told her I'd spent nearly a million for a beautiful Morandi, and she tried to calm me down.

But the story doesn't end there: When I received the authentication (the document that proves it's a genuine Morandi), I discovered they only had a photocopy; the original was missing. I realized now why no one had bid over my offer—and trembled at the idea that it was false. Many months went by before the next meeting of the Fondazione Morandi in Bologna, which meets once a year to authenticate the master's work. When they told me it was original and that this beautiful still life really was painted by Giorgio Morandi, I heaved an enormous sigh of relief!

I've never taken part in person at any auction, I've always bought works on the internet—I hadn't even seen the actual Titian I'm about to tell you about until I bought it.

David Zwirner is perhaps the most famous contemporary art gallery in New York; from there I had purchased photos by Thomas Ruff, a noted German photographer whose portraits are austere and mesmerizing. I didn't expect them to deal in classical art too, and was surprised when I received a link to the preview of an exhibition. There was this magnificent Titian, a real masterpiece. I don't think I've ever felt such a strong desire for a work as then. Over the years I've become more a collector of contemporary than classical art. I had bought various works but literally fell in love with Titian in 2013 at an exhibition in Rome, at the Scuderie del Quirinale, which covered his whole career, his development, his incredible sense of light and color. I had begun to read and study his life: I was fascinated by his sense of humor, his ability to poke fun even at his richest patrons, his entrepreneurial verve. He died at the age of ninety and, unlike many famous painters, had managed to charge extortionate prices for his works. Late Titian is truly magnificent. I then began a long negotiation with the gallery that lasted a year with authentications of authentications, the opinions of some twenty museum directors, and affidavits. I also turned to my friend Matteo Grassi, a classical art expert working between Paris and New York, who confirmed that the painting had been restored by Dianne Dwyer Modestini, the restorer of *Salvator Mundi* whose attribution to Leonardo da Vinci has had a troubled history of confirmation and uncertainty, and was nevertheless sold by auction at Christies in 2017 for $450.3 million, an absolute record, paid by a Saudi prince on behalf of the Abu Dhabi Department of Culture and Tourism.

In the end, not only did I manage to buy my Titian but, to my great satisfaction, I also brought it back to Italy, in the opposite direction to so many works that fly abroad never to return. This was obviously the greatest purchase I have made in my life, but when I look at it each morning as I do my exercises in the sitting room as soon as I get up, I feel the inestimable good fortune of owning such a unique and profound work.

Another work I'm very fond of is a watercolor by Lucian Freud. One day I met his daughter Bella at an exhibition of cover designs for *British Vogue*. I told her I had recently bought a picture by her father, and she reconstructed the whole story of the painting; she told me her father did it in Greece and explained how much he and Francis Bacon influenced each other: they were friends and shared many aspects of their art. Bella and I became friends, so that in 2019 I asked her to organize the interiors and the search for young British artists for our new house in London.

Luca Guadagnino wasn't involved in the London house but has done the interior design for five of my houses. And above all, he's a very dear friend. I've known him for twenty years. We first met at a dinner in Rome and immediately connected. He saw me as a businessman from whom he could learn marketing techniques and get managerial advice, while I adored his taste and admired his manic precision over work. I often went onto his film sets—his fortune is now his reputation—so that last time, when I couldn't get to Boston while he was filming *Challengers*, where Zendaya, the female lead, is at the center of a love triangle in the tennis world, they were both disappointed. But I did manage to follow the filming of *Call Me by Your Name* and *I Am Love* with Tilda Swinton and many others. James Ivory came to the lake with Luca to visit us while he was writing the screenplay of *Call Me by Your Name*.

I think there are many similarities between the role of movie director and that of entrepreneur: Both need to be sure that everything works and must manage their resources so that everyone knows what their task is and carries it out in the best possible way. Luca never leaves anything to chance; if there's a scene in a film involving a legal document for the sale of a property, he goes to a lawyer and has a real document prepared. On the set of the TV series *We Are Who We Are* there's a shot of the morning breakfast that soldiers had, and he found out exactly what they ate, how much they ate, what variety of food, to faithfully recreate the table. When I went to Padua, where Luca was finishing shooting, he told me he was the producer for a film directed by an ex-boyfriend, but that one of the co-producers had disappeared without paying the last installment.

A few nights later, I dreamt that Luca needed half a million euros and when I woke, I thought: "What are friends for if not to help you in your moment of need?" Without Fabio Canè I might still be working at Bain, or more probably in Brazil, making Romagnolo *piadinas*! Realizing that Luca was in trouble and didn't know what to do, I called him and said: "I'll pay that last installment myself." That's how I took a small share in the production of the film *Beckett*. The idea was stimulating, even though I was resigned to losing the money; I thought of it as a gift. I never thought of getting it back, and yet...

And yet, the movie did well; it was beautiful and, thanks to Luca, had a crazy cast starring Alicia Vikander and John David Washington. Netflix bought it, turning it into a success, and I got back the money I put in, plus a capital gain.

Talking once again about cinema, as I mentioned earlier, we restored Federico Fellini's *Amarcord* in 2015 with the Cineteca di Bologna. For me it was a wonderful film—it had won an Oscar forty years before and is so strong and poetic that the word "amarcord" (meaning "I remember" in Romagnolo dialect) has become synonymous with melancholy. We presented the restored version at the Venice Film Festival, and I had the honor to accompany my friend Franca Sozzani, editor-in-chief of *Vogue Italia,* to the first performance.

I was a co-producer of Dea Kulumbegashvili's film *April,* which won the Special Jury Prize at the Venice International Film Festival in 2024. Dea, a Georgian film director who had won many awards for her 2020 movie *Beginning,* made a film that was powerful and at the same time poetic. I am happy to have supported this artist because she has great talent, and I feel more women directors are needed in a profession that until now has been the prerogative of men. I am also a co-producer of the new documentary *Joie de Vivre* by my friend Luca Guadagnino on Bernardo Bertolucci, that Italian director whom Steve Jobs had heard of at the conference at Aspen in 1981, along with Bellini and Pininfarina: It's a kind of magic!

Who knows, maybe it's some sort of revenge after I had been turned down by all the major Hollywood movie companies at the end of my master's degree. Since then, in fact, I have ventured into co-production on many other occasions and have to say I'm really enjoying it.

11

On June 23, 2016, the United Kingdom held a referendum on whether it should stay in the European Union. Those in favor of leaving were 52 percent, while 48 percent preferred to remain. The country was split in half, with the majority of England and Wales voting to go, while Scotland and Northern Ireland were against a divorce.

Next morning, the British were in a state of shock: For those who voted "remain," it felt like a bad dream. They couldn't accept the idea of leaving, and weren't prepared to live in a country that had suddenly become an island again, separated from the rest of the continent to which it had belonged. David Cameron, the prime minister, had felt sure the British would choose Europe when he proposed the referendum, but he accepted the will of the majority and resigned on June 24. The economic crisis and fears about immigration had helped the nationalistic arguments of the "leavers" who advocated closure and isolation from the rest of Europe.

The phenomenon of *Brexodus* began almost immediately: Banks and corporations decided to leave the City, heading for Paris, Frankfurt, Dublin. I, though, decided to move against the flow: in 2015, I had merged with Net-a-Porter, and now was the moment to expand in the very country that many companies were leaving.

I've made these introductory remarks because two important things happened to me in 2017—I met the Prince of Wales as he then was, now King Charles III, a person who would have a major impact on my life; and YNAP and I decided to open a mega Tech Hub in Britain that would give us a powerful technological center in each country, one in Bologna and one in London.

I've always had a fixation about locations. We didn't have stores: we had offices and warehouses. As for the offices, I chose buildings with a splendid view, pleasant surroundings that helped to inspire people. We spent so much time at the computer that it was important to look outside, to see the horizon. In Milan, for example, we had moved to the Navigli, one of the historic and best-loved districts of the city, to an area that had become cool. In the entrance to the building there was a wall screen that showed purchases in real time. It gave details of the clothes being bought—bags, sneakers, hoodies—indicating the place where they had been ordered (Paris, Tokyo, Amsterdam, Sestri Levante). It was wonderful; in an instant you have an exact picture of people's tastes, where they come from, and for what items they choose. Speed was everything: every second was precious, from the moment the order arrived to when it left, so that on the last Black Friday that I spent at YNAP, we reached one order every 0.7 seconds.

My office on the top floor was a large open area with high ceilings and red curtains that could divide the area into multifunctional spaces, including a photographic studio for special projects.

In 2016 we opened a state-of-the-art and totally automated center at Landriano near Milan which, apart from being a gem of innovation, would also save Net-a-Porter from logistical isolation and would enable it to better serve customers outside the United Kingdom.

On June 27, 2017, it was London's turn. We opened the new Tech Hub, a center of innovation that employed hundreds of engineers, scientists, and programmers of all nationalities, in addition to the same number of experts from our twin center in Bologna. It was the first great investment in technology for a company in the luxury sector. We started with an articulated plan in which the technological center was one of the elements: It had been devised to accelerate innovation and to develop the most sophisticated technologies, including artificial intelligence, image recognition, and the creation of technologies for new generation cellphones.

I wanted offices that were modern, sustainable but also visually appealing, and which would communicate the spirit of YNAP. To create them, I commissioned Sir Nicholas Grimshaw, the multiple award-winning British architect famous for his passion for sustainability, whose practice has offices in New York, London, Melbourne, Sydney, Kuala Lumpur, and Doha, and heads a team of over four hundred. I came to know Sir Nicholas through Kerry, who's a close friend of his daughter Chloe, and we often visited the family. I knew his fees were astronomic but decided to risk it all the same. I admired his sensibility and his work—he had completed numerous projects, including Waterloo International Station in London, the Bibliothèque Nationale de France in Paris, and the Master Plan for JFK Airport in New York. I knew of his commitment to sustainability and saw him as a great visionary. He accepted, asked for a sum that was almost symbolic, nothing like what his offices would charge, and transformed seventy thousand square feet at White City, then a fairly rundown part of

London, into a magnificent place, an open space on two floors, with an ultramodern conception, based on collaboration, with piazzas where people could meet and work together, all inspired by design and green planning.

He made extensive use of recyclable materials, especially wood, and introduced around 2,500 plants with total respect for the environment, which was part of his philosophy as well as mine. Back in 2009, in fact, I had started a green initiative, with the launch of YOOXYGEN, a mega project relating to sustainability in the company, and with part of the site devoted to responsible fashion.

Everything was ready; all that remained was the inauguration. I asked Nick to take part and, in front of the deputy mayor, he delivered a magnificent speech in which he said in effect that while all the banks were moving out of London, we were opening a place that would attract talent and create new jobs—another one hundred staff were to be employed on top of the five hundred who already worked for YNAP—and he added that there was a need for brave Europeans like me who headed for London at a time when the English had voted to leave the European Union.

The area known as White City Place was originally the site of the Franco-British Exhibition of 1908 which stood alongside the Olympic Stadium where the first British Olympic Games had taken place. By the 2000s, it was an anonymous area of offices and warehouses when we decided to take part in a redevelopment project with the Royal College of Art, the Soho House Group, and other companies that would later move into this part of London. At the same time we signed a partnership agreement with the prestigious Imperial College of London for the teaching of coding, the basics of programming language, to boys but especially to girls from disadvantaged backgrounds and between the ages of eight and fourteen, thus promoting the importance of digital skills. By the time I left YNAP I had succeeded in promoting coding courses for thousands of young students.

A few months later, through the British Fashion Council, I invited Prince Charles to visit us, and he kindly accepted.

Apart from key events, there are sometimes important moments of empathy, of mutual connection, that happen almost by chance: I've experienced this many times in my life.

We prepared to welcome Prince Charles, together with his consort Camilla, at our new office, which was now in operation. We wanted to tell him about the development of skills relating to artificial intelligence, visual recognition, and research and development, and to illustrate our partnership with Imperial College, but I knew that the prince had no great interest in technology. To break the ice, rather than immerse him in code and in artificial intelligence, augmented reality and virtual reality, I therefore told him I had recently seen many photos of him when he was young.

I had just been to Sicily, to Villasmundo, for the funeral of Giuseppe da San Giuliano, Diego's father. I would never have missed it. I had great respect for the Marchese, he had helped me at the start of YOOX, and above all he was the father of one my best friends, as well as being the most elegant and charming man I had ever met. With the agreement of Diego and his delightful wife Fiona, Giuseppe had bequeathed me a beautiful Aston Martin, like James Bond's in *Casino Royale*. In that house there were also many memories of Prince Charles and Giuseppe, photos of when they were young. I realized they had been good friends, so while we were in the Hub, rather than talking about matters that would have bored him to death, I told him about the Marchese. The prince knew he had died and had sent his condolences to Diego; and so we began an *amarcord* and broke the ice.

And it triggered a sure-fire equation: my friends' friends are my friends too. This creates a kind of immediate empathy, a connection that goes beyond business, beyond technology, beyond roles and titles. In this way I found myself talking with a prince about a friend in common whom we both missed. And from there it was a short step away from comparing notes on style. The prince told me about the shoes he'd had for over twenty years and took good care of; I told him about a pair of John Lobb shoes that I'd cherished for over ten years.... This idea of the longevity of objects, of luxury as "buy less but buy better," is the true sense of sustainability in fashion and the heart of an affinity that we discovered immediately and then more deeply over the years.

Everything started like this. Soon after that meeting, I received a telephone call from his right-hand man, Julian Payne. The prince was inviting me for a weekend in Scotland at Dumfries House.

In the fall I went to his beloved residence in Scotland, which was also the headquarters of the Prince's Foundation (now the King's Foundation), an organization with a twofold purpose: It is involved in training but also in regeneration of local communities. Dumfries House is perfectly restored, with incredible Chippendale furniture and magnificent Murano chandeliers.

NEVER ARRIVE EMPTY-HANDED

I'm from Ravenna, I was brought up by a mother who appreciated good manners: So when I go to someone's house for dinner, I never arrive empty-handed. Yes, but what do you take for a prince? My English wife, Kerry, had read a story in the British press—probably not true—that the prince had a valet whose task it was to put toothpaste on his toothbrush, and the newspapers had made him the subject of ridicule. I therefore decided upon a bold gesture. I'm a fan of the Lorenzi Milano knife shop, an institution of Italian quality since 1967, which sells artisan objects in horn, mother-of-pearl, steel, and silver for the small rituals of everyday life. Well, before leaving Italy I went and bought a present that could arouse displeasure or delight. I packed my tuxedo and left. I remember my arrival in that ceremonial room as if it were today: About fifty guests were gathered, all in kilts, apart from me. I didn't know anyone. I now have a kilt too; I had it made to measure by a Scottish tailor, but I've never worn it. It's in my wardrobe, together with the tuxedo and the hood with the red lining that I use when I dress up as Dracula—my favorite mask, and later I'll tell you why—and an Indian robe that I bought for a wedding: it seems like the wardrobe of a secret agent, with a thousand disguises.

With a glass in my hand, waiting for Prince Charles and the moment to move to the dinner table, I made small talk with some perfect strangers about the weather—the English always talk about the weather just as we Italians always talk about food. It seemed like the scene in a movie: He arrived, looked across at me, and started to wave from a distance. When he approached, we exchanged a few words, then sat down, and when the key moment arrived, I pulled out my gift. If we were on television and not in real life, this would be the peak moment of suspense: I was on tenterhooks, walking a fine line—as so often in my life—between boldness and recklessness (on several occasions it has ended badly for me).

For a prince who obviously has everything, who thinks nothing of the umpteenth object among the thousands of valuable items in his possession, I thought it best to offer something frivolous. It was risky, I knew, but I handed him my wonderful package, which contained...a toothpaste squeezer! And what happened next was what would happen so many times over the coming years. Have a look at the archive of photographs that portray us together: You'll see I always have my ironic little smile, while he seems to be in fits of laughter. The prince found the idea so original, and his butler began to laugh out loud. It had worked!

I was sitting at the table with Patricia Hearst, granddaughter of the publishing magnate William Randolph Hearst, who had come to fame at the age of twenty-one when she was kidnapped by the Symbionese Liberation Army and then became a follower, robbing several banks. She had been convicted, but her sentence was commuted by President Jimmy Carter, and she was released from prison in 1979. She was later granted a pardon by Ronald Reagan and then by Bill Clinton. Patricia, who was now an actress and writer, was sitting beside me when the prince started talking about his enormous love for Italy. "Federico," he said, "invent a project that connects Britain to Italy!"

Once the evening was over, I returned to the cottage they had provided for me and started thinking up an idea. The cottage was in perfect Scottish style with hunting scenes on the walls and wood in the fireplace that I just could not light because there were no firelighters, only eco-friendly kindling and matches. In the end, I called the attendant who lit it effortlessly in two seconds.

Back home, it didn't take me long. I had learned the classical "no sooner said than done" while working with Franca Sozzani, a sense of timing and practicality that doesn't come naturally to the prince but which he admires, to such an extent that he has described me several times as his "secret weapon." (Occasionally, when Maggie asks what my job is, I show off by answering: "I work for the British Crown to save the planet." I feel like 007!) For this project, in the end, all I needed to do was join up the dots without inventing anything. The prince was very interested in the question of education and training which, for me, was pivotal to our company strategies. YOOX is on the front line of sustainability and was the first to launch a platform for green collections. Since 2009 it has introduced the ecobox, packaging in recyclable materials. This appeals to young people, and the average age of our employees is around thirty....

I added the twist of innovation and technology—essential to my business vision—thus creating The Modern Artisan, a capsule collection that uses big data and artificial intelligence to combine craftsmanship and sustainability. The craft of the artisan, a traditional trade, becomes modern and gives young people a new work opportunity. We created a range of men's and women's clothing, designed in Italy by six students at the Fashion in Progress research center at Milan Polytechnic, produced in the United Kingdom by craft workers trained at Dumfries House, all the proceeds of which went to the training programs of the Prince's Foundation. I would become a member of this charity organization three years later. It was the first time that the name of the Prince of Wales had ended up on the label of an item of clothing. Two weeks after going online, once the news had reached the newspapers and TV news channels around the world, we had sold 50 percent: an enormous success!

12

During finite games [...] the players are known, the rules are fixed, and the endpoint is clear. The winners and losers are easily identified. [...] In infinite games, like business or politics or life itself, the players come and go, the rules are changeable, and there is no defined endpoint. There are no winners or losers in an infinite game; there is only ahead and behind. [...]

We will realize that many of the struggles that organizations face exist because their leaders are playing an infinite game with a finite mindset. These organizations tend to lag in innovation, effort, morale, and overall performance.

In stark contrast, the leaders who embrace an infinite mindset build stronger, more innovative, more inspiring organizations. Their people trust each other and their leaders. With an infinite mindset, leaders have the resilience to thrive in an ever-changing world while their competitors fall by the wayside. Ultimately, they are the ones who lead the rest of us into the future.

This passage for Simon Sinek's book *The Infinite Game* perfectly encapsulates my idea of business. You can't run a business if you don't take account of the speed at which the world around you is moving, if you're not ready to turn everything upside down in a flash, and if you're not able to glimpse the first warning signals. You must always remember that the tiniest flap of a butterfly's wing can trigger a hurricane in another part of the world and that an unfinished action can affect your future.

YOOX has remained faithful to its identity but has reinvented itself a thousand times. It was created in 2000 but raced like a hare and sprinted ahead, never stopping. In 2004, the magazine *Time* included it in the list of the "50 Coolest Websites" of the year in its Lifestyle and Culture section. YOOX has triggered an important change in the way in which garments are presented, sold, and purchased; it has helped its customers, who were originally a sophisticated niche, to become a majority. The merger with Net-a-Porter led to the creation of an ecosystem in which discounted and full-price garments were brought together, creating a surprising effect, and many young designers have become big and famous.

Over these years I have often used a formula: C2C+O2O… don't worry, chemistry has nothing to do with it. It means: Content to Commerce plus Online to Offline. It's my vocation to combine shopping and entertainment and to create a close relationship between the physical store and the online store. This has helped me carry the group to success.

I'm convinced there is no conflict between physical and online stores because the customer is one and one alone, regardless of whether they shop on Fifth Avenue or online, and this integration has become the real present and future challenge for the majority of brands.

I certainly don't think the physical store is dead, nor that e-commerce can replace the experience of shopping in a real store—provided the real store can move with the times and find the right degree of technological integration. Nothing, in my view, is completely obsolete. LPs coexist with Spotify, cinema with Netflix, e-commerce with Saturday shopping in city center stores.

I say this because online companies, with a powerful component of innovation, have a built-in imperative: to evolve. They must never look back but must always grasp the real opportunities that lie ahead. I'm too young to talk about traditions, but old enough to have cultivated certain values. These must be open to change while remaining the same. In the words of Joseph Alois Schumpeter, a renowned twentieth-century economist: "Do old things in new ways, this is innovation."

I've always been interested in innovation, in that borderline between unexplored and potential. I love the story of *The Very Hungry Caterpillar* by Eric Carle (to such an extent that my first presentation at the annual summit of Richemont was centered around this analogy), I don't like standing still. I prefer to experience and dream about the future rather than waiting for things to happen. I'm increasingly convinced that young people, technology, and sustainability are the words on which to focus. These are the keys to tomorrow, the greatest challenges and opportunities that we have before us, challenges on which it is essential to work tirelessly, and immediately.

INNOVATION AT THE SERVICE OF SUSTAINABLE FASHION

I have always been involved in the fashion industry, which is one of the world's major pollutants. Often, I have asked myself: How can we break out of this vicious circle? How can we transform the fashion industry—an industry of desire to the nth degree, of frivolity, of transience—into a model of virtue? Can we do something concrete to interrupt this cycle of production, consumption, and destruction of millions of retail garments?

Every year this industry wastes around €500 billion of clothes which, due to the absence of recycling procedures, are thrown onto the garbage dump even before they are sold. Textile production causes around 20 percent of the pollution of clean water, as well as up to 10 percent of CO2 emissions, and it is reckoned that only 2 percent of workers in textile production earn a living wage. The remaining 98 percent, mostly women, find themselves in a situation of extreme poverty. The models of a circular and regenerative chain, however, can contribute toward improving operative efficiency and resilience and thus bring about sustainable growth.

Fashion is a hothouse of creativity, a concentration of ideas and passion, and yet it pollutes, it fills the seas with plastic residues, it incinerates millions of unworn garments, and pushes senseless consumption, especially through fast fashion. At the same time it is also a model for communication. People love it, they follow it, they recognize its value in terms of innovation and identity. Shopping is still, for many, one of the most enjoyable, relaxing, sociable activities that exist—some even call it therapy....

The fashion industry is an incredibly stimulating and economically significant sector, but if it wants not only to prosper but to survive, it needs to put the green economy at the center of its new working models. This is what customers are demanding, especially young people who are saying to us: Save the planet and do it fast.

I take a positive view. If we can slow down some of this excess of fashion collections, this speed of production, this "fashion warming" rather than global warming, there will then be a profound change—and I'm a fan of change. I like novelty, I'm excited by it, unlike so many people who feel anxious about it.

We need concrete actions to put into practice straightaway, not to wave about as marketing, not to be carried out in ten or twenty years. They need to serve as an example, repeatable on a large scale, of what we can do to guide the fashion industry toward practices more harmonious and respectful of nature and of people.

If technological innovation is used with intelligence, it will be a formidable ally in this process of change toward a greener tomorrow.

Sustainable fashion or slow fashion, for me, means first of all finding a garment that you like and want to wear again and again. It's a question of creating objects that can be appreciated throughout your life, and beyond, of being confident that the choices you are making are not harming the planet.

But let's go back for a moment. I began very early to regard sustainability as a pole star that should guide my own thinking as well as that of the Group. On Earth Day in 2009, I decided to launch the YOOXYGEN project (a name invented by a young intern) which included a series of initiatives that my team and I had been developing for over a year to make the whole company increasingly green. The first step was to launch a platform that gave visibility to designers who respected nature. The idea was to help customers purchase in a more responsible way. We began with scouting and supporting sustainable collections, identifying powerful partnerships that might have a positive social impact, and we established a clear definition of what sustainability and circularity meant. The second step was to develop ecoboxes, completely recyclable packaging with no plastic. At the same time, we decided to change the company vehicles, opting for hybrid vehicles, moving then to electric vehicles for deliveries, eliminating plastic from the whole company and thinking toward a real revolution in environmental terms.

This was early, very early, for the fashion sector. Nobody then was talking about respecting nature. We organized a press conference where everything was green, from the contents to the welcome cocktails, and even the journalists took us for Martians; they didn't understand the sense of what we were proposing. It wasn't yet strongly felt.

One person who did believe in it from the very start was Amber Valletta, the beautiful top model I had met years before, when she wanted to create her own line of sustainable clothing. I encouraged and supported her in this startup; she had no distributor, and we promoted her clothes. She has become an ambassador and leading activist for sustainability, and always remembers beginning with us, and that her new career started there.

In February 2020, during Milan Fashion Week, we launched the Vogue YOOX Challenge: The Future of Responsible Fashion in the wonderful former church of San Paolo Converso. Amber gladly accepted my invitation to host the evening.

The project lasted a year and enabled designers and start-uppers to present ideas on the creation of a more sustainable industry: a year after the ten finalists had been selected, it was decided who was the winner, who would be given financial support and mentoring.

Amber and I became friends. We write to each other now and then, and I ask her to tell me how fashion was in the 1980s and 1990s, what those crazy parties were like, and I try to worm the secrets out and relive the irresponsible, free, happy-go-lucky and spontaneous atmosphere they breathed then. There weren't yet the vast businesses, the great conglomerates of today. There was a creative, familiar environment that revolved around the designers and their ideas. Amber is now married to a super-fit man with whom she goes hiking in the Californian woodlands, regularly moving house; each time I want to send her something I need to search out her new address, otherwise the parcels spend months with previous neighbors.

I had an experience similar to the Vogue YOOX Challenge in America. Years ago, I was a jury member of the CFDA/Vogue Fashion Fund, which had the same aims. Each year they organize an event, the CFDA Fashion Awards, for personalities who have excelled in the field of fashion. The leading figure in these initiatives is Anna Wintour, undisputed kingmaker of American and world fashion, editor-in-chief of American *Vogue*, the bible of glamour, since 1988.

Anna is a true authority in the world of glamour: respected, feared, venerated, she determines the success of a collection and its designer. I first met her in New York, in her office, the one so well described in *The Devil Wears Prada* and in the documentary *The September Issue*. She is always perfect, impeccable, and you immediately feel she knows how to manage power. In 2013 we had organized an event with Lena Dunham and Diane von Fürstenberg at Beverly Hills to give awards to selected young American designers. It was a magnificent evening. Anna and I continue to see each other. She often comes to Milan for Fashion Week, though she stays no longer than necessary before flying to Paris, the city she prefers. I've invited her many times to my house, the first time to drink a cappuccino, though it wasn't easy to organize. Her assistant explained to us exactly how she likes it and how she drinks it, and we decided in the end not to take the risk and to order it from Pasticceria Marchesi, a Milanese institution, which makes the best coffee in the city. Anna doesn't take the lift, at least not when she's in Milan—I think she's afraid of getting stuck and her packed diary being interrupted—so she walked up the stairs. Fortunately, I lived on the second floor...

but I wondered what she does in New York, where the lowest skyscraper has at least forty floors, and hope it's a practice that she limits to her travels.

The second time she came to my house was for an event organized by the magazine *W*, when Stefano Tonchi was the editor-in-chief. I remember she was very nice and even went to my daughter Maggie's room to say hello. The last time she tried to contact me was halfway through 2022 but my new assistant, who is unfamiliar with power, told her I was busy and wouldn't be able to call her for at least a week! It wasn't exactly what she expected.

THE IMPORTANCE OF VALUES

Everyone today is talking about digital technology and respect for the environment; they are almost the calling card of the modern era. But technology is a means to an end, not an end in itself. Data, artificial intelligence, virtual reality...they are all important because they allow us to forecast, analyze, and study solutions. We need to have a clear idea about what we want from them. We need objectives and we need to know how to achieve them. The more we love the planet, the more we want to save it, and the more we need to look ahead.

At YNAP we established a program in stages, each part of which was the achievement of an objective and a promise for what we would do after. When we opened the center at Landriano in 2016 and the Tech Hub in London in 2018, we knew that if we wanted to implement a positive climate strategy, we had to reduce our emissions and use 100 percent renewable energy in all our offices and warehouses. In 2020, we reached our target a full year before the objectives we had set ourselves. My final project as CEO of YNAP, once again in 2020, and in a certain sense the legacy I would leave for the coming years, was Infinity. This was a ten-year strategy involving four intervention areas—Circular Business, Circular Culture, Planet Positive, People Positive—each of which was planned with the ambition of providing circular luxury fashion, and of connecting with people who love clothes and accessories that last a lifetime and more. Through these areas, YOOX Net-a-Porter would contribute toward seven of the United Nations' sustainable development objectives in areas such as climate, responsible consumption, and inequality.

In those same years we tried out two pilot Digital Passport projects on various selected garments from our private label and on the whole collection developed for The Prince's Foundation. We put QR codes on each item to allow customers to access a virtual certificate that recounts the journey from production to use, to resale, to reuse, to repair, and to recycling. This is the meaning of circular fashion, which differs from the classic linear journey of production-consumption-disposal.

In many ways, with The Modern Artisan collection, we have taken the first step toward a revolution; we have combined data, craftsmanship, and sustainability. The objective was to equip "modern artisans" with the tools needed to succeed in the digital environment of today, where not only must they excel in their work as creatives and in their manual skills, but they must also understand how to make best use of modern technology and data science. This project can be considered the blueprint of how I think a collection can be devised in the coming years; new luxury is in the hands of young artisans who will create what will become exclusive and desirable tomorrow and beyond.

YOOX declared its values from its first inception. Consumers today choose where to buy on the basis of shared ideas, feelings, passions, ideals. Values, however, are not invented and above all they are not bought. Either you have them, or you don't. Here too, it's a problem of consistency, it's a journey in stages, and the sooner it begins the better it is organized. And ethics, to my mind, has always come first.

I've never forgotten the friends who have helped me, like Kazunori Iwakura, Mihara Yasuhiro, Koji Ono, Holly Brubach, Fabio Canè, and so many others. I've always tried to repay those who have helped me. Fabio, for example, was one of the first to receive YOOX shares in exchange for his loan, and when Mihara had a moment of difficulty, we helped him out by buying much more stock from him and selling it on the site. My business career is studded with gratitude: it's a value in which I firmly believe and, like everyone, when I meet people who turn their backs, who forget what I have done for them, I'm deeply disappointed, but I always try to remember the words of Enzo Ferrari: "Never do good unless you're prepared for ingratitude."

In the group that I founded, 62 percent of employees were women, paid the same salary as men, and over half of middle and senior management were women, with 50 percent of the Executive Committee of YNAP formed by women. I'm a founding member of the Champions of Change Coalition—Global Technology Group that works to promote gender equality in the technology sector, and the number of women in technology in YNAP has reached double that of other tech companies, where there is still a strong predominance of men.

Young people have also been my priority from the time when I founded YOOX: We ourselves were young people addressing other young people, and we gave them the instruments to free themselves from the diktats of traditional fashion. In the company, there were thousands of employees spread everywhere, with an average age of little over thirty, and the same number of staff employed in call centers and logistics: I'm thrilled to have created work for around ten thousand families!

At the same time I tried to encourage emerging talent and conducted a mentoring program for aspiring entrepreneurs coming from typically underrepresented backgrounds. I have already mentioned the coding courses in London, run in conjunction with Imperial College, but from 2016 we did the same in Italy, carrying out digital education programs focused on the teaching of IT through partnerships with such prestigious institutions as the Fondazione Golinelli. The result? The training of over ten thousand young people, mostly young women, in Italy and in the United Kingdom.

I've always been careful to try to respect the sensibility of the people who have worked with me, as well as my customers. In 2016, for example, it was easy to decide to ban furs from all our multibrand sites. Three-quarters of the twenty-six thousand customers we consulted preferred this choice, and I didn't hesitate for one second even though it meant losing tens of millions of euros in sales. After us, hot on our heels, many others followed suit, and I'm proud that the Italian Anti-Vivisection League complimented me on opening the way. Simone Pavesi, head of their Animal Free Fashion group, declared: "The commitment of YOOX Net-a-Porter Group is a significant goal that ought to represent an important example in the fashion world, a tangible signal that the clothing industry can be more sustainable and ethical without necessarily having to resort to products derived from animals." I wasn't forced by any shareholder or board of directors to eliminate furs, I simply anticipated a new customer sensibility—and then, personally, I believe that animal protection is more and more a line of demarcation between right and wrong.

I STAND WITH ELEPHANTS

I have a special relationship, for example, with elephants. I've liked them from when I was a child and, since then, they've cropped up on various occasions, when I've always been happy to do everything possible to protect them. Elephants are cautious, wise, and capture the imagination. I could spend hours watching these giants move with extreme elegance and lightness in their natural habitat. Elephants are magical and play a crucial role in our ecosystem.

In 2017 we dedicated a whole issue of *Porter*—the multiple-award-winning magazine launched in 2014, sold in sixty countries with a print run of 350,000 copies and published by the YOOX Net-a-Porter Group—to the protection of elephants. The supermodel Doutzen Kroes, in association with the Knot On My Planet foundation, had launched a campaign to raise money for the Elephant Crisis Fund, a Save the Elephants and Wildlife Conservation Network initiative, in collaboration with the Leonardo DiCaprio Foundation. The Elephant Crisis Fund helps partners throughout Africa and around the world to stop the killing of elephants caused by ivory trading. We supported it and organized a dinner at The Orangery at Kensington Palace with Naomi Campbell, Cara Delevingne, Natalia Vodianova, Arizona Muse, and various stylists, to collect money and raise public awareness. The campaign had a major impact: All the earnings from *Porter* went to the Foundation.

The second time was when my friend Waris Ahluwalia, the actor in Wes Anderson's films *The Life Aquatic with Steve Zissou* and *Grand Budapest Hotel* and in Spike Lee's *Inside Man,* asked me to help Asian elephants—after he had designed an irreverent line of underwear for YOOX called Dirty in early 2000. Waris, activist, designer, and creative, invited me to sponsor The Animal Ball. It was June 13, 2019, and Prince Charles and Camilla had organized a party at Lancaster House inspired by Truman Capote's Black and White Ball of 1966: everyone had to wear a mask with an animal theme. In the great bestiary I chose the crab because of my great love for the sea. The amount collected for elephants arrived at many millions of pounds—auctions at events like these in England and America reach a very high level and guests are incredibly generous.

On another occasion I worked with King Charles's son, Prince William, on a project for the protection of African elephants. In June 2021 we created a capsule collection for Space for Giants, and all the profits went to this charity that protects the wildlife and landscape of Africa. In short, elephants are my passion, so much so that when I discovered that the last regenerative fashion initiative sponsored by Brunello Cucinelli as part of the task force, which promotes the reforestation of an area of the Himalayas, would help Indian elephants to retrace their traditional corridors which are fundamental in migration and in searching for water, I thought it was a prescient sign and that elephants really were my lucky charm.

AN ITALIAN FAIRY TALE

January 22, 2018, is an important date. Riccardo Luna, one of the leading Italian journalists on technology, writes in his blog: "One in a thousand makes it. And that one in Italy is Federico Marchetti. He's 49 years old and has announced today that the Swiss group Richemont has offered to buy 100 per cent of the shares in YOOX Net-a-Porter (YNAP) valuing it at €5.3 billion. It's not simply financial news: it's a fairytale—they happen every now and then—which tells us much about how innovation works and doesn't work in Italy."

That day I had announced the sale of YNAP to Richemont: it seems like a parable, a fairytale, as Luna says, which seems the stuff of fiction rather than a real and traceable journey. In fact I told my whole story as an entrepreneur on Instagram just as if it were a fairy tale:

> *Once upon a time there was an Italian boy from Ravenna, the city of mosaics and of Dante Alighieri, who one day packed his bags to pursue a dream: to innovate fashion via technology.*
>
> *He created YOOX, a start-up that within a few years became Italy's only tech unicorn and the leader in fashion e-commerce across the whole world, from Europe to America to Japan. The years passed by, and the boy refused to stop his dreaming: next, he traveled to London where he joined forces with his admired rival, NET-A-PORTER, the online luxury brand with which he had dueled head-to-head with from the very beginning. He then made his way to Dubai where the great Alabbar opened the doors to the Emirates.*
>
> *Then, one day the good Swiss giant Richemont decided to make his creation even larger and together they left for China where they met Alibaba and millions of young Chinese people attracted to digital fashion.*
>
> *The boy, who became a Knight of his native realm, was at last satisfied that his dream had come true. And then a real prince appeared, His Royal Highness The Prince*

of Wales, and together they created an innovative and sustainable project to help young people the same age as he was when he started his own adventure.

As you may have gathered, that boy was me and my ambitions became reality. I hope this adventure serves as an inspiration to all those who will never stop dreaming of the impossible or believing in fairy tales.

As the YOOX NET-A-PORTER story continues, I look forward to celebrating its future successes as Chairman as well as writing new chapters of my own.

You can create a startup, make it grow, carry it to the height of success and, when you've reached it, decide to leave it. You can do so because if you're an entrepreneur your first objective must be the success of your company, while your second must be to know at what moment to leave the stage.

And I had understood at that moment that the right thing to do was to accept Richemont's offer and start an exit strategy that was programmed, gradual, considered, and studied in the tiniest detail. I therefore decided immediately that I would not remain beyond the end of my contract, but that I would do everything humanly possible to leave my creation in good order, with a smooth and painless transition.

But what happened from January 22, 2018, to July 23, 2021, the day on which I finally left YNAP, leaving my office for the last time? What did I do in those 1278 days and what projects did I complete?

On March 4, 2020, two years after the sale, and as my contract was coming to an end, I officially announced my succession plan: "As planned, we are in the early stages of implementing a succession plan for the next CEO of YNAP, with me staying on as chairman to ensure a smooth transition and set the new CEO up for success."

On Instagram I also added: *Right before the new millennium, I had a vision fashion would shift online. Against the odds, I followed my instincts and went live before Facebook, before Instagram and before the iPhone. Today the mobile phone represents over €1 billion of our revenues, and we receive 1 billion visits per year across our Group's destinations. If an online shopper is buying luxury right now, the chances are it's coming from us.*

It's been a ground-breaking ride over the past two decades...to be continued! I love YOOX NET-A-PORTER and will give everything I have to guiding our talented teams during this transition and ensuring our Group will thrive in the future. Thanks Johann Rupert and Richemont for your constant trust and support.

Everything seemed ready, set up for a smooth journey, but on March 9 the panorama changed completely: Italy went into lockdown due to the COVID-19 pandemic.

It was a real shock, the country was in lockdown, people were afraid, the prospect seemed bleak, uncertain. I decided then to shut the offices and logistical centers, even though other e-commerce sites remained open. There were no restrictions for online business; many continued, and they obviously increased their trade, while I decided to close the warehouses in agreement with my shareholder. From the business point of view it was a hard decision, with a net loss, but from the human point of view it was the right thing to do. I did it and would do it again.

On April 7 I wrote a letter to all employees in which I explained that I could not abandon the ship in a storm, that I could not leave the people who worked with me at the mercy of events, that I would remain at the group's helm until the waters had calmed and we had reached a safe harbor. The change of management was postponed. The economic and health crisis took priority.

In the order of values, I put health in top place: I wrote various letters, to customers as well as employees, updating them on all the decisions and the course we were taking, and I invited everyone to feel they were part of a community with shared choices and values. "No one must be left behind" is a slogan that the company put into daily practice creating a safe and friendly environment and, as a result, in the company we had 0.1 percent of cases at the end of the year. In practical terms, almost no one took sick.

We efficiently organized distancing, learned to sanitize the areas, introduced new control apps and many management innovations; after a month of zero sales, we re-activated the business, reopened the company, and immediately resumed growth.

At that point I pulled out the succession plan again, and the new CEO was appointed at the end of November: Geoffroy Lefebvre, who had been at Richemont for some time.

Johann Rupert declared: "Richemont's digital journey, since our first investment in Net-a-Porter in 2002 to my encounter with a visionary entrepreneur, Federico Marchetti, that led in 2015 to the creation of the Yoox Net-a-Porter Group, then its acquisition in 2018, has been fascinating in many ways. I would like to thank Federico for his relentless passion, his energy and his drive in shaping the largest player in Luxury Selective Distribution. He has crafted and delivered the vision that has prevailed since 2000 and has inspired so many. I wish Federico all the best for his future career." (*Women's Wear Daily*, December 1, 2020).

From that day, my life changed once again: I was still president of YNAP, knowing that this too was transitory, that it wouldn't last long. My future, in the meantime, took shape. In June 2020, as I have mentioned, Giorgio Armani asked me to give him a hand as his personal *consigliere* on the board of directors. He had never opened the board to people outside the family: How could I say no? Impossible. I felt invested with a symbolic responsibility toward Italian quality, as well as being drawn by the affection I feel toward him.

Then there was Prince Charles, as he then was, who asked me to assist him on questions of sustainability; it was a matter of bringing together utopia and pragmatism, green economy and innovation, technology and reclaiming areas of biodiversity. All these things fit perfectly together. Innovation is at the service of humanity, and humanity studies and pushes forward technological knowledge in the quest for solutions to the most pressing problems.

THE LONG GOODBYE

But we must now leap back again. July 23, 2021, was a great day, the end of a story, and the beginning of an adventure yet to be revealed: I left YNAP. In a letter to the employees, I told them I felt enthusiastic about starting a new chapter in my life but was upset to be leaving them and the company I created, which I had run with passion and devotion for the past twenty-one years and which I still loved as I had on the very first day.

A few days later, on Instagram I wrote: *But now what comes next? I remain an innovator and will continue to invent. I will chair a global task force that will put innovation as the accelerator for a sustainable agenda at the heart of the fashion industry. With the future always uppermost, I plan to use my experience in data, technology and artificial intelligence for the next generation: create new sustainable paths for emerging designers, support promising talents as I've done with many YNAP employees, ensure young tech entrepreneurs succeed, and ensure more girls learn to code. The next generation's vision of the future will take sustainability, innovation and creativity to new heights.*

I remember all the sensations of that period: the feeling of emptiness, no longer having what had been my center of gravity and my absolute commitment, and the euphoria and adrenaline for my new appointments and my new interests. When I went to Bologna to say goodbye to everyone in the warehouse, the place where I had begun and where I found it right to finish, I felt a lump in my throat but was taken by surprise at a long applause from hundreds of warehouse workers, something that moved me deeply and I'll never forget.

In a certain sense, YOOX was like a child for me, but it was time to let it go its own way. At this point I'd like to talk about Maggie, my real child, who is now a young teenager. When you become a father, you discover a new form of love you have never felt before. It's an unconditional feeling that consists of protection and care, happiness and trepidation. It's a secret link that unites you indissolubly for your whole life. I melt before her, though I don't imagine I'm the only father to feel this. Before she was born, Kerry and I had compiled a list of names that worked well in both Italian and English, such as Agata, but then I saw her—Kerry was still under the anesthetic after the caesarean birth—and instinctively decided it would be Margherita. She now prefers Maggie, as I've already mentioned, but we laugh when I tell her I was inspired by the pizza, one of her favorite dishes.

During the twenty-one years that I was running YOOX and then YNAP, when I wasn't traveling for work, I tried to spend as much time as I could with her. We had breakfast together in the morning, and I read her a book in the evening—yes, a printed book, there's no comparison!—before she went to sleep, clutching me, in her little bed. We follow Formula One Grand Prix races that we both love, and we like fishing together in exotic countries: Once she even caught a shark! Then there are things that she likes but I don't, such as skiing, whereas I'm a beach boy.

I have a weakness for Maggie, I've always shown her off to all and everybody; she's my priority and one of the reasons why I left my first "child" YOOX. I wanted to find even more time to devote to her.

Maggie is intuitive and creative, but at the same time very rational. Every now and then I see an entrepreneurial urge in her: She likes inventing mini businesses with her classmates such as the sale of customized stickers, or she offers to help me when I give advice to certain private equity ventures when they ask my opinion about buying a company. On one occasion it was a brand of sneakers and thanks to her—she knows all about them—I discovered that their models were copies. The private equity venture then decided not to go ahead, saving many millions of euros. On other occasions we joke and think of doing a startup together, such as robot pets—pets which are machines even though they don't seem to be.

She still has time to grow up and to choose, whereas I have decided to work now for the future of young people, to fight for the environment, so that generations like Maggie's don't have to pay too high a price for our mistakes. I know that at some point she'll fly from the nest, but wherever her passions and inclinations take her, I will support her. One day she'll be an adult, she'll live her own life, she'll be free and independent knowing I'll always be there beside her.

I did the same with YOOX; having followed it from its inception to when it had reached majority, I knew it was now able to continue its journey without me.

The idea of leaving with a well-devised succession plan, announced eighteen months before, put on hold due to COVID and then resumed in the fall of 2020 with the appointment of the new CEO, had now reached its completion. Everything was set.

Richemont's top management behaved very decently, as ought to happen between shareholder and entrepreneur, and sadly often doesn't. They surprised me by arriving from Geneva so that we could toast the succession all together. These too are values: for both sides to part from each other with fairness and respect.

During a live interview on Sky TG24, when asked what I would do next, I said: "I'm certain about what I won't do. I've learned this over the years, and also recently: I won't be an employee. I left investment banking partly because I had seen certain injustices that I didn't like. When I came back from the United States, I worked for a consultancy company and didn't much like that either. Then finally I invented YOOX: my company, my project. I certainly don't see myself going back, I don't see myself going back to being employed. I like the DNA of the entrepreneur too much, and therefore the only thing I can really do is help others or have a project of my own." I've ended up indeed "defending" the planet for the King of England, because at that point I had already decided: the question of sustainability is the keystone that will make all the difference. E-commerce has become everyday life. Is there still something to be invented in that sector? Certainly yes, but it's now a fully-fledged business. Whereas on questions of ecology, of circularity, and of young people, I think there's much work to be done and we really are at the beginning.

I recently read a fable, *L'assemblea degli animali* (*The Assembly of the Animals*) by Filelfo, a little book that tells how nature has rebelled against mankind and the animals come together to explain that we had to change direction and become more respectful.

> *Last comes the raven: that's what the Italian had written in his book. And he, the raven, was arriving last at the great assembly of animals. He was late and couldn't forgive himself for it. It doesn't happen often, in the life of a bird, to witness such an event. The last of his ancestors to have taken part in a great assembly was remembered many generations before, when the sky was not yet crossed by great mechanical birds created by humans and the lights of the cities didn't dazzle the nights making it difficult to find their way with the stars. At one time humans used ravens to interpret the omens and they observed their flight paths to guide their own actions. They still believed that what is high up is also low down and what is low down is like what is high up. And that all things are one single thing, which can be called nature. But humans now no longer look at the sky. Over the world they had raised a cloud of dust and smoke and stenches that covered the approaching spring breeze, just like the first gusts of winter winds at the autumn equinox, confusing so many migrating birds, making them change their plans, delaying arrivals and departures and transforming the routes south into those tangles of congested expressways that humans*

> *took to move about frantically from one place to another without the raven managing to understand the hidden reasons for that vain and constant escape from themselves. Breathless and worried about his lateness, the raven tried to fly as quickly as he could to reach the appointed place, that secret place, the same for millions of years, that all animals know because they learn it when they come into the world.*

Little by little, Filelfo writes, they all arrive: the lion, the whale, the eagle, the mouse...a dog and a cat too. The meeting is urgent: The ecological crisis cannot be ignored any longer, the Earth needs to be saved from humans. To save it, after long discussions, the animals decide to send a terrible warning: an epidemic. But they will soon discover that, to save the Earth from humans, they must first save humans from a much older evil: Humans have forgotten culture and are in danger of forgetting nature. It's a contemporary tale, full of warnings, and I hope we will all choose to act more responsibly.

Everyone now talks about sustainability, but most people don't really know what it is. Worse still, there is much too much greenwashing. According to investigations by the European Commission which has studied hundreds of web sites and "environmental" claims, 42 percent are "exaggerated, false or deceptive." What is more, in over half of the cases, "the company did not provide sufficient information for consumers to judge the claim's accuracy." It's not enough to say that a garment or accessory is made with recycled materials for it to be sustainable; the procedure is more complex. We need to move from a linear to a circular economy, to move away from the current business model, for example, by using products longer. Green raw materials, traceability thanks to new technologies.

That is what consumers are asking: 57 percent want to do more sustainable shopping, but they don't know where to do it and how to recognize it. And this is exactly what I'm working on.

Despite recent political events pushing in the opposite direction, the trend is now set and can no longer be stopped. Wastage is beginning to leave space for a new sensibility that is more attentive toward saving, to the reduction of thoughtless purchasing, to a more careful choice. We will throw away less food, less clothing, we will revalue vintage and reduce garbage. We will leave more space for well-being, for traveling and spirituality, we will do less shopping and more distance working, we will live in greener cities, we will make less use of automobiles and will learn to make objects last longer.

If I think about young people, I see them enthusiastic and worried. Worried about their futures, because they don't know how to integrate into society and be recognized, but at the same time I see them eager for change. They want to be independent, to challenge the rules, to create a job rather than to find one. They think about startups that are involved with social issues, the environment, or services for the community. They want to find a new way of working, of living, of loving. And we can guide them, help them to avoid making the mistakes that our generation has made.

Young people are ready for change. They have shown resilience and an urge to fight for the environment, they have taken to the streets, they have listened to Greta Thunberg. There are now millions of them, and they demand respect. I love the company of young people, which is why in September 2021 I accepted the appointment for a one-off six-month course entitled Creating a Startup in the Digital and Sustainable Economy at my old university, the Bocconi in Milan. I taught students how to create a digital and sustainable startup, I explained how the defense of the environment will be one of the priorities that can no longer be ignored and that if they work in this way, they will be able to obtain financing—we are talking about billions of dollars for market opportunities in sustainable development by 2030. When I accepted the appointment, I told the rector: "I intend to use my experience in big data, in technology, and in artificial intelligence for the future generation. To give support to the most promising talents, to promote the success of young tech entrepreneurs, to ensure that many more young women students learn the job of coding. The vision of the next generation will bring innovation, sustainability and creativity to a new level."

It was a remarkably interesting experience because the students were attentive, curious, they involved me in their projects, asked me countless questions on how I began and the obstacles I faced, and found many ideas for their own business futures. I saw many reactions and concrete proposals, and I encouraged them to create the next unicorn by founding a techno-sustainable startup, because we need many more techno entrepreneurs and creative minds that think green.

13

We need to wind the tape back to the end of the 1960s. From the end of World War II, thanks also to the Bretton Woods agreement, the economy soared, and as affluence increased, so did the great problems linked to pollution, at first imperceptibly and then more visibly. One material in particular—plastic—was spreading more and more and would bring a far-reaching change to our planet. It's everywhere. It's the symbol of new mass consumption. Colorful, indestructible, pliable, economical—it became the symbol of modernity and began to appear in fashion and in design. It was impossible to stop the spread of a material that the whole world liked so much that global production of plastic would increase from 15 million tons in 1964 to 100 million in the mid-1970s, reaching 460 million today. And this leap forward would bring an increase in the production of waste, which has more than doubled, so that it has now reached 353 million tons. Every year, 8 million tons of plastic end up in the oceans and, if the current trend continues, it is estimated there will be more than 150 million tons of plastic in the seas by 2025, meaning that we will find more plastic than fish in the oceans.

The world in the early 1960s was intent on growth and nobody worried about the environment. Save for a few notable exceptions.

"We are faced at this moment with the horrifying effects of pollution in all its cancerous forms.... There is the growing menace of oil pollution at sea, which almost destroys beaches and certainly destroys tens of thousands of seabirds. There is chemical pollution discharged into rivers from factories and chemical plants, which clogs up the rivers with toxic substances and adds to the filth in the seas. There is air pollution from smoke and fumes discharged by factories and from gases pumped out by endless cars and airplanes." This is 1970, and the speaker is a twenty-two-year-old, Charles, Prince of Wales and future king, who after going to Strasbourg with his father, Prince Philip, to a conference on the protection of animals, spoke at Cardiff at a conference on the countryside. It was his first speech on the climate emergency.

I was one year old. I never thought I would meet and come to know him. I never imagined I would work with him on the objective that is my priority, today more than ever, but also that of all of us—to save the planet. I challenge anyone to find a person so far-sighted: King Charles was a pioneer for the environment and has never given up, from the 1970s up to the last project he founded (the SMI—Sustainable Markets Initiative) and those we have shared together on sustainable fashion and underlining the importance of respect for the environment. The SMI, launched on the occasion of the meeting of the World Economic Forum at Davos in 2020, follows the principles of Terra Carta, a ten-point declaration (with graphics designed by Sir Jony Ive) that invites private individuals to give central importance to nature, people, and the planet in the creation of value. Some have accused him of eccentricity, some have laughed about him talking to trees, some have joked about his eco-spiritualism, and his book *Harmony*, and his organic farms, but I can state that he is a person with genuine feelings, a big heart, and a real passion for nature.

Many still know nothing about his dedication, and young people are often amazed when I tell them he's been a champion of sustainability for many years.

After The Modern Artisan project, which I mentioned earlier, my relationship with him has continued and grown from year to year. From then, everything began to flow naturally, a series of increasingly ambitious activities that have the planet at heart, such as the fashion task force, which he asked me to set up. I'm the only Italian to preside over one of his task forces, as well as being a member of his boards of directors—that of Highgrove, a country house with fabulous grounds and gardens that produce organic vegetables sold also by Fortnum & Mason. I am also a trustee of his Foundation and appointed to manage his charitable activities. At the task force, I have managed to involve a limited number of courageous and enlightened CEOs of top luxury brands, including Armani, Cucinelli, Chloé from Richemont, major groups like Puig and Prada, Stella McCartney and Gabriella Hearst, two forerunners of sustainability. It's a highly diversified group because I think diversity can help people to learn more quickly from each other.

In October 2021, during the G20 meeting in Rome, the Prince of Wales, as he then was, gave a speech before the various heads of state and said: "The planet's health today will dictate the health, happiness, and economic prosperity of generations to come. Hence our overwhelming responsibility to generations yet unborn. After very nearly fifty years of trying to raise awareness of the growing climate and environmental crisis, I'm at last sensing a change in attitudes and the buildup of positive momentum." He also asked them to listen to young people, "who see you, ladies and gentlemen, as the stewards of the planet," and expressed the hope that leading entrepreneurs would swiftly implement production aims following a greater respect for nature: "Some three hundred of the world's top CEOs from every sector of the economy including financial services and representing well over sixty trillion dollars of assets under management have joined my Sustainable Markets Initiative and demonstrated how acutely sensitive they are to the way both consumers, who control more than sixty percent of global GDP, and shareholders now demand changes in the way businesses behave."

"We must now translate fine words into still finer actions," he concluded. "As the future of humanity and nature herself are at stake, it is surely time to set aside our differences and grasp this unique opportunity to launch a substantial green recovery."

On that occasion I took him a white truffle from Alba in Piemonte, the first of the season. I had great difficulty finding one and took it to Rome in a chill bag—which reminded me of the one my mother would fondly give me containing homemade cappelletti during my first years at university—and I had to explain what was inside to the staff at the embassy so they wouldn't think it was a bomb. He adored the truffle and even wrote me a letter telling me how delighted he had been.

In short, after all, I might be the Italian who brings gifts, but I think it's a way of creating a connection that goes beyond formality.

That same day, at the British Embassy in Rome, we presented our Digital Passport, a technology-based system that enables producers, designers, retailers, online platforms, and resellers to provide complete transparency and traceability on products they sell and gives customer access to reliable information on how clothing and accessories are designed, manufactured, and distributed. The commitment to implement it, together with the adoption of a protocol on circular data, was unanimously agreed on by members of the Task Force.

Everyone began gradually to implement it and the road map provided that all the others would also comply over the next twelve to eighteen months, in advance of the European Commission who, in March 2022, made it compulsory for all textile brands within five years. When I heard about this decision, I thought: "We started well before, it's always better to get there early than to be subjected to it at the last minute."

Then we set up a program of regenerative fashion in collaboration with Marc Palahi, scientist and CEO of Circular Bioeconomy Alliance. What does it mean? It means going back to the beginning of the production chain, adopting innovative processes and methods such as new cultivation techniques, new methods of irrigation, and applying principles of biodiversity for the reclamation of land impoverished by intensive cultivation and by chemical fertilizers. It means going to where the fashion process first begins in order to produce organic materials guaranteeing respectable and fairly paid work for local populations. It's rather like what Brunello Cucinelli did with our Himalaya Project to restore desolate landscapes and revive the craft skills of communities, improving the local economies of cashmere, cotton, and silk. And this initiative too, like the Digital Passport, is tangible, with over a million trees planted, and thousands of nomadic people who have guaranteed work. These are initiatives that really can change the way things are done.

In February 2023, with Brunello, we presented the initial results of the project to King Charles at Buckingham Palace: The first five kilos of cashmere had arrived at Cucinelli's factory in Perugia from the Himalayas and the experts had judged the quality to be excellent, so that it could be used in the finest knitwear, leaving so much space for scalability of production and the prospect of a major impact on that area and its populations.

WORKING FOR THE CROWN

On behalf of my Task Force, I took part in two meetings of the COP, Conference of the Parties, attended by the countries that had signed the United Nations framework convention on climate change. The first time was in Glasgow in November 2021. During those days, as I walked the streets between one meeting and another, I saw a surge of young people in bright colors parading with provocative placards and chanting clear and direct slogans. I was so fascinated by these peaceful demonstrations that on the return flight to Milan I thought that things were beginning to change at last. The agendas of governments and the private sector had begun to line up with young people's protests. I felt satisfied because it seemed we were close to our target and would be moving ahead fast. And yet, a year later, at the COP27 in Egypt, it seemed we had taken a step backward because, as Greta Thunberg says, there was still too much *blah blah blah,* even though we had presented some very concrete projects there.

I saw the prince again several times, he invited me to his private residence at Birkhall, in Scotland. I remember a long walk we took in his grounds: He knew every tree by its name, with incredible expertise and natural interest. There is also an Italian corner: a Paneveggio spruce, it was one of my Christmas presents. They call these trees *alberi di risonanza* because they produce a perfect sound. Stradivarius himself, it seems, would visit the *foresta dei violini* to personally choose the wood for the soundboards. This sapling brings together Charles's two great passions: nature and music. After my first presumptuous gift, the toothpaste squeezer, I came to know him better....

That day, at Birkhall, we had lunch together. The only problem is that he doesn't eat lunch, and I therefore had Prince Charles watching me as I ate. A surreal situation: he dines in the evening, while at midday he drinks juiced fruit and vegetables. He sipped from a large glass, while for me he'd had two or three things prepared. I'm a pescatarian, whereas he doesn't like fish—they don't cook it particularly well in Britain—though we once dined together and had it served to us, and he politely ate it.

On that occasion I was so embarrassed that at a certain point I even forgot my etiquette and, instead of using a knife and fork, put the cheese on the cracker and picked it up with my hand, causing him to smile.

THE STRESS OF DRESS CODE

In all our meetings I've often had to cope with formality and dress code. I now almost always dress in an Armani cashmere sweatshirt and track pants and a pair of plastic Adidas shoes recycled from the oceans, but I'm sometimes involved in ceremonial occasions that dictate a different elegance. For example, I received an invitation from the prince on which "smoking jacket" was written. I didn't know what it meant, so I did a search on the internet and discovered that it's a colored velvet jacket worn during evenings spent in the countryside in the smoking room. I therefore split an Armani tuxedo, took the velvet jacket and, rather than the tie, I matched it with an ascot tied at the neck—something that I never do. When he saw me, the prince—who was dressed sublimely with a perfect combination of matching colors—guessed that maybe I hadn't properly understood the instructions or had interpreted them in my own way, but he smiled kindly at me, also because not even the other dinner guest, Edward Enninful (former editor-in-chief of *British Vogue*), was dressed in the prescribed outfit.

Nor is it the first or the last time that I get the dress code wrong. I often turn up without a jacket in places where it is required. Once I was due to take tea with an English lady at the London Ritz, but they wouldn't let me in because I had no tie.

But the gaffe over which I felt the greatest embarrassment goes back to 1995, at a dinner at the house of Giorgio Armani. At that time, as I have mentioned, I was working for Lehman Brothers and in a relationship with Giorgio's niece Roberta. I was there as her companion (though I felt galled when they introduced me as "the boyfriend of") and, when we entered the sitting room, I saw that Richard Gere was one of the guests. I couldn't believe it!

I remember every moment of *American Gigolo*: California, the sun, the convertibles, and above all the star's shirts and jackets in their various shades. Even then I was fascinated by that wardrobe and the way fashion can create a personality. In short, I had perfected my own way of dressing, and I too had found various garments I particularly liked: high-neck sweaters and shirts with Korean collars. It was summer and I had come to dinner with the linen shirt I was very proud of. What a shame that Gere, when he saw me, told me the collar wasn't Korean but Chinese, and that the Chinese had invaded Tibet which he had been actively involved in defending for years. He added that I ought to be careful about symbols, even in my clothing!

Returning to Charles, when Queen Elizabeth died at Balmoral, I took my pen and paper and wrote to the King. Our way of communicating over the years has in fact been by letter, more or less one every two months, written by hand. I didn't want to send the traditional, though heartfelt, condolences. All deaths are sudden, even those that are natural, those that you ought to expect. For a son to lose his mother is deeply painful, even if he knows she is old or sick. To break that bond is almost unimaginable. I therefore wrote about mothers, about these universal figures that cross boundaries and speak to people's hearts. I identified with his pain, also because—as I think happens to everyone—I'd like to banish that idea, and foolishly imagine it will never happen to me, and that my mother will always be here beside me.

A few months later he invited me for tea at Buckingham Palace. I arrived a few minutes early and, at five o'clock precisely, I was shown into his study, full of fountain pens. The tea table was magnificent, laid with countless items: scones with spectacular clotted cream, sandwiches, various cakes and desserts. I broke the ice by giving him a birthday present, a book on Transylvania.

Here I must digress, because Transylvania is another of those series of "coincidences" that connects various events in my life. I've already mentioned that I like dressing up as Dracula: I make up my eyes, put gel in my hair, put on my tuxedo and my cape, and look just like Bela Lugosi's character, so much so that I seriously frighten my neighbors. But that's not all. The first coincidence is that Kerry was born near Whitby, where Bram Stoker began writing his novel *Dracula*: he drew inspiration, it would seem, from the abbey ruins, from that chilly windswept North Yorkshire promontory, and from a book he had found in the town library. The story tells of a sixteenth-century prince named Vlad Tepes, known as Dracula, whose practice, it is said, was to impale his Turkish enemies. The second coincidence is that King Charles himself is descended from the same Vlad III Basarab, a fifteenth-century Romanian voivode, prince of Wallachia. Charles has properties in Transylvania and had invited me in May of 2022 to spend a few relaxing days there. Sadly, Kerry tested positive for COVID on the evening before we were due to leave, so we had to cancel. Imagine what might have happened if I hadn't found out in time and had gone to Transylvania, putting the Queen's Platinum Jubilee at risk, infecting Prince Charles and maybe Queen Elizabeth herself during all the celebrations!

We were sitting at the tea table. I told him I'd started using green ink for the letters I wrote to him, and he said that English admirals used it once upon a time. I told him then that, after Cucinelli, Giorgio Armani had decided to invest a large sum in a regenerative agricultural project, in Puglia, and to focus on cotton, the material that his company used most. We'd discovered there had been a vast production of cotton in southern Italy until fifty years ago, which was then entirely abandoned because it was replaced by polyester. The idea was to reintroduce the old cotton tradition in Puglia, regenerating the soil and giving work and prosperity to the local populations. And Giorgio Armani immediately embraced this idea, being a champion of all things Italian.

On June 5, 2023, to mark World Environment Day, the Armani Group, in collaboration with the fashion task force of the Sustainable Markets Initiative and with the Circular Bioeconomy Alliance, therefore announced the Apulia Regenerative Cotton Project, which focuses on the development of cotton in agroforestry cultivation. This is what Giorgio Armani had to say:

> *In fashion, everything begins from the material: all my designs start with the choice of fabric. And it was by experimenting and using non-traditional fabrics that I revolutionized fashion. But the textile industry is one of the sectors with the greatest impact on the planet and that is an issue that cannot be neglected. Our commitment with the Sustainable Markets Initiative is to drive positive change: it is a bold and innovative project and one that is particularly meaningful for me and my company. Actively participating in the development of agroforestry regenerative cotton, especially on Italian soil, is an important step and will also have a real impact on local*

> *communities. Once a utopia, regenerative fashion finally begins to assume a tangible form.*

The aim is to demonstrate that it's possible to increase landscape diversity, soil fertility, water saving, and ecosystemic services connected to biodiversity, producing at the same time cotton at a lower environmental impact thanks to the use of agroforestry systems: a real revolution if the first to do it is Armani, who is taken as an example by the whole sector.

Now I come to think of it, I've been working for years with two kings: King Charles III, and Giorgio, the king of fashion, who are not only recognized authorities at world level but also have many points in common, including care for the environment and sustainable development.

King Giorgio, then, is one of the few designers to embody two characteristics that don't always coexist: creativity and entrepreneurial capacity that, in him, become inseparable and difficult to replicate. In his case, the right side of the brain, which controls creative and artistic activities, combines perfectly with the left side, which is the seat of logic. Armani has a rational mind that holds strategies and numbers but at the same time creates ideas, clothes, accessories, furniture, hotels, and many other fascinating objects. For someone like me, who is seen above all as a businessman, he has been a beacon and a spiritual guide because, even though I don't design clothing, all the same, to invent so many new things, I too have often called on my right hemisphere and my creativity.

King Charles was pleasantly impressed by Armani's commitment, and I realized he had invited me to tea in order to give a personal thank you.

My afternoon tea at Buckingham Palace reached its climax when he began to prepare it himself. It was a true ceremony. As he followed meticulously every stage, I asked: "May I help you, Sir?" (etiquette requires that after the first time, when you must call him "your majesty," you can safely use "sir," and I confess that the occasional "Charles" has slipped out), but he replied: "No, no, no." I later discovered it was a custom also of the queen, a kind of ritual. When I left, I immediately called my mother and told her everything, sending her into fits of laughter.

Once again on the theme of coincidences, one day, at a Ferrari event—cars that I love for their combination of technology and beauty—I meet Jony Ive, the man from Apple who designed the iPhone, the iPod, iPad, iMac, MacBook Air, Apple Watch, and AirPods: a true genius.

We chatted all evening—he, I, and Marc Newson, the partner with whom he founded LoveFrom, a superlative design agency. We discovered that we had various things in common, including a friendship with King Charles. Jony had recently designed the coronation crest, full of symbols: the rose for England, the thistle for Scotland, the daffodil for Wales, and the shamrock for Northern Ireland, framed by a red and blue emblem. But we also have Lake Como in common, where Marc lived as a child and has many recollections. For a tech guy like me, Jony is a point of reference, and I can never thank him enough for having designed the iPhone, so central to my business. Without such a revolutionary object I would never have achieved what I have done. From there, a fine friendship developed.

I followed the first moves of King Charles with affection, I watched him in the months after the death of Queen Elizabeth, and I sensed his reactions. I saw that the grief over his mother's death loomed heavily over the joy of becoming king. The first part of his life had certainly been different from what lay ahead, but the monarchy is a calling to which you must respond, and he has waited a long time for it to happen.

ONE DAY AS KING

On April 3, 2023, I received an email from Lorna Spence, head of ceremonial events for the Royal Household, inviting me to the coronation of King Charles and Queen Camilla, and to inform me that an official invitation would arrive by post. The days went by, I saw photographs on the internet and in the newspapers, of the invitation designed by Andrew Jamieson, decorated with heraldic themes, flowers, birds, insects, and a homage to the late Queen, but mine didn't arrive. Maybe it was because there are several public holidays in Italy around April and May, or maybe it was because that's how the postal system works these days, so I wrote to Lorna to find out what had happened. She assured me it had been sent in early April and would arrive any day now. I asked her to send another to my London address, but she guaranteed that I needed only to turn up and someone would let me in. I insisted, and when I reached London four days before the event, I found a yellow admission ticket that gave me access to Westminster Abbey. I was convinced that was the end of the adventure, but it had only just begun.

Kerry and Maggie, meanwhile, had joined me for the weekend—they wanted to be with me for the celebration even though it was a personal invitation and could not be extended—but since our house was some distance from the center, and London would be closed off, we decided to spend two days at the Café Royal, an old hotel on Regent Street where I stayed when I was in London for YNAP.

Even though the King had allowed freedom over dress code, this time I decided it was right to reverse the rules; I didn't want to be the unconventional nerd, I wanted to try real British formal elegance. Before I left, I sought the advice of my friend Brunello Cucinelli, who sent me his tailor from Solomeo, first to Milan and then to London for a first and a second fitting. The result was sublime: a half morning dress in extremely light pearl-gray woolen silk twill with perfectly matching tie and waistcoat. I'd never had a suit like this in my life. And thanks to Brunello I felt a bit of a king myself.

For my choice of gift for the coronation, I chose to combine his passion for plants with that for watercolors. A present for a king, as for anyone else, needs to be thought out. I obviously couldn't give him a silver platter or, even less, a teapot. On Friday, May 5, I delivered to Clarence House an album containing collections of Italian vegetable seeds, from the Roman artichoke to the Calabrian onion, the Tuscan black cabbage, the Sicilian caper, the Ligurian borage, as well as basil, licorice, and amaranth. I felt the book was just right for another reason: It was an adventure within an adventure or, if you prefer, an appointment with destiny. Why? Because it was the result of a series of coincidences that fit perfectly together.

For the seeds, I called Marco Bay, a landscape architect who'd been dealing with the plants on my balcony in Milan. He told me he was at a horticultural fair at that moment and there were some wonderful Italian seeds. He offered to get some for me. The seeds were a good start, but how would I package them? At this point Kerry suggested creating an album of watercolors and thought of Fiona Corsini, Diego's wife who, like her husband, was an enthusiastic watercolorist and created them most poetically.

Fiona painted various vegetables, suggested inserting the seed envelopes inside, and in this way created a little gem. But the coincidence is that thirty years earlier, Charles had been to Sicily, to the house of the marchese, Diego's father, with his watercolor instructor, and the photos I had seen at his house, and which portrayed them together, were of that same period.

On Saturday, May 6, there was a clear blue sky in London. I awoke at 6:00 a.m., got ready, left at 7:15, and set Google Maps. The directions to the security checkpoint at Westminster Abbey said nineteen minutes. I had plenty of time before the doors closed at 8:30. I began walking, but I was stopped just after Piccadilly Circus and told I couldn't go that way. I pleaded with the security guards to let me through and after a lengthy discussion I succeeded. The same story was repeated several times at other roadblocks, and I finally reached St. James's Park. It seemed I'd almost reached my destination when under Big Ben a disagreeable police officer gave me a sharp no, on parliamentary orders. Things looked bad; I was about to miss the coronation. What could I do? The policeman wouldn't listen, retracing my steps was unthinkable, time was passing. I moved on and found another guard who this time had a blue badge, for diplomatic guests. Not only did he let me pass, but he went further, letting me cross the avenue where the royal procession was awaited.

At 8:25 I entered Westminster Abbey at last. I was sweating—I also had a bad cold and was dosed with paracetamol—and now discovered the seats weren't numbered: King Charles had decided that it was first come first served, and too bad for those who arrived late. He didn't want hierarchies; he opted for a more democratic organization. So I sat in the fourth or fifth row, next to Edward Enninful, who had also just arrived, probably expecting to be given a place in the front row like in the fashion shows. But we were in the central nave, close to the entrance for the heads of state and royalty, and we had a good view of all that was going on.

It was cold inside the church, and nine degrees outside—it was May in London! And so, as the ceremony began, I started dreaming of a warm bath and the tea with ginger, lemon, and honey that I would savor on my return to the hotel.

It seems incredible: I first met the King in 2018, when he was still the Prince of Wales, and today I was here to witness a piece of history—there were very few Italians, just President Mattarella, his daughter, and me. The coronation of King Charles III is the first in modern times, when the monarch has to deal with new criteria: openness, inclusivity, speed, sustainability. And where everything ends up on social media almost before it happens. He wants a kingdom in tune with his beliefs and with the changing world: multicultural and conscious of diversity. Allow me to say that King Charles is a revolutionary man, for even at this coronation he chose to put meritocracy before aristocracy: what you do is more important than what you say, action wins above *blah blah blah*. His sensibility and his concern for the protection of nature can become the British monarchy's true modernizing feature.

The atmosphere was solemn, the ritual perfect, all was synchronized, elegant, with an ancient aura and at the same time simple, fluid. Behind the organization, I could recognize his touch, his scrupulous attention to detail. Everything reflected him, from the ethical choice of holy oil that had come from Jerusalem but was cruelty free—containing no excretions from the glands of small mammals or ambergris from the intestine of whales, which had both been used in past coronations—to the invitations on recycled paper. I studied him during the ritual: He had the serious expression that he assumes when concentrating. Camilla was at ease, Kate looked beautiful. I saw Harry pass, alone, seated further behind his brother William, who stooped to kiss the King during the ritual: Was that anticipated? I didn't know, but I found it very human. I was struck by others present, more than the royals: It was a multicultural gathering, the King's desire to have representatives from other religions was an important choice. Charles seemed emotional as he received the scepter from Baroness Floella Benjamin, and that was when I asked myself: But am I really here? How has an untitled businessman like me ended up among kings and queens, snatching an invitation from one of the aristocrats who complain each day in the English tabloids that they haven't received one themselves? The answer certainly lay in the relationship that Charles and I had created from the first day we began working together, and which had strengthened over the years. All the same, everything seemed surreal.

Meanwhile the ceremony proceeded exactly to script: The King was austere, focused, the smile came only when the choir began an anthem, and I too felt a pang of emotion.

It was drizzling when we left, I had forgotten my umbrella, but Edward, who had a lunch at Fortnum & Mason with Katy Perry, who would be singing tomorrow at Windsor Castle, gave me a lift to my hotel, fortunately just a few yards from the restaurant.

As soon as I was back at the hotel, the telephone rang. It was Edward, who apologized for not having said it in the car, and invited me for lunch with Katy and other celebrities. "Thanks," I replied, "but I can't, I'm desperate for a hot bath…send my regards to Katy Perry." I felt I needed to recover my strength. I didn't want to sicken any further, seeing that Kerry and I were invited to Jony Ive's house that evening to celebrate the King, and the next day I would be going to the Coronation Concert where I could see and applaud the singer just the same.

CONCLUSION

American and Italian, technological and human, rational and passionate, mathematical and unpredictable, warm and cool. It's been said so many times that you can't be everything, you need to transmit a clear unambiguous message, you need to decide what is most important. But what if you discover that the key to modernity lies in the simultaneous presence of more than one spirit? If it turns out that the new humanism is a blend of technology and passion and is the true guiding light toward a more habitable and virtuous future?

A distinguishing feature of my adventure has been the blending of differences, the attraction of opposites, extraneous beings that get to know and admire each other. I started out with a name, YOOX, that seemed meaningless and yet those four letters in fact contained so much: Between the female and male chromosomes are technology and the symbol of the infinite, humanism and technology coexisting in harmony.

In the early years of this century, it seemed impossible to find a resting place between two extremes. Putting your faith in the digital future and all its implications meant putting ideas about humanity to one side. I have always rejected this dichotomy; the magic formula that has accompanied me throughout my life—creativity and innovation fused together—has enabled me to guide fashion into an unknown terrain, that of the internet and of artificial intelligence, without ever losing the sparks of imagination that can only come from the human mind.

Once back from America, imbued with all the teachings I had absorbed during my MBA, I wanted to try out the speed of the net, the power of meritocracy, and my capacity to develop a new startup out of nothing. I could have embraced the model emerging from Silicon Valley. I could have created an ascetic and perfect entity, focused solely on numbers and performance. But that wasn't what I wanted to do. I had something else in mind and was sure I could achieve it.

When I put together the first clothes for my e-commerce site, what caught the eye was the mix and match, the blend of styles, of colors, of different lines and designers, sometimes light years different from one another, yet so attractive if mixed and regenerated by a new perspective. I decided from the very start that my beacon, but also the beacon for everyone with whom I would work and every client who would visit the site, would be creativity, the freedom to see things without prejudices or preformed ideas.

I returned to Italy to found my company because I knew Italy was the only country that would give me the stimulus and the passion to make it a success in the way I dreamed, with a human touch that no machine can yet produce.

Italy is a special country. Our skills are recognized everywhere, and our lifestyle is imitated and copied throughout the world. We know how to create great businesses while enjoying ourselves, we know how to commit ourselves to the very limit in what we believe, but we also want to feel our hearts beat, we want to experience emotions and nurture them. I've always been firmly convinced that the typically Italian touch, that mixture of practicality, craftsmanship, and savoir faire, the ability to devote ourselves generously to our work but also to friendship, to feelings, can make all the difference.

In the introduction to their book *Sprezzatura: 50 Ways Italian Genius Shaped the World*, Peter D'Epiro and Mary Desmond

Pinkowish write: "*When Castiglione advises his ideal courtier to do everything with a certain sprezzatura, he is providing suggestions on how to do things that are practical (even writing a love sonnet has a practical end in mind) and, most important, he is urging that they be done with a stylishness and panache that make them look easy. This 'aesthetic pragmatism' has its roots in Italy's incomparable tradition of craftsmanship throughout the ages and is still evident in the country's flair for design, whether of clothes, furniture, utensils, buildings, railway, tunnels or custom-made automobiles.*"

Made in Italy philosophy has shown that bravura is pure humanity, commitment, devotion, achievement of standards of perfection without ever forgetting our own origins, our own culture, our own DNA.

Italy has long been a cradle of creativity, ingenuity, and humanism, shaping not only its own destiny but also the broader course of Western civilization. The Romans were not merely conquerors; they were master innovators who developed engineering and architectural solutions that transformed the ancient world. Roads, aqueducts, bridges, and urban planning projects were executed with astonishing precision, many of which remain standing today. From the engineering marvels of ancient Rome to the intellectual and artistic explosion of the Renaissance, which was above all a new way of thinking and portraying the world in its entirety, we remained centered on functionality and beauty. I like to remember the example of Filippo Brunelleschi. The son of a notary, his training was in mathematics. After starting out as a goldsmith, in 1401 he competed for the commission to produce the doors of the Florence Baptistry, but the project was awarded to someone else. Between 1402 and 1404 he went to Rome with Donatello to study the city's works. In 1418, when the competition was announced for the building of the dome on

Florence's cathedral, Santa Maria del Fiore, Brunelleschi decided to present his own project. It was turned down several times and then, when finally accepted, took him sixteen years to build. He had to convince the cathedral's guild of masons to cast aside their doubts, guaranteeing the stability of the structure, building a crane, and constructing moveable scaffolding. But it was the beginning of a revolution and marked the birth of modern architecture. The dome today is still regarded as Europe's most important and innovative building since the Roman period. But what does Brunelleschi teach us? That the only way to innovate, the only way to change the present and look toward the future, was through daring to do what no one else had done before, bringing together his studies in optics, engineering, architecture and above all his sense of beauty. Brunelleschi wasn't the only one. In the Renaissance we find Leonardo da Vinci, Michelangelo, Raphael, Titian, Botticelli, Donatello—artists who have left a legacy and whose works continue to intrigue art lovers because they bring together humanism, innovation, and creativity.

But what does it mean to be creative in business today? People talk about the ability to create with intelligence, with imagination, about having sensitivity, producing ideas, being original, redefining and restructuring skills and experiences. The ingredients for obtaining this result, as we might imagine, are many and varied, especially in the millennium in which we live, where so many things around us are programmed for continual renewal and where ingenious ideas seem increasingly more difficult to formulate.

The slogan "business is business" has been commonly used for years. Allow those who know how to use numbers, those who handle money, to get on with their work. Profit is their number one priority. But doing business over recent years has become a much more complex operation. In order to remain competitive, to be visible, to be noticed, and above all to be loved by their customers, companies have one imperative. They need to move ahead, never stopping. It's often important to respond unexpectedly, find new solutions, think in a completely different way, start from way off, reverse the data, reject certain assurances, and rely on totally casual associations of ideas. In other words, you need to innovate, be one step ahead, avoid treading the same beaten paths. And to do this, you need creatives. You must go looking for them, pick them out, involve them in the production processes, giving them all the power they need. Innovation requires original thought, it involves doing things never done before, for only in that way can you look ahead and develop a business that is planted in the future, rather than in the past. You need the courage to listen to those who dream, those who pursue happiness, enjoyment, passion, those who know the power of emotions and don't focus on profit alone.

I've given carte blanche to creatives; I've left them free to develop ideas, to propose projects that are crazy, sometimes impracticable, but always stimulating, and which stir astonishment and surprise. I've asked them to attempt things they've never done before: I've asked musicians to become designers and film directors to become interior designers. I've always had great respect for creativity and culture as integral parts of my business, not as two distinct objects. In my view it's important that people in business look upon creatives as their allies and that artists and designers are integrated into the company in a perfect and equal alliance.

When I imagined my company, I thought of it as a magical box where customers, having once entered, were entertained, captivated by an object, where they returned because each day was different, full of surprises: music, cinema, art, shopping merged into something unique that was to be found in no other e-commerce site in the world. At the same time, behind the scenes, there was a sophisticated technology, where the algorithms calculated billions of prices, perfectly tracing the demand curve of customers who could try clothing on their own avatars in virtual dressing rooms, and where artificial intelligence was indeed teaching style to machines.

I have chased innovation throughout my life, I have dreamed of the future, at times I have imagined it so clearly that I could almost touch it. Technology has always been—and more now than ever before—a precious ally, the perfect traveling companion, capable of simplifying complex processes, of transforming intuition into practicable and beneficial reality. Digital technology has enabled me to carry fashion onto Planet Internet at a time when buying clothes online seemed like Star Trek. And today, in my new commitment in the field of sustainability at the service of His Majesty King Charles, I still see technology as a valuable tool for innovation, as an arrow for my bow, rather than an uncontrollable weapon. In 2000, for example, I wanted to carry all brands, one by one, onto the web. Now, with the Digital Passport, I'm pressing the accelerator on the traceability and sustainability of clothing and am certain that within five years every single company will be obliged to reveal to their customer the whole history of the item of clothing they are buying and how to prolong its life. Just a couple of years after I proposed it to the task force that I chair, the passport was already in the shops attached to some of the clothing on sale. It will go viral. When consumers are at last informed, are aware, and can choose according to their values, there can be no more turning back. Innovation is a precious ally in reversing the course of climate change, and the planet will be saved thanks to the talent human beings have to dream, to imagine, and to adopt solutions hitherto unseen.

In a world that is moving toward artificial intelligence, I like to think that we humans are unique and irreplaceable and that, instead of "artificial," we should be calling it "Augmented Intelligence," as if it were a prosthesis, an extension of our brain, at our complete disposal.

AI is now revolutionizing our daily lives, our way of working and of thinking. Robots are now able to run autonomously, voice assistants are our interfaces, and algorithms are omnipresent and all-powerful. The first temptation would be to step aside, to leave space for technology, to believe that innovation by itself will produce new innovation that will be in a position to replace us, be better than us, and that our input will become superfluous. Some might think that one day it will be enough to operate whatever machine we have at our disposal to create objects and satisfy needs. In other words, we run the risk of feeling useless and less innovative than a robot.

But when everything is robotized, when the new Coco Chanel becomes a fanciful programmer (maybe she's already been created), when clothes are designed by algorithms, printed in 3D and delivered to our homes by drone, when on looking at them we realize they are anonymous and identical, we'll go looking for a small artisan who uses her or his inventive and creative talent to produce a single small "masterpiece," and everything labeled "made by humans" will have an enormous value. When all we talk to are discs recorded and modulated by artificial intelligence, we'll go looking for a friend with whom we can chat face-to-face. And when we're tired of digital platforms and other inventions that will gradually appear with their metallic sounds, we'll go salvaging books like rare objects, authenticity will become the most precious commodity, and we'll make peace with our own complexity. Technology will proceed along with our humanism:

Sometimes their paths will overlap, at other times they'll go off in different directions. There will be an alternation in which our peculiarities will become a jewel to be preserved and transmitted. We do not respond to a binary code. We are beings who look to the future and know the past. We have the advantage of emotions and sensibilities that no automation will ever manage to replace.

I'd like to recall the words of the Italian philosopher Luciano Floridi, which I find illuminating: "The computer plays chess better than we do, but it's not knowing how to play chess that makes us exceptional, it's perhaps the urge to play it, the fact that we'd like to win, or that I don't play so well when I'm playing with my niece because I want her to win."

And so, this story begins and ends in Ravenna, my hometown, the last capital of the Western Roman Empire before its fall in 476 AD, an historical crossroads between the ancient Roman world and the new medieval era.

I began as a boy in a seaside town, sleeping in one corner of my parents' bedroom, but escaping each night through the window, in my dreams, to see where my imagination might take me. Never in my wildest thoughts did I imagine returning home one day in April 2025 in the company of the King of England. But it happened. It was perhaps, to some extent, because he'd heard me talking with obvious pride about my hometown at just the right moment, that King Charles decided to pay a visit to Ravenna, after a visit to the Vatican and a meeting with the Pope. It was his only other stop in Italy. And at the end of the day, as I stood next to him in the Basilica of San Vitale staring up in wonder at the mosaics that evoked a deep blue starry night sky, we were just two people awed by a timeless masterpiece, created by human creativity.

The end

BIBLIOGRAPHY

Shawn Achor, *The Happiness Advantage: How a Positive Brain Fuels Success in Work and Life,* Crown Currency, 2010.

Shawn Achor, "The Happy Secret to Better Work," TEDx Talk at Bloomington, February 1, 2012.

Debora Attanasio, "'La luce finale è lontana, dobbiamo agire': l'appello definitivo sull'ambiente del principe Carlo al G20," in *Marie Claire,* October 31, 2021.

Paul Auster, "Random Notes—September 11, 2001, 4 PM," in Ulrich Baer, *101 Stories: New York Writes After September 11,* New York University Press, New York, 2002.

Jeff Bezos, *Invent and Wander: The Collected Writings of Jeff Bezos,* Harvard Business Review Press, 2020.

Rhys Blakely, "Fashion's Best Kept Secret," in *The Times,* September 22, 2004.

Kerry Capell, "Yoox: Discounted Luxury. This e-tailer thrives by selling designer duds cheap," in *Bloomberg BusinessWeek,* December 30, 2002.

Eric Carle, *The Very Hungry Caterpillar,* World Publishing Company, Cleveland, 1969.

Jackie Daly, "The unconfined genius of Luca Guadagnino," in *How To Spend It—The HTSI autumn design special 2022,* in *Financial Times,* October 5, 2022.

Peter D'Epiro and Mary Desmond, *Sprezzatura: 50 Ways Italian Genius Shaped the World,* Anchor, 2007.

Salvatore Ferragamo, *Shoemaker of Dreams*, Crown Publishers, 1985.

Filelfo, *L'assemblea degli animali. Una favola selvaggia*, Einaudi, Turin, 2020.

Luciano Floridi, "The good web—some challenges and strategies to realise it," speech given at The Web Conference 2018, Lyon, April 25, 2018.

Luciano Floridi, *Pensare l'infosfera*, Raffaello Cortina Editore, Milan, 2020.

Global Plastic Outlook, OECD, 2022.

Luca Guadagnino, *Salvatore—Il calzolaio dei sogni*, documentary 2020.

Alessandro Guerriero, *Dressing Ourselves*, Charta, Milan, 2005.

Carl Gustav Jung, *Synchronicity: An Acausal Connecting Principle*, Princeton University Press, 1960.

Kevin Kelly, "We Are the Web," in *Wired*, August 1, 2005.

Young Kim, *A Year on Earth with Mr. Hell*, Ubu Gallery, New York, 2021.

Riccardo Luna, "Breve storia di Federico Marchetti che ha trasformato un milione e mezzo in 5,3 miliardi," in *Agi—Stazione Futuro*, January 22, 2018.

Charles Mackay, *Extraordinary Popular Delusions and the Madness of Crowds*, Richard Bentley, London, 1841.

Enrica Morini, *Storia della Moda—XVIII-XXI secolo*, Skira, Lausanne, 2017.

Phaidon Editors, *By Design: The World's Best Contemporary Interior Designers*, Phaidon, London, 2021.

Pino Pignatta, "Yoox, quell'azienda senza amore," in *Famiglia Cristiana*, June 3, 2015.

The Prince of Wales, Tony Juniper, Ian Skelly, *Harmony: A New Way of Looking at Our World*, HarperCollins, New York, 2010.

Proceeding of the National Academy of Sciences (PNAS), 2022.

Jeremy Rifkin, *The Third Industrial Revolution: How Lateral Power Is Transforming Energy, the Economy, and the World*, St. Martin's Press, 2011.

Brooke Roberts-Islam, "How Yoox Net-a-Porter Is Using Artificial Intelligence to Revive Artisan Craft," in *Forbes*, November 12, 2020.

Joseph A. Schumpeter, *Theory of Economic Development*, Transaction Publishers, New Brunswic1983.

Klaus Schwab, "The Fourth Industrial Revolution. What It Means and How to Respond," in *Foreign Affairs*, December 12, 2015.

John Seabrook, "The Geek of Chic. How Federico Marchetti brought e-commerce to fashion," in *The New Yorker*, September 10, 2010.

Oliver Shah, "Business of Fashion Ruffled by 'Bias' Allegations," in *The Sunday Times*, June 28, 2020.

Horacio Silva, "The Italian Jobber," in *The New York Times*, October 15, 2010.

Simon Sinek, *The Infinite Game*, Penguin, 2019.

Lina Sotis, "Quando la moda arriva on line," in *Corriere della Sera*, January 18, 2005.

Luisa Zargani, "YNAP Group names CEO," in *Women's Wear Daily*, December 1, 2020.

World Economic Forum, Ellen MacArthur Foundation, and McKinsey & Company, *The New Plastics Economy: Rethinking the future of plastics* (2016).

ACKNOWLEDGMENTS

I want to thank everyone who helped make my crazy Italian-American dream a reality.

First, my parents, who were models of integrity, consistency, and unwavering guidance. Without my mother, especially, I would never have gotten to where I am.

I certainly must thank my partner Kerry, who supported me through everything. My daughter Maggie, my kindest critic who never lets me get away with anything. I also thank my lifelong hometown friends who are always there and who still know how to laugh and have fun together like when we were kids.

I thank my original YOOX team—a group of young, nonconformist, enthusiastic, provocative, hardworking, and experimental people. Many of us came from Romagna, our land and the place we love, and against the odds achieved great success. It fills me with joy that many of them have also found professional success after YOOX, becoming investors, venture capitalists, professors, and prominent designers themselves.

A heartfelt thank you to Elserino Piol, who believed in me from the very beginning—without him, I never would have been able to get started. And a grateful thank you to Johann Rupert, who allowed me to finish on a high note.

Last, but certainly not least, I owe a great deal to Daniela Hamaui, who collaborated with me on the writing of this book. I deeply admire her intellect, integrity, and her incredible writing talent. I'd also like to thank my outstanding translator Richard Dixon, who in the midst of working on many high-profile projects found time for a whimsical, fun book like mine.

ABOUT THE AUTHOR

Photo by David Needleman

Federico Marchetti, tech entrepreneur and a pioneer in digital fashion, founded the world's first lifestyle e-commerce destination, YOOX, in 2000. In 2015, he led a merger with Net-a-Porter to create the world leader in online luxury fashion, shifting the shopping habits of millions of people. In 2018 his company was bought by Richemont, one of the world's leading luxury groups, for a $6 billion transaction value.

In 2020, he became the first non-family member to join the Giorgio Armani Board of Directors. In 2021, the Prince of Wales, now King Charles III, asked Marchetti to lead The Sustainable Markets Initiative's Fashion Task Force, which includes brands such as Chloé, Armani, Brunello Cucinelli, Gabriela Hearst, and Prada. He is also a trustee of The King's Foundation.

Marchetti graduated from Bocconi University in 1993 and obtained his Master's degree from Columbia Business School in 1999.

In 2017, his work was recognized by the President of the Italian Republic, who knighted him as a Cavaliere del Lavoro.